REA

D1328539

A Tale of Two Leagues

A Tale of Two Leagues

How Baseball Changed as the Rules, Ball, Franchises, Stadiums and Players Changed, 1900-1998

by
RUSSELL O. WRIGHT

McFarland & Company, Inc., Publishers
Jefferson, North Carolina, and London

To Brian Keith Wright

Library of Congress Cataloguing-in-Publication data are available
ISBN 0-7864-0712-3 (library binding : 50# alkaline paper) ∞

British Library Cataloguing-in-Publication data are available

Manufactured in the United States of America

*McFarland & Company, Inc., Publishers
Box 611, Jefferson, North Carolina 28640
www.mcfarlandpub.com*

Acknowledgments

The primary sources for this book were the tenth edition of *The Baseball Encyclopedia* published by Macmillan and the fifth edition of *Total Baseball* published by Viking. Data for 1997 and 1998 came primarily from *USA Today Baseball Weekly* published by Gannett Co., Inc.

Many other reference sources, primarily of a narrative historical nature, were used as background for this book. They are far too numerous to mention, and most provided only a small piece of additional or new information. But I do want to acknowledge the series of books written by William Curran about the fundamental aspects of the game (fielding, hitting, and pitching). These books are written in a thoughtful, nearly scientific way, and they provide much useful (and credible) information about the development of the game from the late 1800s through the first three decades of the twentieth century.

I also want to acknowledge the positive impact on everyone of three events from the 1998 season: the wonderful home run record chase of Mark McGwire and Sammy Sosa that electrified the whole country; the new record for American League wins posted by the New York Yankees; and the decision of Cal Ripken, Jr., to end his record streak of consecutive games played. The key element in each of these events was not just the 70 home runs hit by McGwire and the 66 hit by Sosa, nor the 114 wins by the Yankees, nor the final tally of 2,632 consecutive games played by Ripken. What made them all especially memorable was the high degree of professionalism exhibited by McGwire, Sosa, and Ripken as individuals, and the "old pro" feel of the Yankee team that relied not on superstars but on competent professional team performance to win day after day.

The pursuit of these records greatly increased the level of enthusiasm for the game in 1998, and the professionalism of the key performers proved once again that the "good old days" are right.

Contents

List of Figures

Part II: Offensive Measures

Part III: Defensive Measures

List of Chronologies and Tables

Part I: The Chronologies

Part IV: Leaders and Records (Tables)

Preface

Each of my prior baseball books planted the seed for a subsequent book, and this book follows that pattern. My first book, *The Evolution of Baseball*, uses measures averaged over the five and ten year periods in each decade to show how the game evolved. It identifies leading teams for key measures, shows how teams cycled between winning and losing periods, and presents home run records both on the road and in the various stadiums of each team.

My next book, *The Best of Teams, the Worst of Teams*, selects the best teams for each franchise during the century and identifies their key players. It lists highs and lows for many measures (not only key measures) for all teams (not only the leaders) for peak years and all-time five year peak periods (not only five and ten year periods arranged by decades), and summarizes highs and lows for each team for the measures and ranks them in comparison with the other teams.

My second book ends in 1994, but dramatic changes in the style of play (especially in home runs and strikeouts) began with the expansion of 1993. Thus, my third book, *Crossing the Plate*, focuses on the results of these changes (which culminated in the home run chase of McGwire and Sosa in 1998) and traces their origins to the designated hitter rule of 1973. It compares the 1993–1997 period to other periods of high offense and summarizes and ranks the peak years in the century for each league and each team on both a per game and total year basis.

The 1993–1997 period had much off-field activity. Baseball moved one mile up to Denver, new divisions created a wild card in the playoffs, the 1994 World Series was canceled, interleague play began, and realignment for the 1998 expansion moved the Milwaukee Brewers to the National League.

The heated discussions about interleague play and realignment were a prime trigger for the present book. Much was said about abandoning a century of tradition and losing statistical continuity. But the true tradition of baseball is change. It has been "traditional" to change the rules, the ball, the franchises, and the stadiums in which the franchises play. Off-field changes such as increasing the player pool by opening the majors to black players have been equally significant.

This book shows that some combination of the factors listed in the preceding paragraph have changed literally *every* year from 1900 through 1998 (changes before 1900 were even more numerous). Some changes were small and some huge, but their combined effect on statistical continuity were as great (or greater) than those that will occur as a result of interleague play or realignment.

1

The 1920 rule change banning "trick" pitches and the associated change of putting clean balls into play much more often caused a sharp break in statistical continuity for hitting and pitching for all years prior to 1920. The strike zone change of 1963 and the reversal of the change and the lowering of the mound in 1969 created breaks in continuity on both sides of the 1963–1968 period. The adoption of the designated hitter rule by the American League in 1973 broke statistical continuity with prior years in the league as well as with comparisons between the leagues, and the beginning of play in the mile high city of Denver did the same thing 20 years later in 1993.

Thus, objecting to a loss of statistical continuity due to realignment or interleague play is objecting to a loss of something that either no longer exists or never did exist, depending on one's point of view. There is a perception among many that baseball is a sport that has changed relatively little in this century, but this perception is wrong. Adopting interleague play and realigning the leagues simply continue the ongoing changes of the century.

What is needed to put the arguments about such issues into context is a concise reference of changes in the rules, the ball, the franchises, the stadiums, and the player pool, and the effect these changes had on the style of play. This book meets that need. In Part I it shows when key rules were set at today's levels (e.g., strikes at 3 and balls at 4) and the changes that came after (e.g., banning trick pitches in 1920, creating the DH in 1973, and changing the strike zone). It describes the development of the ball and tells which changes were real and which only rumors. It shows when franchises were created or moved, lists which stadiums they played in when, and describes changes in the player pool. It also shows that changes of this type happened literally every year after 1900.

Parts II and III show the effect of the changes in Part I on specific measures. Averaging measures over periods of time give excellent overviews, but averaging sometimes hides a key year of change. The best way to show variations in the battle between offense and defense is to use yearly changes in such league measures as runs, home runs, batting average, stolen bases, strikeouts, walks, errors, and double plays. This is what I do in Parts II and III. The teams that led each league and the majors for each measure in each year are also shown.

Part IV then summarizes the leaders, showing which teams led most often for which measures. Part IV also shows which teams dominated specific measures in different parts of the century, and it summarizes all-time league and team records for each measure. Finally, Part IV compares the game before and after the designated hitter and forecasts what we can expect in the future.

The Introduction provides the background needed to use the book fully. Much of the information in this book does not exist in any previously published source, and much of the rest of it cannot be found gathered in a single source. I wish I had this book on hand when I wrote my prior books.

Introduction

Nearly all the comparisons in this book are on a league basis and thus the data is shown on a per game basis. As I have pointed out in my prior books, using data on a per game basis is the only way to compare leagues in different time frames, because both the number of teams and the number of games player per team can vary over time. With the adoption of the 154 game schedule in 1904, the number of games played in both leagues were reasonably consistent in each season except for the reductions in 1918 and 1919 resulting from World War I. But this changed with the advent of expansion in 1961 and the introduction of the 162 game schedule. The unfortunately high number of strikes in subsequent years also produced differences in the total number of games played in a given season.

Further, even in the same year, one league can play more games than the other, especially after 1961 when expansion produced a number of years when the leagues had a different number of teams (as they did in 1998). Thus, comparisons between leagues are meaningful only on a per game basis. In any event, knowing there were a record 2,742 home runs hit in the American League in 1996 is not nearly as useful as knowing that the average number of home runs per team per game in the American League in 1996 was 1.21.

However, when per game averages are calculated over a period of years, all years are considered equal regardless of the number of games played. For example, per game records for a decade are determined by adding the per game values for each year and dividing by ten. This gives a different result than adding totals for the decade and dividing by the total number of games played in the decade. Making all years equal avoids giving extra weight to years when a higher than usual number of games was played.

As noted in the Preface, the book consists of four parts: The Chronologies, Offensive Measures, Defensive Measures, and Leaders and Records. Part I begins with The Chronology of Rule Changes, a summary of changes in the rules that tracks the development of the game since its origin in the 1840s. These changes are selected and presented in a way that makes it easy to grasp their significance and to find them quickly when they are needed again. Although initial rules were recorded in 1845, the chronology begins with the convention held in 1857 that is credited with defining the rules that formed the basis for the game as we know it today. A summary at the end of the chronology identifies the rule changes that had the greatest effect on the way the game is played.

The second chronology in Part I shows key events in the development of the ball. Few things had as much impact on the way the game was played early in the century as the development of the ball, and nothing in baseball has been surrounded by as much as misinformation as that development. Much of that misinformation still exists, and this chronology will help correct this problem. It is shown clearly that there was no such thing as a secret "lively" ball that was responsible for the huge increase in offense in 1920. There was a true lively ball patented in 1909, tested in 1910, and made the official ball (with much publicity) in 1911. The rule changes of 1920 brought its effect back again by forbidding the practice of doctoring the ball. Pitchers began the practice before the turn of the century, and they developed it to a high art after the impact of the lively ball in 1911. Further, there was a change in procedure in 1920 that had nothing to do with the rules or the development of the ball, but it may have been the single most important change in terms of the surge in offense. This was the instruction to the umpires to put new balls into play much more often after Ray Chapman was killed by a discolored muddy ball on a drizzly day in August of 1920.

This chronology also shows how "what everybody knows" about the ball is so often incorrect. Even in the late 1800s players said they could tell the difference between the balls used in different leagues simply by touch. The reality is that the balls were made by the same company in the same factory and the only difference between the balls was the label showing for which league it was the "official" ball. The American League and National League used identical balls until 1931, but sportswriters still claim today that the "lively" ball introduced into the American League in 1920 was then introduced into the National League in 1921 by that league's manufacturer. The first time the leagues used different balls was at the request of the National League for the 1931 season, when they decided they wanted fewer home runs. They succeeded in greatly reducing offense in their league in 1931 (and for the next two years), but when the fans declined as well the National League went back to the American League ball in 1934. This chronology will enable a reader to learn much about the true development of the ball as well as how that development related to changes in the style of play in the first part of the century.

The third chronology in Part I lists milestones in the establishment of the franchises. It starts in 1900 with the National League's reduction to 8 franchises from the 12 they had in 1899 (those 8 franchises remained unchanged until 1953). This chronology adds the formation of the new American League in 1901 and then traces the development and movement of franchises in both leagues through 1998. The chronology starts with a summary of the leagues that were formed since professional baseball players started their first league in 1871. This puts the staying power of the National and American leagues in context. The original 16 franchises that existed in 1901 had grown to 30 in 1998.

Following the franchise chronology, the stadium chronology lists the stadiums each of the 30 franchises played in during the century. This includes moves into new stadiums when franchises moved to new cities as well as moves to new stadiums within the same city. The chronology does not attempt, however, to show the many modifications made in each stadium while it was occupied. Moves to new stadiums had obvious effects on the style of play both for the team playing there and the teams that visited them. But in many cases the modifications made to existing stadiums had an equal or greater affect. As stands were expanded to add capacity, home runs were usually made easier because the stadiums were fixed within city blocks and stands could only be added inward. The construction of second decks in such places as Tiger Stadium and Shibe Park further reduced home run distances as the second decks overhung the lower decks. Further, the addition of screens or the relocation of home plate in many parks were specifically done to make it either harder or easier to hit home runs.

The chronology of yearly changes that ends Part I takes many of these stadium changes into account when showing how some combination of changes in the rules, the ball, the franchises, the stadiums, and the player pool took place literally every year during the century. There were usually more changes in a given year than those listed in this chronology, but only a few changes are chosen each year due to space limitations. It is not always possible to tell if the changes listed had the most substantial effect on play on the field that year, but they do show that at least one or more such changes happened every year.

Part II shows how the changes of Part I affected runs, home runs, batting average, and stolen bases. These measures are shown graphically by year so that a change in offense due to a change in the rules or the ball can be tied directly to the year in which the new rule took effect or the new ball was used. For example, the decision of the National League to use a different ball in 1931 caused a dramatic drop in runs as shown clearly in Figure 2-4. Similarly, Figure 2-13 shows that the record batting average in the National League in 1930 reflected a reasonable progression of batting average increases leading up to 1930 rather than an isolated event that mysteriously took place in 1930. Using yearly results is the key to understanding cause and effect in events such as these.

Ten graphs are used for each measure to show each year from 1900 through 1998. The scale of each graph reflects the high and low points for the measure in the century. This makes it possible to determine the exact value of the measure in each year as well as the relative value in terms of the highs and lows for the century. For example, the level of runs in Figure 2-7 during the death of offense in the 1963–1968 period can be seen to be near "dead ball" levels even though Figure 2-7 is far from Figure 2-1 showing "dead ball" period results.

The graphs also show the leading team for the measure for each year in each league. For example, Figure 2-4 shows the Yankees led the American League in runs in 1936 when the league set its all-time record for runs. A glance at the figure shows the Yankees led the league in runs every year but two in the 1930s. This provides a good insight into the way the Yankees dominated the league in the 1930s. The leading teams are selected based on runs per game, but within a single year (rather than across decades) the per game leader usually agrees with the total year leader more than 95 percent of the time. However, this means that sometimes the leaders will not agree with those shown in the two leading encyclopedias which determine leaders based on yearly totals. Further, the data in these encyclopedias do not always agree with each other nor with previous editions of the same encyclopedia. Thus, data for both the leaders and the leagues may vary from that shown in your favorite encyclopedia.

The team leading the majors in a measure is shown in bold. Using Figure 2-4 again as an example, it can be seen that the American League leader also led the majors in runs every year. This shows how the American League dominated the National League in the 1930s. The leaders are shown by the name of the team at the time it was the leader. For example, the (now) Baltimore Orioles are shown as the St. Louis Browns when they were league leaders before 1954, when the Browns moved to Baltimore and became the Orioles. The same is true for the Washington Senators and the Minneapolis Twins before 1961.

Part III follows the same format as Part II in showing how strikeouts, walks, errors, and double plays varied during the century as the changes described in Part I took place. Strikeouts and walks indicate the ebb and flow of the battle between pitcher and hitter, while errors show how fielding skills have improved constantly since the game began. In the 1800s errors outnumbered hits, and scores in the 20s were common. Errors fell steadily during the century and are still declining today, even though they are already 70 percent lower than in the early 1900s. As explained in Part III, earned run average (ERA) has essentially no meaning in terms of comparisons over the century unless the role errors play in determining ERA is understood. The decline in errors does not, however, mean a constant increase in double plays. Double plays declined from their peaks near 1950 as baserunners declined due to the great increase in strikeouts and a decline in walks. Growing strikeouts negate better fielding in producing double plays.

Part IV has tables showing which teams dominated which measures before and after the designated hitter. The top overall leaders for the century come from the original 16 teams as expected because these teams existed much longer than the expansion teams. But showing results before and after the DH give the expansion teams a chance to compete over a shorter period. All-time team and league records are shown, and splitting league results by time frames shows that the AL led the NL in most measures before 1945 while the NL led the AL in the 27 seasons between 1946 and 1972. But in the 26 seasons after the DH arrived in 1973, the AL has dominated the NL by unprecedented ratios.

Part I
The Chronologies

Chronology of Rule Changes

The basic written rules are generally accepted to be those issued by the Knickerbocker Base Ball Club of New York City in 1845. But a convention held in 1857 substantially expanded and changed those rules, and they changed nearly yearly thereafter until well into the 1900s. The rate of change decreased in this century, but many changes greatly affecting play on the field have continued to be made. The key milestones in the development of the rules are those relating to the location of the pitcher relative to the batter; the number of balls and strikes; the strike zone; and the condition of the ball. The ball is such a key issue that it has its own chronology. The key rule changes since 1857 are:

1857--The construction of the ball is defined.

1863--A pitcher's box is defined with the front line 45 feet from home plate.

1865--Balls must be caught on the fly (rather than one bounce) to be an out.

1872--The ball is set at its present weight and size.

1874--The batter's box is introduced.

1881--The pitcher's box is moved back to a distance of 50 feet.

1884--The pitcher is now permitted to throw overhand.

1887--The first strike zone is defined as no higher than the shoulder and no lower than the knee (this will not change until 1950). Also, starting this year, the batter can no longer call for a preferred pitch.

1888--The batter is out after three strikes.

1889--A walk is defined as four balls. The number of balls and strikes have varied greatly since the first set of rules, but now both will remain unchanged.

1890--The first rule forbidding discoloration of the ball appears.

1893--The pitcher's plate (mound) is set at its present distance of 60 feet, 6 inches (in 1895 the mound itself will be set at its present size of 6 by 24 inches). Moving the pitcher back is a dramatic change and batting averages soar to record highs. As a small compensation, bats with one flat side are now illegal.

1900--Home plate is changed from a 12-inch square to its present five-sided shape with the longest side being 17 inches wide. It has been unchanged since.

1901--A foul ball now counts as a strike up to strike two (National League).

1903--The American League accepts the foul strike rule the National League adopted in 1901, and the height of the pitcher's mound is regulated for the first time and is set at 15 inches. The foul strike rule produces hitting declines and increases pitcher strikeout-to-walk ratios in each league in the year it is adopted.

1909--A patent is issued for the cork-center ball.

1920--The rule forbidding the application of foreign substances to the ball is greatly expanded, and all "trick" pitches are forbidden (some spitball pitchers are permitted to continue under a "grandfather" clause). This rule and associated changes outlined in the chronology of the ball produce a huge surge in offense.

1950--The rule book was substantially rewritten mainly for the purpose of clarification. But the strike zone was redefined. The 1887 rule had been reconfirmed in 1907, but in 1950 the strike zone was defined as being between the batter's armpits and the top of his knees. This was a smaller strike zone than before. Walks were at record highs at the time, but, contrary to what would be expected, walks declined as the 1950s progressed. However, offense increased and the National League set its all-time home run record in 1955.

1963--In an effort to reduce home runs, the strike zone was defined as being "from the top of the shoulders to the bottom of the knees." The rule makers said they were just going back to the pre-1950 strike zone, but the original strike zone of "no higher than the shoulder and no lower than the knee" is not necessarily the same as "the top of the shoulder to the bottom of the knees." The 1963 definition defines the largest possible zone. The rule makers also ignored the fact that runs were in a long-term decline in spite of high home run levels. The result was the death of offense in the 1963-68 period with runs and batting averages falling back to (or below) the levels of the "dead ball" days.

1969--The strike zone changed to match the 1950 wording of "between the armpits and the top of the knees." Also, the height of the pitcher's mound was reduced to 10 inches (five inches below the level set in 1903). Some felt the mound change was more significant than the strike zone change because it was believed the prior rule regarding mound height was loosely enforced and many mounds were higher than the 15 inch maximum. The 1969 rule gave the umpires a method to better enforce the height restriction.

1973--The American League, still in a runs drought in spite of the 1969 changes, adopted the designated hitter rule. The National League declined to adopt the rule (National League hitting had recovered much better after the 1969 changes than had American League hitting). The American League adopted the rule as an experiment, but it was made permanent in 1975.

1988--In what was called a "clarification," the strike zone was defined as the area between a line at the midpoint of the top of the shoulders and the top of the uniform pants and a line at the top of the knees.

1996--The top of the strike zone is still defined as a line at the midpoint of the top of the shoulders and the top of the uniform pants, but the bottom of the strike zone is now a line at the hallow beneath the kneecap. Depending on the way the batter stands at the plate, this may be an increase in the strike zone.

1998--Controversy over the strike zone continues. The actual strike zone has always been whatever an individual umpire felt it was. Of all the strike zone rule changes, the biggest difference on the field came after the 1963 change. Strikeouts increased and offense decreased dramatically in the 1963-68 period. But while strikeouts decreased moderately for a few years after the 1969 reversal, offense did not increase until much until later in the 1970s. By then the designated hitter rule was in force in the American League.

The strike zone controversy probably will never go away. The consensus today is that umpires do not call the high strike but do widen the strike zone. Strikeouts continue to set new records but walks are also at high levels. It's not clear if the difference between the "real" strike zone and the one called on the field has much effect on the "big swing" approach most hitters take today.

Since the American and National leagues agreed on common rules in 1903, the rule changes that had the greatest impact on the style of play came in 1920, 1963, and 1973. Banning trick pitches and "doctoring" of the ball in 1920 helped produce a great surge in offense that lasted for almost 20 years. The change in the strike zone in 1963 put pitchers fully in charge from 1963 through 1968, but the reversal of the change in the strike zone and the reduction in the height of the mound that came in 1969 did not return offense to where it was before 1963. However, the designated hitter rule in 1973 not only produced an increase in offense in the American League over the next 25 years, it meant the leagues would play under different rules for the first time in 70 years.

Chronology of the development of the ball--The main issue in the development of the ball is the supposed introduction of a "lively" ball in 1920. The style of play changed so much after 1920 that the game is known as the "dead ball" era before 1920 and the "lively ball" era after. But a more accurate designation for the eras before and after 1920 would be the "dirty ball" and "clean ball" eras. In the late 1800s, manufacturers called the ball they sold to the major leagues a "Professional Dead Ball." This differentiated it from the "nickel rocket" sold to schoolboys. The "Dead Ball" designation was gone by 1900, but the generic term "dead ball" remained once many writers decided a "lively ball" was introduced in 1920. In fact, the only lively ball ever put into play came not in 1920 (or after), but in 1910 when the cork-center ball first appeared.

The chronology for the ball also starts with the convention held in 1857 to modify the rules. But the key events in the development of the ball were changes in manufacturing techniques (which were always well publicized) and the great change that took place in 1920 in deciding when to put new balls into play.

1857--The ball must weigh 6-6.25 ounces with a circumference of 10-10.25 inches. It must be made of India rubber and yarn and the cover must be made of leather. It is furnished by the challenging team and becomes the property of the winner as "a trophy of victory."

1861--The ball is reduced to 5.5-5.75 ounces and 9.5-9.75 inches. It is now within 0.5 ounces and 0.5 inches of its permanent weight and dimensions.

1866--Benjamin Shibe and Alfred J. Reach establish the A. J. Reach company in Philadelphia to make baseballs. Shibe would later be a key executive of the Philadelphia A's (after whom Shibe Park would be named) and Reach was at the time a famous baseball player who gave the new company credibility.

1872--The ball must weigh 5-5.25 ounces and be 9-9.25 inches (this weight and size has remained unchanged for over 125 years). It must contain one ounce of vulcanized rubber in mold form. If it becomes ripped or otherwise unfit for play in the umpire's opinion, he calls for a new ball only at the end of a complete inning. A ball is expected to last for a full game unless it is lost. Balls hit into the crowds around the field or in the stands are returned into play.

1874--For consistency the yarn used in the ball is required to be wool.

1876--The National League is founded and the Reach company wins the contract to supply the "official" ball by offering to supply it at no charge.

1878--The A. J. Spalding company, named after the famous pitcher who was a major figure in the formation of both the Chicago White Stockings (later the Cubs) and the National League, wins the contract to supply the ball by offering to pay the league a dollar a dozen. Spalding sub-contracts the job to the Mahn Company and later to Reach. The American Association (AA) decides that the Mahn ball is unsatisfactory after using it in 1882, and the AA switches to Reach for 1883. The AA ball gets a Reach label and the National League ball a Spalding label. Some players claim they can tell the Spalding and Reach balls apart by touch, but the balls are separated at the factory only for labeling.

1890--For the first time the rules forbid discoloring the ball by rubbing it with soil or other material. In 1897 the rule is modified to impose a fine of five dollars on the offending player. The umpire is permitted to replace the discolored ball with a new one if the captain of either team requests it.

1901--The American League is formed and offers to make Reach the official supplier of its ball if Shibe backs a franchise in Philadelphia (the AA had disbanded in 1892). Spalding now owns a controlling interest in Reach and agrees to the plan. Once again Reach is the supplier for both major leagues. The only difference is the label and the red and blue stitches used in the American League ball as opposed to the red and black stitches used in the National League ball.

1909--Shibe is granted a patent for the cork-center ball. This was part of his intensive effort to develop balls that would hold their shape for a whole game. He was the first to treat the yarn with rubber cement for that purpose in 1883, and he installed machines to wind the yarn more consistently in 1901 (and to boost his output). The cork-center ball was tested in 1910 and declared the official ball in 1911 with a burst of publicity. The ball turned out to be more lively (although that was not the reason for its development), and offense soared in 1911 and 1912. Pitchers responded by intensifying their use of "trick" pitches (the spitball had long been their best weapon but many other trick pitches were refined and developed), and offense fell off through the rest of the decade.

1916--On June 29 the Cubs and Reds played a nine-inning game with just one ball. The condition of the ball at the end of the game was not noted.

1920--Responding to the crowds who came to see Babe Ruth hit home runs in 1919, the rules were changed before the 1920 season to eliminate trick pitches. These included the spit ball, the shine ball, the mud ball, and the emery ball. It was forbidden to rub the ball with soil or apply "rosin, paraffin, licorice, or any other foreign substance to it." Some spitball pitchers were exempted by name for a year (the exemption was extended in 1921 to the end of their careers). The list of forbidden practices gives a good idea of how balls previously degraded as the game progressed, especially when as few balls as possible were used.

On August 16 in the Polo Grounds, Ray Chapman of the Indians was hit in the left temple by a pitch from Carl Mays of the Yankees on a gray, overcast, drizzly day. The ball was wet and muddy and Chapman seemed to lose sight of it. He died the next morning. The result was that umpires were instructed to put new balls into play much more often. By 1929 the average number of balls used per game was near 100. This was one key to the "lively" ball of the 1920s.

It's likely that improved winding machines and a better grade of wool available from Australia after WWI improved the resilience of the ball in 1919. It's also possible that the cover was slightly undercut, which sunk the stitches a little. This put pitchers at an even greater disadvantage when they lost their trick pitches in 1920. They complained greatly as new balls were put into play much more often, claiming the balls were too "glossy" and hard to grip, especially with lower stitches. Strikeouts fell sharply and batting averages soared.

1920, 1925, and 1929 Tests of the Ball--In 1920 some balls Babe Ruth hit for home runs were sent to the National Bureau of Standards. The bureau was uniquely qualified to test them because they tested balls in 1917 to determine the best government buys for servicemen. The bureau found no difference between the balls of 1917 and 1920. In 1925 the University of Columbia compared balls from 1914, 1923, and 1925 and found no lively ball. In 1929 *Scientific American* got similar results for balls from 1924 and 1929. They pointed out that balls lose some resilience every time they are hit, thus confirming that increased offense is an expected result of putting new balls into play much more often.

1926--Reach introduces the cushioned-cork-center ball. This was another improvement aimed at a more consistent and serviceable ball and was advertised as such. When hitting in 1926 declined from its 1925 level, there was an article about a "conspiracy" to deaden the ball. Such stories disappeared when Ruth hit 60 home runs in 1927 and hitting surged to new highs in 1929 and 1930.

1930--The National League set an all-time major league record with a batting average of .303. But the American League, partly due to the 1929 stock market crash, instructed its umpires to slow a little the introduction of new balls into the game to reduce the costs of supplying balls for the season. The National League adopted the change in 1931, although both leagues later dropped the idea.

1931--In their spring meeting, the National League decided to use a ball with a new cover and raised stitches. Their intent was to reduce home runs, but runs also fell dramatically. The American League went along with the raised stitches but did not adopt the new cover. For the first time the leagues used different balls. National League hitting overall declined sharply in the 1931-33 period, but the American League showed a relatively small effect.

1933--In December the National League, frankly stating they wanted a more lively ball, agreed to use the American League ball in 1934. But the Yankees continued to set all-time run scoring records and the American League remained a "hitter's league" while the National League was seen as a "pitcher's league."

1943--For a time poorer quality synthetic materials were used due to the needs of the war effort. But the degree to which this affected the game is unclear because of the decline in average skills due to the drafting of players.

1975--The rules permit cowhide as well as horsehide covers. This is the final act for Spalding. Cost reduction efforts had led to the cheaper cowhide as well as offshore assembly in Haiti in 1973. Spalding states they will stop making major league balls after the 1976 season, the same year Rawlings takes over.

1998--With the ball now required to meet such tests as rebound velocity, roundness after pounding, and compression distortion, "secret" changes are more unlikely than ever. But surges in hitting nearly always start "juiced ball" claims, while declines are most often credited to great pitching. Among conspiracy buffs, only hitters seem to need help from the dark side to have a great year.

Chronology of the establishment of the franchises--To put the chronology in context, the "major" leagues that existed from 1871 onward were:

1871--National Association. Lasted from 1871 through 1875.

1876--National League. Franchises came and went, but after being reduced from 12 in 1899 to 8 in 1900 they stayed the same until 1953.

1882--American Association. Lasted from 1882 through 1891.

1884--Union Association. Only season was 1884.

1890--Player's League. Only season was 1890.

1901--American League. After peace with the National League was declared in 1903, the eight American League franchises remained the same until 1954.

1914--Federal League. Only seasons were 1914 and 1915.

The National League was founded 25 years before the American League, but in terms of franchises that still exist somewhere today, they were established only one year apart (1900 and 1901). The chronology from 1900 forward is:

1900--The National League reduces to eight franchises in Boston, Brooklyn, Chicago, Cincinnati, New York, Philadelphia, Pittsburgh, and St. Louis. There will be no changes until Boston moves to Milwaukee in 1953.

1901--The American League under Ban Johnson declares itself a major league. When the National League refuses to accept it as such, war is declared in the form of player raids and franchises moves. The eight American League franchises in 1901 were in Baltimore, Boston, Chicago, Cleveland, Detroit, Milwaukee, Philadelphia, and Washington.

1902--The Milwaukee franchise is moved to St. Louis in the American League, and when it is announced that the Baltimore franchise will move to New York for the 1903 season, the National League sues for peace.

1903--The leagues agree on the location of franchises, common rules on the field, the cessation of player raids, and the resolution of conflicting player contracts. The American League now has franchises in Boston, Chicago, Cleveland, Detroit, New York, Philadelphia, St. Louis, and Washington. There will be no changes until St. Louis moves to Baltimore in 1954.

1953--First season for the Milwaukee Braves who move from Boston.

1954--First season for the Baltimore Orioles who move from St. Louis and change their name from the Browns to the Orioles.

1955--First season for the Kansas City A's who move from Philadelphia.

1958--First season for the Los Angeles Dodgers and San Francisco Giants who move from Brooklyn and New York respectively.

1961--The American League expands and the 162 game season begins with the addition of the Los Angeles Angels and the new Washington Senators. The old Washington Senators move to Minneapolis and become the Minnesota Twins.

1962--The National League expands and starts a 162 game season with the addition of the Houston Colt .45's (later the Astros) and the New York Mets.

1966--First season for the Atlanta Braves who move from Milwaukee. The Angels move down the freeway from Los Angeles to Anaheim after changing their name to the California Angels just before the end of the 1965 season.

1968--First season for the Oakland A's who move from Kansas City.

1969--The American League expands again and splits into two divisions with the addition of the Kansas City Royals and the Seattle Pilots. The National League does the same and adds the Montreal Expos and the San Diego Padres.

1970--First season for the Milwaukee Brewers who move from Seattle after only one year as the Pilots and change their name to the Brewers.

1972--The new Washington Senators move to Texas and become the Texas Rangers. To keep the divisions balanced, the American League puts the Rangers in the West Division and moves the Milwaukee Brewers to the East Division.

1977--The American League expands for the third time and adds the Seattle Mariners and the Toronto Blue Jays.

1993--The National League expands for the third time and adds the Florida Marlins and the Colorado Rockies.

1998--First season for two more expansion teams, the American League Tampa Bay Devil Rays and the National League Arizona Diamondbacks who are located in Phoenix. In the first step of realignment, the Milwaukee Brewers move to the National League.

The American League now has 14 franchises in Anaheim, Baltimore, Boston, Chicago, Cleveland, Detroit, Kansas City, Minnesota (Minneapolis), New York, Oakland, Seattle, Tampa Bay, Texas (Arlington), and Toronto.

The National League now has 16 franchises in Arizona (Phoenix), Atlanta, Chicago, Cincinnati, Colorado (Denver), Florida (Miami), Houston, Los Angeles, Milwaukee, Montreal, New York, Philadelphia, Pittsburgh, San Diego, San Francisco, and St. Louis.

Although 6 have moved, the 16 franchises of 1903 still exist in 1998.

Chronology of the stadiums--The chronology shows the stadiums occupied by each franchise since 1900. Starting with the American league it lists the teams rather than the cities in alphabetical order. This gives the best continuity because many franchises have moved to different cities, but none have disbanded since 1900. Many stadiums have had undergone substantial refurbishment, but primarily only the dates of movement to a new stadium are listed here. The names are those most commonly associated with the stadium during its lifetime.

A's--The A's began in Philadelphia's Columbia Park in 1901 and shifted to Shibe Park, the first concrete and steel park in the majors, in 1909. They moved to Kansas City in 1955 and played in Municipal Stadium there until moving to Oakland in 1968. They have played in the Oakland Coliseum since 1968.

Angels--In 1961 the Angels started in minor-league Wrigley Field in Los Angeles and helped set what was then the all-time record for home runs in one park in one year. They moved to Dodger Stadium in 1962 and then to Anaheim Stadium (The Big A) in 1966 where they have been since. The stadium was rebuilt in 1998 and renamed Edison International Field (the Big Ed).

Blue Jays--The Blue Jays played in Toronto's Exhibition Stadium from their start in 1977 until they opened their flashy SkyDome in June 1989.

Devil Rays--The St. Petersburg ThunderDome was built a decade ago to attract baseball to the Tampa Bay area. The Devil Rays fulfilled the dream by opening in 1998 in what is now (substantially upgraded) Tropicana Field.

Indians--The Indians used League Park from 1901 through 1946, sharing dates with Municipal Stadium from 1932 onward. They moved permanently into Municipal Stadium in 1947 and them moved to Jacobs Field (The Jake) in 1994.

Mariners--Since their 1997 start the Mariners have played in the Kingdome. A new stadium with a retractable roof will open during the 1999 season.

Orioles--After moving from Milwaukee in 1901 and becoming the St. Louis Browns, the Orioles/Browns played in Sportsman's Park from 1902 through 1953. Following their move from St. Louis in 1954, the Orioles played in Baltimore's Memorial Stadium until Camden Yards opened in 1992.

Rangers--As the new Washington Senators, the Rangers/Senators played one year in old Griffith Stadium in 1961 and then moved to RFK Stadium in 1962. They left for Texas in 1972, becoming the Rangers and playing in Arlington Stadium until "The Ballpark at Arlington" opened in 1994.

Red Sox--After starting at Huntington Grounds in 1901, the Red Sox have been in Fenway Park since 1912. But a new Fenway may be in the works.

Royals--From 1969 through 1972 the Royals played in Municipal Stadium in Kansas City, replacing the A's who had moved to Oakland. The Royals moved to the new Royals Stadium (later Kauffman Stadium) in 1973.

Tigers--Although the stadium itself has changed greatly, the Tigers have played in the same location since 1901. The stadium was Bennett Park in 1901, Navin Field in 1912, Briggs Stadium in 1938, and Tiger Stadium in 1961. The Tigers will begin play in a brand new Tiger Stadium in 2000.

Twins--In Washington, the Twins/Senators played in American League Park for two years and then in National League Park/Griffith Stadium from 1903 through 1960. After moving to Minneapolis and becoming the Twins in 1961, they played in Metropolitan Stadium until the Metrodome opened in 1982.

White Sox--The White Sox played in Chicago's South Side Park from 1901 until they moved into Comiskey Park, the new "palace" of baseball, in July 1910. They moved across the parking lot to the new Comiskey Park in 1991.

Yankees--After moving to New York from Baltimore in 1903, the Yankees played in Hilltop Park. They shared the Polo Grounds with the Giants from 1913 through 1922, but the Giants evicted the Yankees when Babe Ruth outdrew the "home" team. Yankee Stadium was built across the river from the Polo Grounds in 1923, and the Yankees have been there since except for two years in Shea Stadium (1974 and 1975) while Yankee Stadium was being redone. But falling debris in 1998 may well lead to a new Yankee Stadium.

Astros--The Astros began as the Houston Colt .45's in 1962 and played in Colt Stadium which had been built strictly for temporary use. The Astros moved into the famous Astrodome in 1965 and have been there ever since. A new stadium downtown at Union Station is now underway.

Braves--The Braves played in Boston's South End Grounds before moving to Braves Field in August 1915. They left for Milwaukee in 1953, and played in Milwaukee County Stadium until 1966 when they moved to Atlanta-Fulton County Stadium. What would become Turner Field was built across the parking lot for the 1996 Olympics, and the Braves began play in Turner Field in 1997.

Brewers--The Brewers began in the AL 1969 expansion as the Seattle Pilots playing in Sick's Stadium. They fled to Milwaukee in 1970 to play in County Stadium (empty since the Braves left). In the 1998 realignment they moved to the NL, and they plan to move into brand new Miller Stadium as well in 2000.

Cards--Through 1919, the Cards played in Robison Field, a park that was as bad as the Phillies' Baker Bowl. In 1920, the Cards joined the Browns in Sportsman's Park. After the Browns moved to Baltimore in 1954, the Cards refurbished the park and named it Busch Stadium after their owner. A brand new Busch Stadium was built in 1966, and the Cards have been there ever since.

Cubs--From 1901 through 1915 the Cubs played in Chicago's West Side Grounds. When the Federal League disbanded after the 1915 season, the owner of the Chicago entry in the Federal League was permitted to buy the Cubs, and he moved them into his park (Weeghman Park) in 1916. The Cubs have been there ever since although the park has been substantially modified and had its name changed to Wrigley Field after its most famous subsequent owner.

Diamondbacks--In their first season of 1998 the Diamondbacks played in the Bank One Ballpark in Phoenix, the newest stadium in the majors that year. It features a retractable roof and natural grass.

Dodgers--In 1901 the Dodgers played in Washington Park in Brooklyn, and they moved from there to newly built Ebbets Field in 1913. In 1958 they moved to Los Angeles, playing in the oddly modified Los Angeles Memorial Coliseum. In 1962 they went from the ridiculous to the sublime and moved into beautiful Dodger Stadium where they have been ever since.

Expos--The Expos began in 1969 in Jarry Park, the worst park in the majors since Baker Bowl closed in 1938. Jarry Park was meant to be temporary, but it lasted until 1977 when the Expos moved into Olympic Stadium (built for the 1976 Olympics). It was to have a retractable dome, but the roof balked so much at moving it was made permanent. A new stadium circa 2001 is hoped for.

Giants--The Giants played in the same location in New York from 1901 onward, although the final version of the Polo Grounds was rebuilt after a fire in 1911. The Giants moved to San Francisco in 1958 and played two years in minor league Seals Stadium before moving into windy Candlestick Park (now 3Com Park) in 1960. Their new downtown PacBell Stadium opens in 2000.

Marlins--The expansion Marlins joined the NFL's Miami Dolphins in 1993 in Joe Robbie/Pro Player Stadium, a park that reflects the compromise.

Mets--The expansion Mets spent 1962 and 1963 in the old Polo Grounds until moving into new Shea Stadium in 1964, and they are still there.

Padres--Born in the 1969 expansion, the Padres shared San Diego Stadium with the San Diego Chargers. The park was renamed Jack Murphy Stadium ("the Murph") in 1981, but after being redone for the 1998 Super Bowl it was renamed Qualcomm Stadium. A new downtown stadium is planned for 2002.

Phillies--The Huntington Grounds where the 1901 Phillies played later became Baker Bowl, the worst park in the majors. After some stands collapsed in 1938, the Phillies joined the A's in Shibe Park. When the A's left in 1955, the Phillies took over Shibe Park/Connie Mack Stadium. The Phillies moved to brand new Veterans Stadium in 1971 and still play there today (with the NFL Eagles).

Pirates--The Pirates were in Exposition Park in 1901 and played there until moving to Forbes Field in June 1909. In June, 1970 they moved into Three Rivers Stadium. Their new PNC Park is scheduled to open in 2001.

Reds--The Reds played in the same place from 1901 until 1970, but the park changed greatly around them. Its most lasting name was Crosley Field (home of the first NL night game in 1935). The Reds moved to Riverfront Stadium (now Cinergy Field) during 1970, and a new stadium is planned for 2003.

Rockies--In 1993 the Rockies began in modified Mile High Stadium, an ugly compromise like the 1958 LA Coliseum. But Coors Field, an attractive park still featuring lots of high-altitude home runs (and big crowds), opened in 1995.

Chronology of yearly changes--As explained in the Introduction, this list identifies some of the changes occurring every year from 1900 through 1998.

1900--National League reduces from 12 to 8 franchises.

1901--AL begins play and raids NL players; NL adopts foul strike rule.

1902--AL Milwaukee franchise moves to St. Louis; Hit batter awarded first.

1903--AL/NL make peace, player raids stop; AL adopts foul strike rule; AL Baltimore franchise moves to New York; Senators move to Griffith Stadium.

1904--152 game schedule; Fences 235 feet minimum, 90 feet behind home.

1905--World Series made permanent after Giants refuse to play in 1904.

1906--Umpires put in control of game balls after Connie Mack feeds "soft" ones to opposing hitters and hoards "hard" ones for his batters.

1907--Catcher shin guards appear; Rule forbidding defaced balls reaffirmed.

1908--Pitchers specifically forbidden to deface balls, but all such rules continue to be broken; Spitball techniques peak as runs hit record lows.

1909--Shibe Park and Forbes Field first stadiums built of concrete and steel.

1910--Initial test use of cork-center ball; Comiskey Park opens.

1911--Cork-center ball declared official ball; Polo Grounds rebuilt.

1912--Fenway Park opens; Navin Field (Tiger Stadium) rebuilt.

1913--Ebbets Field opens; Yankees move into Polo Grounds with Giants.

1914--Federal League begins and starts player raids.

1915--Last year for Federal League; Braves Field opens.

1916--Cubs move to what will become Wrigley Field.

1917--WWI drafts begin to affect major league rosters.

1918--Drafts increase and season ends abruptly on September 1 due to WWI.

1919--Babe Ruth goes to outfield; Bill Doak glove developed; Schedule cut.

1920--All "trick" pitches outlawed; New balls put into play much more often in mid-August; Cards move to Sportsman's Park; Doak glove mass produced.

1921--New balls in play all year; Umpires use river mud to remove gloss.

1922--Work begins to move stands back at Wrigley Field for more capacity.

1923--Yankee Stadium opens; Ruling permits one-piece bats only.

1924--Leagues agree on World Series in 2-3-2 cycle with alternate openers.

1925--A's add left field stands including second deck with overhang.

1926--Cushioned-cork-center ball introduced; Pitchers permitted resin bags.

1927--Comiskey Park adds second decks and reduces foul lines.

1928--Signing players under 17 banned; Inner fences built in Braves Field.

1929--Browns install outfield screen in Sportsman's Park to cut home runs.

1930--No more bounce home runs in AL, and NL agrees at end of season.

1931--NL uses ball with new cover and raised stitches, AL keeps old cover.

1932--Indians split schedule between League Park and Municipal Stadium.

1933--NL decides to adopt AL ball for the 1934 season to increase offense.

1934--Home plate in Comiskey Park moved out to increase home runs.

1935--Reds host first NL night game; A's add 22 feet to right field wall.

1936--The Tigers add double decks in right field with an overhang.

1937--Bleachers redone at Yankee Stadium/Wrigley Field (ivy also added).

1938--Phils move to Shibe Park; Tigers enclose field; Reds move home plate.

1939--First AL night game at Shibe Park; Glove measurements limited.

1940--Fenway Park bullpens built to help Ted Williams hit home runs.

1941--Draft trims player pool in minors, Hank Greenburg key loss in majors.

1942--WWII draft begins to seriously affect most major league rosters.

1943--Ball with (inferior) synthetic materials used due to WWII needs.

1944--Players as young as 15 are signed as WWII draft decimates rosters.

1945--Top players slowly return from WWII; Dodgers sign Jackie Robinson.

1946--Reds install screen to increase home runs; Raids by Mexican League.

1947--Robinson to majors; Indians fulltime in smaller Municipal Stadium.

1948--Negro National League disbands as blacks move to major leagues.

1949--First black players in All-Star game as integration of majors grows.

1950--Smaller strike zone starts this year; "Bonus baby" rule changed.

1951--Reds play full year without screen (which will go up again in 1953).

1952--Korean War begins to affect rosters as Ted Williams is activated.

1953--Braves move to Milwaukee; Last year for Pirates' "Kiner's Korner."

1954--Browns now Baltimore Orioles; Cards redo renamed Busch Stadium.

1955--A's go to Kansas City; Phils redo what is now Connie Mack Stadium.

1956--Phils make final right field wall cut; Senators continue size reductions.

1957--Dodgers play eight games in Jersey City after playing seven in 1956.

1958--Dodgers move to Los Angeles; Giants move to San Francisco.

1959--Dodgers reduce Coliseum right-center distance to increase home runs.

1960--Candlestick Park opens (becomes 3Com Park in the 90s).

1961--Old Senators become Minneapolis Twins; New Washington Senators and LA Angels born (new total home run record set in Wrigley Field in LA).

1962--NL expansion adds Astros/Mets; Dodger/RFK Stadiums open.

1963--Larger strike zone leads to death of offense for next five years.

1964--Shea Stadium opens; Free agent draft approved in December.

1965--Astrodome opens; A's try "pennant porch" before 1966 "spite screen."

1966--Braves go to Atlanta; Angels to Anaheim; New Busch Stadium opens.

1967--Visits to the mound before the pitcher must be removed are limited.

1968--Kansas City A's go to Oakland (and to largest foul ground in majors).

1969--Smaller strike zone; Lower mound; Royals/Pilots/Expos/Padres start.

1970--Seattle Pilots now Milwaukee Brewers; Three Rivers and Riverfront Stadiums open in Pittsburgh and Cincinnati respectively.

1971--Phils open Veterans Stadium; Giants enclose/enlarge Candlestick.

1972--New Washington Senators become the Texas Rangers.

1973--Designated Hitter rule used by AL; Royals Stadium opens.

1974--Yankees move to Shea Stadium while Yankee Stadium is rebuilt.

1975--DH now permanent; Free agent decision; Balls can use cowhide.

1976--Yankees return to rebuilt Yankee Stadium; First free-agent draft.

1977--Seattle Mariners/Toronto Blue Jays start play; Olympic Stadium opens.

1978--Giants replace carpet with grass; Rangers add upper deck.

1979--Inner eight-foot fence installed at Shea Stadium.

1980--Anaheim Stadium now fully enclosed and triple-decked.

1981--Season split in middle of year due to strike.

1982--Metrodome opens in Minneapolis; Padres move home plate back.

1983--All players must wear batting helmets (some 1982 players excepted).

1984--Bats to be thrown out if grip improvement material exceeds 18 inches.

1985--Astrodome fences moved in to increase offense.

1986--DH will be used only in AL parks in World Series.

1987--Plans set in motion to add lights to Wrigley Field for the 1988 season.

1988--Strike zone "clarified" in rules; First night game at Wrigley Field.

1989--Toronto SkyDome opens in June.

1990--Home plate moved in Kingdome changing outfield distances.

1991--New Comiskey Park opens in Chicago.

1992--Camden Yards opens in Baltimore.

1993--Colorado Rockies (Denver) and Florida Marlins (Miami) start play.

1994--The Ball Park at Arlington/Jacobs Field open; Strike stops season.

1995--Ongoing strike delays start of season; Coors Field in Denver opens.

1996--Strike zone re-clarified; Coliseum redo makes A's open in Las Vegas.

1997--Interleague play begins with no DH in NL parks; Turner Field opens.

1998--Tampa Bay Devil Rays/Arizona Diamondbacks start; Brewers to NL.

Part II
Offensive Measures

Runs by Year

Figure 2-1 shows runs per game by year for the American and National leagues from 1900 through 1910. The scale of the graph includes the highest and lowest values of runs per game in the century. The same scale is used for all decades so it is possible to see at a glance how runs in one decade compare to the highs and lows for the century. For example, in its first year of 1901, even in the "dead ball" era, the AL averaged 5.35 runs per game, a mark only six percent below its all-time high of 5.67 set in 1936 (Figure 2-4).

The exact values of runs per game for each year are shown below the graph together with the teams that led each league. Teams that led the majors are shown in bold. The list of leaders shows which teams were best during the decade. For example, the Tigers of Ty Cobb led the AL 4 years in a row at the end of the decade. The Yankees and Red Sox are the only other teams to lead the AL as many as 4 times in a row. The Dodgers hold the NL and major league record at 5 from 1949 through 1953. The Pirates of Honus Wagner topped the NL most often during the 1900-10 period.

Runs per game in the NL fell between 1900 and 1901 due to the adoption of the foul strike rule for the 1901 season and the player raids by the AL. The AL adopted the foul strike rule for the 1903 season, and runs decreased between 1902 and 1903 accordingly (the NL bounced back in 1903 when the player raids ceased). Runs fell in both leagues after 1903 due to the increasing use of the spitball and the decline of errors (Figure 3-21). Fewer errors meant fewer runners reaching first base and fewer advancing on the basepaths.

In the NL, runs per game fell to 3.33 in 1908, the low point for the century. The AL fell to 3.44 runs per game in 1908, but that was still higher than the 3.41 runs per game recorded by the AL in 1968 (Figure 2-7). The low point in 1968 ultimately led to the designated hitter rule in 1973.

The widespread use of the spitball (and other doctored pitches) after 1903 was not the only reason runs were low in the first decade. An equally important reason was the fact that one ball was expected to last the full game. Balls hit into the crowds around the field were retrieved and put back into play. By the end of most games the ball was dark and lumpy. The cork-center ball, patented in 1909, was meant to be more durable (and unavoidably more lively) under these circumstances. It was tested during the 1910 season and proclaimed as the official ball in 1911. Runs increased in 1910 and soared in 1911 (Figure 2-2).

Figure 2-1. AL/NL Runs Per Game 1900-10

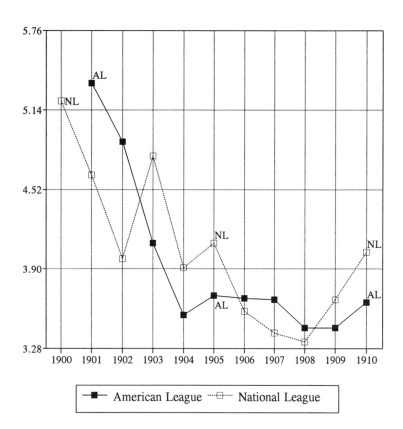

Year	AL Runs/Game	AL Leader	NL Runs/Game	NL Leader
1900	--	--	5.21	**Dodgers**
1901	5.35	**White Sox**	4.63	Cards
1902	4.89	**A's**	3.98	Pirates
1903	4.10	Red Sox	4.78	**Pirates**
1904	3.54	Indians	3.91	**Giants**
1905	3.69	A's	4.10	**Giants**
1906	3.67	Indians	3.57	**Cubs**
1907	3.66	**Tigers**	3.40	Pirates
1908	3.44	**Tigers**	3.33	Giants
1909	3.44	Tigers	3.66	**Pirates**
1910	3.64	Tigers	4.03	**Cubs**

Figure 2-2 shows runs per game by year for the American and National leagues from 1910 through 1920. The scale of the graph includes the highest and lowest values of runs per game in the century. The same scale is used for all decades so it is possible to see at a glance how runs in one decade compare to the highs and lows for the century. The exact values of runs per game for each year are shown below the graph together with the teams that led each league. Teams that led the majors are shown in bold.

The fulltime use of the cork-center ball in 1911 caused a surge in runs that lasted through the 1912 season. However, pitchers reacted to the new lively ball by substantially increasing their efforts to doctor the ball in any way possible. The spitball continued to be the pitch of choice, but a wide range of additional substances were applied to the ball and its surface was cut and defaced regularly. One ball was still expected to last the whole game, which helped pitchers in their effort to deaden the ball. Runs declined in 1913, and player raids by the new Federal League in 1914 and 1915 helped to reduce runs farther due to the dilution of talent. Runs fell nearly to the levels of the 1906-09 period by 1916, and the effects of WWI helped to keep them there through 1918. But runs climbed in the AL in 1919 as Babe Ruth began a revolution in home runs that would affect run scoring in baseball for the rest of the century.

As a fulltime outfielder in 1919, Babe Ruth broke all existing home run records and led the AL in runs (as he did through 1924) after Ty Cobb (4 times) and Eddie Collins (3 times) had been the leaders earlier in the decade (the Tigers and A's each led the AL 3 times). The 1919 White Sox, who won the pennant (and became the Black Sox by throwing the World Series), led the majors in runs over the Giants, who led the NL in 1919 for the 7th time in the decade (George Burns of the Giants led the NL in runs 5 times in the period).

This surge in runs made 1919 the best run scoring year for the AL since 1912, and even the NL had its best year since 1914. A short schedule was in place in 1919 because owners feared the forced early shutdown of 1918 due to WWI would affect 1919 attendance. But the AL had its second best attendance ever in 1919 and the majors had the highest total since 1911. The response to the exploits of Babe Ruth led to the 1920 rule changes eliminating doctored pitches, and the unfortunate death of Ray Chapman led to new balls being put into play much more often after mid-August. Babe Ruth and the AL set new records for home runs and attendance respectively in 1920 as the AL scored more runs in 1920 than in any year since it adopted the foul strike rule in 1903 (Figure 2-1).

Runs rose also in the NL in 1920, but the 1920 mark was well below the league peaks set earlier in the century. Many NL hitters were still concentrating on the level swing that was key to playing for one run, while AL hitters were copying the Babe Ruth approach of swinging from the heels and uppercutting the ball. The NL caught on to the new style in 1921.

Figure 2-2. AL/NL Runs Per Game 1910-20

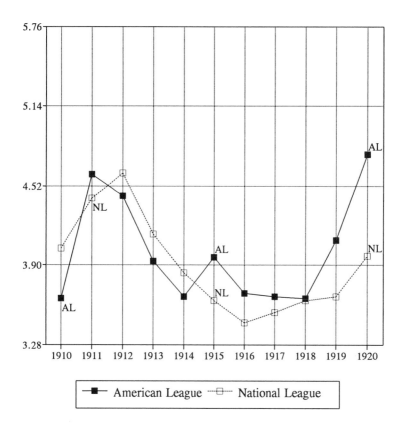

Year	AL Runs/Game	AL Leader	NL Runs/Game	NL Leader
1910	3.64	Tigers	4.03	**Cubs**
1911	4.61	**A's**	4.42	Giants
1912	4.44	Red Sox	4.62	**Giants**
1913	3.93	**A's**	4.14	Cubs
1914	3.65	**A's**	3.84	Giants
1915	3.96	**Tigers**	3.62	Phillies
1916	3.68	**Tigers**	3.45	Giants
1917	3.65	**White Sox**	3.53	Giants
1918	3.64	Yankees	3.62	**Reds**
1919	4.09	**White Sox**	3.65	Giants
1920	4.76	**Indians**	3.97	Giants

Figure 2-3 shows runs per game by year for the American and National leagues from 1920 through 1930. The scale of the graph includes the highest and lowest values of runs per game in the century. The same scale is used for all decades so it is possible to see at a glance how runs in one decade compare to the highs and lows for the century. The exact values of runs per game for each year are shown below the graph together with the teams that led each league. Teams that led the majors are shown in bold.

As described in the text accompanying Figure 2-2, NL hitters began to copy the Babe Ruth style in earnest in 1921, and the NL actually topped the AL in scoring in 1922 and 1923 (the NL also passed the AL in home runs in 1922 and led the AL for the rest of the decade). The AL regained the lead in runs in 1924 and held it until the NL surged ahead again in 1929 and 1930.

Much has been made of the performance of the NL in 1930 when the league set its all-time record for runs and batting average. It has been claimed that there was a "lively" ball introduced in the NL in 1930. But the NL increase in runs between 1928 and 1930 was less than the increase that occurred between 1920 and 1922. The cushioned-cork-center ball was introduced in 1926, but offense declined between 1925 and 1926 in both leagues. The NL declined in 1931 after ordering a change in the ball, but the AL did not fully match the change and set its all-time high in runs in 1936. There was nothing magical about 1930. It was just another statistical peak in a time of high offense.

In the 9 seasons between 1922 and 1930, the AL led the NL in runs 5 times while the AL leader led the majors in runs 6 times. The Yankees led the AL and the majors in runs 4 times between 1922 and 1930 (Babe Ruth led the AL in runs 6 times in the decade), even beating out the 1930 Cards who set an all-time NL team record that year. The Yankees led the AL in runs 27 times in the century and led the majors 19 times. Both marks are the best in baseball. The Cards led the NL in runs 14 times in the century (second to the Giants who led 20 times), but the Cards led the majors only once when they were the best war-time team in baseball in 1944. Rogers Hornsby played for the Cards when he led the NL in runs 4 times in the decade (other NL runs leaders in the period include Kiki Cuyler who led 2 times and the Waner brothers who each led once).

Similarly, the Yankees and Giants led their leagues in runs 5 times each between 1920 and 1930, but the Yankees led the majors all 5 times while the Giants led the majors only in 1924. This was typical of the way the Yankees dominated baseball in the 1920s (and 1930s). The NL was comparable to the AL in runs (and superior in home runs) in the 1920s. But no team could consistently score runs (or hit home runs) like the Yankees. The Yankees continued their domination in the 1930s even after Babe Ruth was gone. The AL peaked in runs in 1936 while the NL became the inferior league in spite of reversing in 1934 its disastrous 1931 decision to change the ball (Figure 2-4).

Figure 2-3. AL/NL Runs Per Game 1920-30

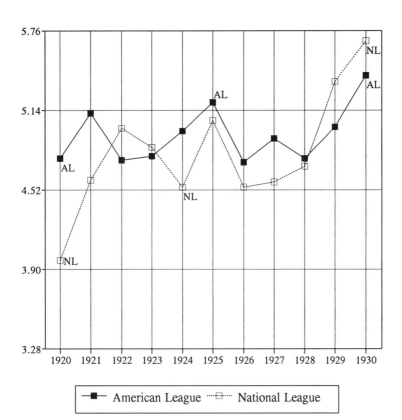

Year	AL Runs/Game	AL Leader	NL Runs/Game	NL Leader
1920	4.76	**Indians**	3.97	Giants
1921	5.12	**Yankees**	4.59	Giants
1922	4.75	**Browns**	5.00	Cards
1923	4.78	**Indians**	4.85	Giants
1924	4.98	Tigers	4.54	**Giants**
1925	5.20	Browns	5.06	**Pirates**
1926	4.73	**Yankees**	4.54	Cards
1927	4.92	**Yankees**	4.58	Giants
1928	4.76	**Yankees**	4.70	Pirates
1929	5.01	Tigers	5.36	**Cubs**
1930	5.41	**Yankees**	5.68	Cards

Figure 2-4 shows runs per game by year for the American and National leagues from 1930 through 1940. The scale of the graph includes the highest and lowest values of runs per game in the century. The same scale is used for all decades so it is possible to see at a glance how runs in one decade compare to the highs and lows for the century. The exact values of runs per game for each year are shown below the graph together with the teams that led each league. Teams that led the majors are shown in bold.

After reaching its all-time peak for runs in 1930, the NL ordered a new ball in 1931 with raised seams and a new cover in an attempt to reduce home runs. The AL went along with the raised seams but not the new cover. Offense declined slightly in the AL, but it fell dramatically in the NL. Runs declined by 21 percent in the NL between 1930 and 1931, and by 1933 they were down 30 percent from 1930. The 3.97 average for the NL in 1933 was its lowest mark since the league recorded the same mark in 1920. The AL scored 1.03 runs per game more than the NL in 1933, a difference that remains the largest ever between the leagues.

The NL owners voted to change to the AL ball for the 1934 season, and runs in the NL increased by 18 percent between 1933 and 1934. But the Yankees of the 1936-39 period were the most dominant team ever in baseball, and they drove the AL to its all-time high in runs in 1936. The poor performance of the NL in the 1931-33 period had already tagged the NL as the "pitcher's league," and the Yankees of the 1936-39 period reinforced the popular concept that the AL was the "hitter's league" (in some circles the NL became the "curveball league" and the AL the "fastball league").

The Yankees led the AL in scoring 8 times in the 11 seasons between 1930 and 1940, and the Tigers led the league the other 3 years. Both teams led the majors in scoring each time they led the AL in scoring. Before the designated hitter arrived in 1973, the AL led the NL in scoring 42 times while the NL led 30 times. The difference between the leagues was the period from 1931 through 1942 when the AL led the NL in scoring 12 straight years. Individually, Lou Gehrig led the AL in runs 4 times in the period while newcomers Joe DiMaggio, Hank Greenberg, and Ted Williams led one year each. In the NL, Chuck Klein led or tied 3 times and Arky Vaughan led 2 times.

In spite of the great performance by the Yankees in the 1930s and the 1934 reversal of the NL decline, both leagues reached 1940 at relatively low scoring levels. The AL in 1940 was at its lowest level since 1928, breaking a string of 12 straight years at or above 5.0 runs per game. Excluding its big dip in 1934, the NL in 1940 was at its lowest level since 1920. Pitchers had been slowly recovering from the sudden loss of their pitching tools in 1920, and although home runs remained near historically high levels, runs were primed to decline. By the middle of WWII runs were near "dead ball" levels again (Figure 2-5).

Figure 2-4. AL/NL Runs Per Game 1930-40

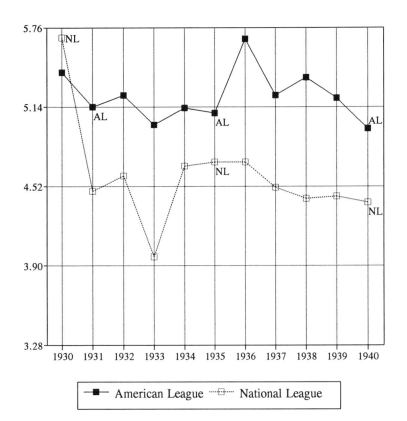

Year	AL Runs/Game	AL Leader	NL Runs/Game	NL Leader
1930	5.41	Yankees	5.68	Cards
1931	5.14	Yankees	4.48	Cubs
1932	5.23	Yankees	4.60	Phillies
1933	5.00	Yankees	3.97	Cards
1934	5.13	Tigers	4.68	Cards
1935	5.09	Tigers	4.71	Cubs
1936	5.67	Yankees	4.71	Pirates
1937	5.23	Yankees	4.51	Cubs
1938	5.37	Yankees	4.42	Reds
1939	5.21	Yankees	4.44	Cards
1940	4.97	Tigers	4.39	Pirates

Figure 2-5 shows runs per game by year for the American and National leagues from 1940 through 1950. The scale of the graph includes the highest and lowest values of runs per game in the century. The same scale is used for all decades so it is possible to see at a glance how runs in one decade compare to the highs and lows for the century. The exact values of runs per game for each year are shown below the graph together with the teams that led each league. Teams that led the majors are shown in bold.

Runs in 1940 were in decline in both leagues (Figure 2-4), and runs fell farther after 1940. The effect of WWII was small in 1941 as Ted Williams became the last hitter to exceed .400 and Joe DiMaggio captured the attention of the whole country with his 56 game hitting streak, but the draft had a much stronger effect in 1942. The combination of the draft and the poorer materials available for use in the ball in 1943 resulted in the lowest level of runs in the majors since 1918 when WWI was having its maximum impact.

The NL rebounded higher than the AL from the 1943 lows, but runs fell again in 1946 even though the players (and record numbers of fans) were back from WWII by then. The Giants sparked an upturn in runs in 1947 when they set what was then the all-time major league home run record (and was the NL peak until 1997). The new talent pool made available by the breaking of the color line by Jackie Robinson helped the upturn continue through 1950 (when the strike zone was changed in favor of hitters). The AL averaged over 5.0 runs per game in 1950 for the first time since 1939, but no one suspected at the time that the 5.0 mark would not be topped again until 1994.

The Red Sox set an all-time team record for runs in 1950 (in the majors only three Yankee teams from the 1930s ever scored more). The 1950 Red Sox also are the last team in the majors to have a team batting average above .300. The 1940s marked the emergence of the Red Sox as a great run scoring team. They led the AL in runs 7 times between 1941 and 1951 with Ted Williams leading the league 5 times (the Yankees led 4 times with unknown Snuffy Stirnweiss leading the AL twice in the war years). The Red Sox joined the Tigers and Yankees as the only AL teams to lead in runs 4 consecutive years (1948 through 1951).

In the NL the Dodgers emerged as a great scoring team. Topping the Cards, who led 3 times with Stan Musial leading twice, the Dodgers led the NL in scoring 8 times between 1941 and 1953, doing it 5 times in a row from 1949 through 1953. They are the only team in the majors to do so (even the Colorado Rockies have not been able to top that record). Pete Reiser, Arky Vaughan, Eddie Stanky, and Pee Wee Reese all led the NL once for the Dodgers in the period. The Dodgers became a pitching team after moving to Dodger Stadium and have led the NL in runs only twice since 1955.

The Red Sox and Dodgers helped their leagues leave the 1940s at a high point in 1950, but the 1950s produced a much different result (Figure 2-6).

Figure 2-5. AL/NL Runs Per Game 1940-50

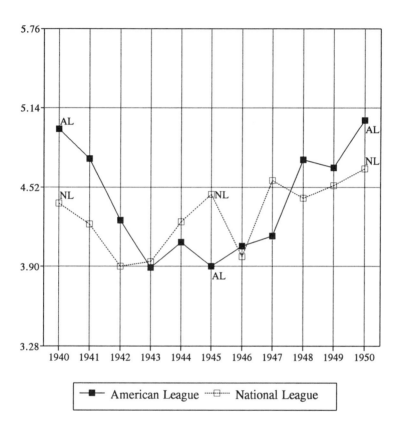

Year	AL Runs/Game	AL Leader	NL Runs/Game	NL Leader
1940	4.97	**Tigers**	4.39	Pirates
1941	4.74	**Red Sox**	4.23	Dodgers
1942	4.26	**Yankees**	3.90	Cards
1943	3.89	Yankees	3.94	**Dodgers**
1944	4.09	Red Sox	4.25	**Cards**
1945	3.90	Yankees	4.46	**Dodgers**
1946	4.06	**Red Sox**	3.98	Cards
1947	4.14	Yankees	4.57	**Giants**
1948	4.73	**Red Sox**	4.43	Giants
1949	4.67	**Red Sox**	4.53	Dodgers
1950	5.04	**Red Sox**	4.66	Dodgers

Figure 2-6 shows runs per game by year for the American and National leagues from 1950 through 1960. The scale of the graph includes the highest and lowest values of runs per game in the century. The same scale is used for all decades so it is possible to see at a glance how runs in one decade compare to the highs and lows for the century. The exact values of runs per game for each year are shown below the graph together with the teams that led each league. Teams that led the majors are shown in bold.

The 1950 strike zone change favoring hitters may have helped the AL reach 5.04 runs in 1950, but AL runs fell after 1950 and the NL topped its 1950 level only in 1953. Walks also fell from record highs in 1949 and 1950 (Figure 3-15) even though the strike zone change favored higher walks. Home runs hit what were then record levels in both leagues leaving the impression that the decade was a time of high offense. But run scoring in the 1950s does not support this perception. NL runs peaked in 1953 when the Dodgers finished their run of five straight years as the NL's highest scoring team. The Dodgers also set an all-time NL record in 1953 for runs scored in a five year period, topping the record set by the Giants in the 1927-31 period. The NL set its still standing home run record in 1955, but runs declined from the 1953 level and have not topped it since. By 1960 NL runs were at their lowest level since 1952.

AL runs were also lower in 1960 than in 1950. The Yankees led the AL in runs 6 times in the period (Joe DiMaggio led the AL in 1951 and Mickey Mantle led 5 times afterwards). But after 1960 the Yankees would lead the AL in scoring only 4 more times. The Yankees would continue to be winners in future decades, but other teams would become the leaders in scoring runs. The period of Yankee offensive dominance that began in the 1920s would end in the early 1960s. The Dodgers also had their last hurrah as a high scoring team in the 1950s with Duke Snider leading 3 times. Stan Musial led the NL twice and new names such as Frank Robinson, Willie Mays, and Hank Aaron showed up on the leader's list.

The level of home runs being hit in the 1950s blinded the owners to the fact that pitchers were once more beginning to dominate hitters. Strikeouts were soaring (Figure 3-6) and batting averages (Figure 2-16) had fallen a little below the already low levels of the 1940s. From 1957 onward runs were clustering very close to the line marking a level of 4.30 runs per game. This was below the level reached by both leagues in 1911 and 1912 (Figure 2-2) after the surge in offense that resulted from the introduction of the cork-center ball. Except for the years during and just after WWII, the AL in 1958 scored its lowest level of runs since Babe Ruth started the home run revolution in 1919.

This overlooked decline in runs in the late 1950s helps to explain why the seemingly small change in the strike zone in 1963 (Figure 2-7) had such a devastating effect on scoring runs. The careful balance between hitter and pitcher was suddenly tilted strongly in favor of the pitcher in 1963.

Figure 2-6. AL/NL Runs Per Game 1950-60

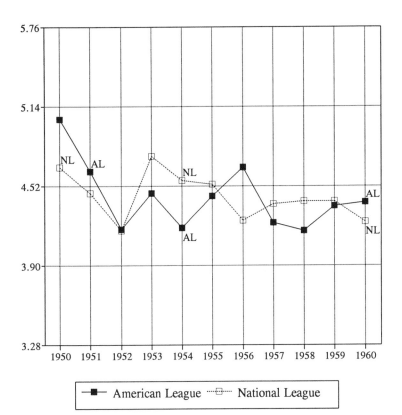

Year	AL Runs/Game	AL Leader	NL Runs/Game	NL Leader
1950	5.04	**Red Sox**	4.66	Dodgers
1951	4.63	Red Sox	4.46	**Dodgers**
1952	4.18	Indians	4.17	**Dodgers**
1953	4.46	Yankees	4.75	**Dodgers**
1954	4.19	**Yankees**	4.56	Cards
1955	4.44	Tigers	4.53	**Dodgers**
1956	4.66	**Yankees**	4.25	Reds
1957	4.23	Yankees	4.38	**Braves**
1958	4.17	**Yankees**	4.40	Giants
1959	4.36	Indians	4.40	**Reds**
1960	4.39	**Yankees**	4.24	Pirates

Figure 2-7 shows runs per game by year for the American and National leagues from 1960 through 1970. The scale of the graph includes the highest and lowest values of runs per game in the century. The same scale is used for all decades so it is possible to see at a glance how runs in one decade compare to the highs and lows for the century. The exact values of runs per game for each year are shown below the graph together with the teams that led each league. Teams that led the majors are shown in bold.

As shown in Figure 2-6, runs in 1960 were near a low point for the 1950-60 period. Expansion in the AL in 1961 led to a small increase in runs that year, but the NL expansion of 1962 produced a small decline in runs in 1962. The strike zone change in favor of pitchers in 1963 (Table 1-1) immediately moved runs in both leagues down to their lowest levels in decades. In the AL, runs in 1963 reached their lowest level since 1945. Except for 1943 and 1945, runs in the AL in 1963 were at their lowest level since 1918. No exceptions were needed in the NL. Runs in 1963 in the NL reached their lowest level since 1919.

Pitchers became even more dominant after 1963. Runs in the AL fell steadily and hit an all-time league low in 1968. Only the all-time twentieth century low of 3.33 runs per game by the NL in 1908 (and its mark of 3.40 runs per game in 1907) fall below the AL level of 3.41 runs per game in 1968. The NL also declined in 1968 to 3.43 runs per game, its third lowest mark in the century. The combined level of runs in 1963 lead only 1908, a year when the cork-center ball and Babe Ruth were still unknown. Considering the improvement in the ball and the change in the style of play, 1968 was the deadest of all the "dead ball" years in the century. The 1963-68 period truly marked the death of offense.

The owners tried to return pitchers and hitters to a point of balance in 1969 by reversing the 1963 strike zone change and lowering the mound. Runs increased in both leagues in 1969, although neither league did much better than return to their highs for the 1963-68 period. Runs in the AL increased by a small amount in 1969, but in the NL that year runs rose to their highest level since 1962 (which in turn was the league's best since 1955.) This difference between the AL and the NL after the 1963-68 period would have a profound effect on the decision to use the designated hitter in 1973.

The death of offense in the 1963-68 period also produced some new runs leaders in both leagues. The Twins led the AL in 1963 for the first time in the century, and they led the league 4 times in the 7 years between 1963 and 1969. This was primarily due to Harmon Killebrew who was also leading the Twins to their best home records in this period. The Braves, who had led the NL for the first time in 1957, led the league and the majors in runs in 1964 and 1966. NL teams, demonstrating the league's superiority over the AL in the period, led the majors in runs 6 of the 7 years between 1964 and 1970. This would change dramatically after the DH was introduced in 1973 (Figure 2-8).

Figure 2-7. AL/NL Runs Per Game 1960-70

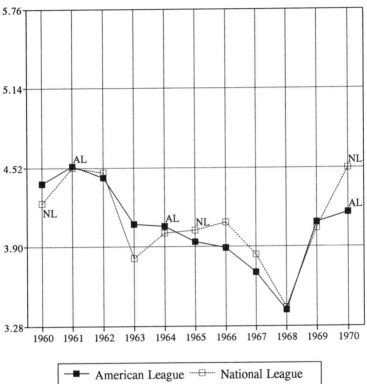

Year	AL Runs/Game	AL Leader	NL Runs/Game	NL Leader
1960	4.39	**Yankees**	4.24	Pirates
1961	4.53	**Tigers**	4.52	Giants
1962	4.44	Yankees	4.48	**Giants**
1963	4.08	**Twins**	3.81	Cards
1964	4.06	Twins	4.01	**Braves**
1965	3.94	Twins	4.03	**Reds**
1966	3.89	Orioles	4.09	**Braves**
1967	3.70	**Red Sox**	3.84	Cubs
1968	3.41	Tigers	3.43	**Reds**
1969	4.09	Twins	4.05	**Reds**
1970	4.17	Orioles	4.52	**Giants**

Figure 2-8 shows runs per game by year for the American and National leagues from 1970 through 1980. The scale of the graph includes the highest and lowest values of runs per game in the century. The same scale is used for all decades so it is possible to see at a glance how runs in one decade compare to the highs and lows for the century. The exact values of runs per game for each year are shown below the graph together with the teams that led each league. Teams that led the majors are shown in bold.

Runs rebounded in 1970 from their lows of the 1963-68 period, but the recovery did not last past 1970. Runs fell in both leagues in 1971, and then held steady in 1972 in the NL. But runs fell to 3.47 runs per game in the AL in 1972. This was the lowest level in AL history except for the lows of 1907 and 1908 and the all-time low of 1968. Deciding it had had enough of the imbalance between pitching and hitting, the AL voted to adopt a designated hitter rule as an experiment for the 1973 season. The experiment was to be reconsidered in 1975, and it was made permanent that year. The NL did not agree to the rule partially because NL runs were above record lows in 1972, and they increased from their 1972 levels in the 1973-75 period. As a result the leagues played under different rules in 1973 for the first time since 1902. Further, the AL regained dominance over the NL in scoring runs and hitting home runs.

Except for 1967, NL teams led the majors in runs every year from 1964 through 1976. This was the best such performance for the NL in the century. But 1974 was the last year the NL led the AL in runs per game. The use of the DH produced a 23 percent increase in runs per game in the AL between 1972 and 1973, and the AL topped the NL in runs in 1973 for only the second time since 1965. The NL came back to lead the AL by 0.05 runs per game in 1974, but the AL has led the NL in every year since. The AL has also led the NL in home runs per game in every year since the DH was adopted in 1973. The Twins took over the major league lead in runs per game in 1977, and AL teams have led the majors in runs per game every year since except for the 1990 Mets (Figure 2-9). In the NL Pete Rose led in scoring 3 times and Keith Hernandez led twice in the period. In the AL only Carl Yastrzemski led as many as 2 times.

By the end of the decade the AL was steadily increasing its lead over the NL. In 1979 the AL scored 4.67 runs per game, its highest level since 1950 and 35 percent above its low point of 1972. The NL, on the other hand, averaged 4.14 runs per game for the last five years of the decade (1975 through 1979), exactly the same mark they averaged in the 1940-44 period when the effects of WWII were driving runs down in both leagues. By declining to adopt the DH, the NL had insured that it would be looking up at the AL indefinitely in terms of offense. Further, the NL was now struggling to stay above an average of four runs per game, and before another decade had passed the NL would find itself back in "dead ball" days (Figure 2-9).

Figure 2-8. AL/NL Runs Per Game 1970-80

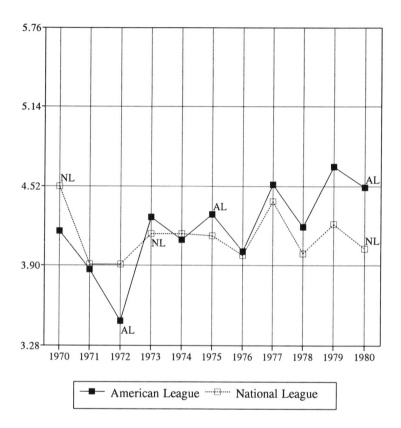

Year	AL Runs/Game	AL Leader	NL Runs/Game	NL Leader
1970	4.17	Orioles	4.52	**Giants**
1971	3.87	Orioles	3.91	**Pirates**
1972	3.47	Red Sox	3.91	**Astros**
1973	4.28	A's	4.15	**Braves**
1974	4.10	Red Sox	4.15	**Dodgers**
1975	4.30	Red Sox	4.13	**Reds**
1976	4.01	Yankees	3.98	**Reds**
1977	4.53	**Twins**	4.40	Phillies
1978	4.20	**Brewers**	3.99	Dodgers
1979	4.67	**Angels**	4.22	Pirates
1980	4.51	**Tigers**	4.03	Cards

Figure 2-9 shows runs per game by year for the American and National leagues from 1980 through 1990. The scale of the graph includes the highest and lowest values of runs per game in the century. The same scale is used for all decades so it is possible to see at a glance how runs in one decade compare to the highs and lows for the century. The exact values of runs per game for each year are shown below the graph together with the teams that led each league. Teams that led the majors are shown in bold.

Runs fell in both leagues in 1981 due to the mid-year player's strike. Runs rebounded in 1982 and climbed to a peak in 1987. There is no clear reason for the 1987 peak, but cries of a conspiracy to sneak a lively ball into play were heard once more. However, there were no cries of a conspiracy to deaden the ball when runs fell off sharply in 1988. People familiar with statistics know that all processes have "runs" in which a steady increase (or decrease) in the item being measured occurs before the normal average level is regained. The AL averaged 4.47 runs per game in the 1980s and the NL 4.08. The 1987 peak was about 10 percent above average in both leagues, a reasonable value for any decade. The key feature in 1987 was a surge in home runs. The AL set what was then its all-time record for home runs per game in 1987, and the NL had its best year since 1961 (Figure 3-9).

The AL scored its highest level of runs since 1950 in 1987, and the NL had its best year since 1970. But in 1988 the AL was down by 11 percent and the NL by 14 percent. The 3.88 runs per game averaged by the NL in 1988 was its lowest since 1968, and except for 1963 and 1967 in the 1963-68 period, the lowest in the NL since 1919. It was also the beginning of a period (1988 through 1992) when the NL looked like it had returned to the days before 1919 in terms of runs, batting average, and double plays (the latter being a good measure of activity on the basepaths). Only the advent of expansion to the mile high city of Denver in 1993 would pull the NL out of its doldrums (Figure 2-10).

In 1990 the NL was closer to the AL in runs than in any year since 1976. The 1990 Mets became the first NL team since the 1976 Reds to lead the majors in runs (the Mets are still the last NL team to do so). The Mets led the NL 4 times in the period, but Ryne Sandberg of the Cubs and Tim Raines of the Expos were at the top most often in runs. Similarly, the Tigers and Red Sox led the AL (and the majors) in runs three times each in the 1980s, but Rickey Henderson, moving between the A's and Yankees, led the AL 5 times in runs with Paul Molitor of the Brewers leading twice. Wade Boggs of the Red Sox did lead once and tie Henderson once for the lead.

The Red Sox, Tigers, and Mets would be replaced by expansion teams as runs leaders in the 1990s. The Mariners, born in 1977, took over the AL lead in 1996, and the Rockies, born in 1993, became the top hitting team in the NL by a wide margin only two years after their birth (Figure 2-10).

Figure 2-9. AL/NL Runs Per Game 1980-90

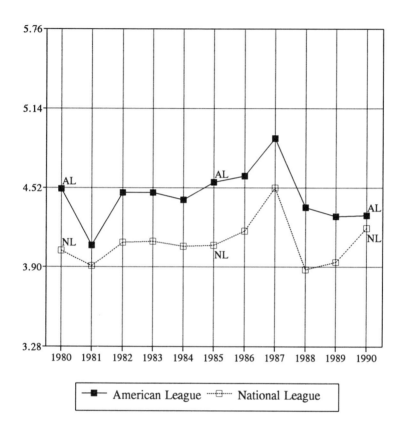

Year	AL Runs/Game	AL Leader	NL Runs/Game	NL Leader
1980	4.51	**Tigers**	4.03	Cards
1981	4.07	**Red Sox**	3.91	Phillies
1982	4.48	**Brewers**	4.09	Braves
1983	4.48	**White Sox**	4.10	Braves
1984	4.42	**Tigers**	4.06	Cubs
1985	4.56	**Yankees**	4.07	Cards
1986	4.61	**Indians**	4.18	Mets
1987	4.90	**Tigers**	4.52	Mets
1988	4.36	**Red Sox**	3.88	Mets
1989	4.29	**Red Sox**	3.96	Cubs
1990	4.30	Blue Jays	4.20	**Mets**

Figure 2-10 shows runs per game by year for the American and National leagues from 1988 through 1998. The scale of the graph includes the highest and lowest values of runs per game in the century. The same scale is used for all decades so it is possible to see at a glance how runs in one decade compare to the highs and lows for the century. The exact values of runs per game for each year are shown below the graph together with the teams that led each league. Teams that led the majors are shown in bold.

Figure 2-10 shows the impact of expansion in 1993. Before 1993 the AL averaged 4.35 runs per game for the 1988-92 period, a little lower than the 4.40 it had averaged since the birth of the DH in 1973. The NL averaged 4.00 runs per game from 1988 through 1992, 8 percent below the AL for that period. But if the decades between 1910 and 1990 are split evenly into 5 year periods, the only periods lower for runs per game than the 1988-92 period in the NL are the 1965-69 and 1915-19 periods. The NL had a batting average of .246 in 1989, the third lowest year in the 80 seasons since 1909. In 1991, the NL averaged only 0.79 double plays per game, the lowest in the league since 1919 in spite of the much better fielding in 1991. The NL had returned to "dead ball" days.

Everything changed in 1993. Runs per game increased by 16 percent in the NL between 1992 and 1993, moved up a little in 1994, and then settled at an average of 4.63 from 1994 through 1998. This was 19 percent above the 1992 low and 16 percent above the average for the 1988-92 period. Only the 1926-30 period, when the NL set its all-time 5 year record of 4.97 runs per game, can top the 1994-98 period. Results in the AL were similar even though it did not play a direct role in the 1993 expansion. Runs climbed 9 percent between 1992 and 1993 and climbed another 11 percent between 1993 and 1994. The AL averaged 5.12 runs per game from 1994 through 1998. This was 19 percent above 1992 and 18 percent above the average for the 1988-92 period. Only 5 year periods selected from the 1930s, when the AL set its all-time runs per game records, can top the 5.12 runs per game averaged by the AL in the 1994-98 period.

The primary reason for the surge after 1993 was the arrival of a critical mass of hitters who grew up with the DH (and aluminum bats) and were used to taking big swings at any point in the count. It was the second coming of the Babe Ruth effect except that this time pitchers set all-time highs for strikeouts rather than all-time lows. Pitchers had not lost their tools as they had after 1920, but hitters were willing to strike out frequently as long as they drove in plenty of runs in the bargain. The NL, the only baseball league in the world not using the DH, still benefitted greatly from the generation that grew up with the DH. The NL also got extra boosts from arcade baseball in Denver and the start of interleague play that put the DH in the NL for part of the year and took it away from the AL. But the AL, experts in the use of the DH, continued to outscore the NL by 11 percent while setting all-time home run records (Figure 2-30).

Figure 2-10. AL/NL Runs Per Game 1988-98

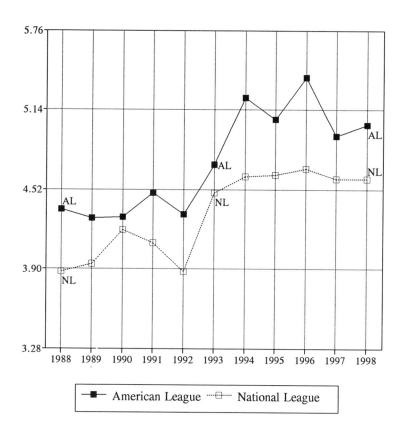

Year	AL Runs/Game	AL Leader	NL Runs/Game	NL Leader
1988	4.36	**Red Sox**	3.88	Mets
1989	4.29	**Red Sox**	3.94	Cubs
1990	4.30	Blue Jays	4.20	**Mets**
1991	4.49	**Rangers**	4.10	Pirates
1992	4.32	**Tigers**	3.88	Pirates
1993	4.71	**Tigers**	4.49	Phillies
1994	5.23	**Indians**	4.62	Reds
1995	5.06	**Indians**	4.63	Rockies
1996	5.39	**Mariners**	4.68	Rockies
1997	4.93	**Mariners**	4.60	Rockies
1998	5.01	**Yankees**	4.60	Astros

Figure 2-11 shows batting average by year for the American and National leagues from 1900 through 1910. The scale of the graph includes the highest and lowest values of batting average in the century. The same scale is used for all decades so it is possible to see at a glance how batting averages in one decade compare to the highs and lows for the century. The exact values of batting average for each year are shown below the graph together with the teams that led each league. Teams that led the majors are shown in bold.

More hits produce both more runs and higher batting averages, but runs and batting averages do not necessarily track each other across the decades. Decreasing walks and errors, for example, mean fewer runs for the same number of hits. Increasing home runs, however, can mean more runs for the same number of hits. And a big swing intended to try to hit home runs can reduce total hits and thus batting averages while runs are maintained at relatively high levels. All of these effects took place between 1900 and 1998.

Even though the first decade of the century belongs to the "dead ball" era, both leagues started out with high batting averages. The NL level of .279 in 1900 just misses the league's top ten list for the century, and the AL's level of .277 in its first year of 1901 makes the league's top 20 list. The adoption of the foul strike rule by the NL in 1901 and the AL in 1903 produced substantial drops in batting average from the previous year. This is an excellent example of how a seemingly simple rule change can greatly affect play on the field.

Except for the rebound in 1903 by the NL when the AL stopped its player raids, batting averages in both leagues generally declined through the rest of the decade due to the increasing use of the spitball and other "doctored" pitches. The fact that one (increasingly dark and lumpy) ball was meant to last the whole game was another reason for the decrease in batting average through the decade.

Both leagues hit a low of .239 in 1908. The AL was slightly lower than the NL in 1908, but .239 represents the all-time low for the NL in this century. The AL reached an all-time major league low of .230 in 1968 (Figure 2-17), but the AL also hit .236 in 1967 and .239 in 1972. Repeating its 1908 dip in 1972 was a major factor in the adoption of the DH rule by the AL in 1973.

The Giants and Pirates led the NL in batting average during the decade, with the Giants leading both the league and the majors four times. Honus Wagner of the Pirates was the prime individual leader for the NL. The Indians and Tigers led the AL with Nap Lajoie leading the Indians in the middle of the decade. Ty Cobb hit only .240 in his rookie year of 1905, but by 1907 Cobb led the Tigers to three straight batting average titles as well as three straight pennants.

The cork-center ball was selectively tested during the 1910 season. The NL had a sharp increase in batting average in 1910, and when the cork-center ball was declared the official ball for the full 1911 season both leagues surged to their highest averages since adopting the foul strike rule (Figure 2-12).

Figure 2-11. AL/NL Batting Average 1900-10

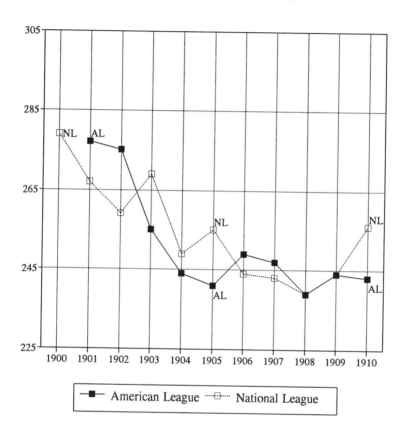

Year	AL Batting Avg	AL Leader	NL Batting Avg	NL Leader
1900	--	--	279	**Dodgers**
1901	277	**Yankees**	267	Dodgers
1902	275	**Indians**	259	Pirates
1903	255	Red Sox	269	**Reds**
1904	244	Indians	249	**Giants**
1905	241	Indians	255	**Giants**
1906	249	**Indians**	244	Cubs
1907	247	**Tigers**	243	Pirates
1908	239	Tigers	239	**Giants**
1909	244	**Tigers**	244	Pirates
1910	243	A's	256	**Giants**

Figure 2-12 shows batting average by year for the American and National leagues from 1910 through 1920. The scale of the graph includes the highest and lowest values of batting average in the century. The same scale is used for all decades so it is possible to see at a glance how batting averages in one decade compare to the highs and lows for the century. The exact values of batting average for each year are shown below the graph together with the teams that led each league. Teams that led the majors are shown in bold.

The new cork-center ball caused a surge in hitting in 1911. Ty Cobb and "Shoeless Joe" Jackson both hit over .400, the first time in the century two batters had done so in the same year (Cobb won 9 batting titles in the 1910-20 period, while the best in the NL was 2 each by Jake Daubert and Edd Roush). However, pitchers reacted to the new lively ball by substantially increasing their efforts to doctor the ball in any way possible. The spitball continued to be the pitch of choice, but a wide range of additional substances were applied to the ball and its surface was cut and defaced regularly. One ball was still expected to last the whole game and this helped pitchers in their effort to deaden the ball.

This extra effort by pitchers produced a decline in batting averages by 1913, and player raids by the new Federal League in 1914 and 1915 helped to reduce averages farther due to the dilution of talent. Batting averages stabilized at these lower levels as averages remained nearly constant from 1914 through 1917. There was a slight increase in 1918 in spite of the effects of WWI, and then averages climbed in 1919 as Babe Ruth began his revolution in home runs. The new rules in 1920 that created a much cleaner ball to hit enabled the AL to set what was then a league record in batting average, while the NL had its best mark since 1900, the year before it adopted the foul strike rule.

The A's were the premier team in baseball in the first part of the decade, and they led the league in batting average 5 straight years from 1910 through 1914, leading the majors 3 times. The Giants led the NL 4 years in a row and led the majors in the 2 years the A's did not. Until the Rockies were born, only the Red Sox had been able to win as many as 4 consecutive batting average titles since the A's and Giants set their records (the Red Sox did it from 1987 through 1990). The Rockies made it 4 straight in 1998 (Figure 2-20), and they may lead the NL every year indefinitely unless the NL adopts the designated hitter.

Ironically, the A's have led the AL only a total of 8 times in batting average, ranking 6th on the league's leader list (Table 4-3). They last led the league in 1968, and the only other years they led after 1914 were 1925 and 1932. The Giants have led the NL a total of 13 times, but after 1930 they led only in 1962 and 1993. The Giants did, however, set the all-time major league record at .319 in the league's record year of 1930 (Table 4-10).

As high as the record of the 1930 Giants seems, hitting over .300 as a team became a routine event in the decade after the rule changes of 1920.

Figure 2-12. AL/NL Batting Average 1910-20

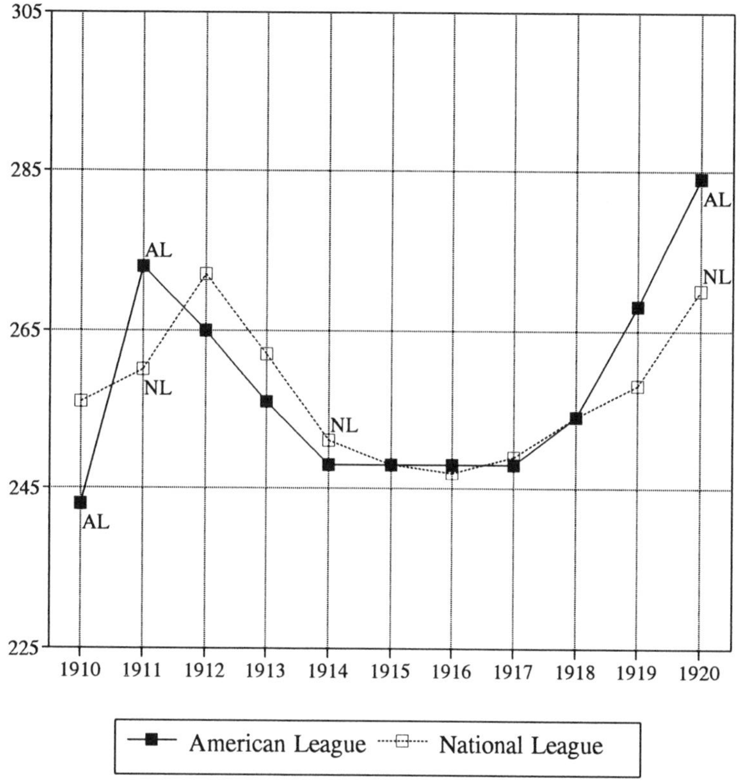

Year	AL Batting Avg	AL Leader	NL Batting Avg	NL Leader
1910	243	A's	256	**Giants**
1911	273	**A's**	260	Giants
1912	265	A's	272	**Giants**
1913	256	**A's**	262	Giants
1914	248	A's	251	Dodgers
1915	248	**Tigers**	248	Cards
1916	248	**Tigers**	247	Dodgers
1917	248	Tigers	249	**Reds**
1918	254	Indians	254	**Reds**
1919	268	**White Sox**	258	Giants
1920	284	**Browns**	270	Cards

Figure 2-13 shows batting average by year for the American and National leagues from 1920 through 1930. The scale of the graph includes the highest and lowest values of batting average in the century. The same scale is used for all decades so it is possible to see at a glance how batting averages in one decade compare to the highs and lows for the century. The exact values of batting average for each year are shown below the graph together with the teams that led each league. Teams that led the majors are shown in bold.

The 1920 rule changes (banning trick pitches and having new balls introduced into play much more often) left pitchers relatively helpless in the 1920s because key tools had been removed from their tool kit. Strikeouts in each league fell to the lowest levels since the adoption of the foul strike rule (Figure 3-3). Runs and home runs soared, but while runs would reach high levels again in the 1930s and 1990s, and home runs would regularly increase making the 1920s look like a "dead ball" decade, batting averages would never again approach the levels reached in the 1920s once pitchers adapted to the loss of their tools.

The AL immediately reached its all-time high batting average in 1921. Averages clustered around the .285 line the rest of the decade, but the AL never exceeded the .292 league average reached in 1921 (1925 was actually almost one full percentage point below 1921). The NL matched the AL in batting average during the decade, but there was a NL surge in 1929 that led to a peak in 1930 when the NL set the all-time major league record of .303. Much has been written about this 1930 record concerning speculation that there must have been some sort of extra-lively ball used in 1930. But the rate of increase from 1928 to 1929 was actually about 50 percent larger than the rate of increase from 1929 to 1930. The year 1930 was simply the NL's statistical peak for the period.

The Tigers set the all-time AL team record in 1921 with an average of .316 (Table 4-10). This is not far below the .319 of the 1930 Giants. Farther, 4 teams in the AL exceeded .300 in 1921, not grossly different from the 6 NL teams that did so in 1930. A total of 33 teams hit over .300 in the 10 years from 1921 through 1930, an average of 3.3 teams per year. Thus, it was not uncommon for teams to exceed .300 in this period. Individually, Rogers Hornsby hit over .400 three different times between 1920 and 1930, while George Sisler did it twice and Ty Cobb, Harry Heilmann, and Bill Terry each did so once. But only Terry (.401 in 1930) did it after 1925. Essentially the NL reached its peak in totally dominating pitchers nine years after the AL and at a somewhat higher level.

Although Hornsby won 7 batting titles and Heilmann 4, the team leaders were well scattered during the period. The Pirates led their league 4 times with the Tigers, Yankees, and Giants leading 3 times each. Seven other teams also got to be league leaders at least once in the decade. This confirms that the rise in batting averages was widespread in the 1920s as pitchers struggled to regain their balance. The 1930s would mark their return to a more competitive position.

Figure 2-13. AL/NL Batting Average 1920-30

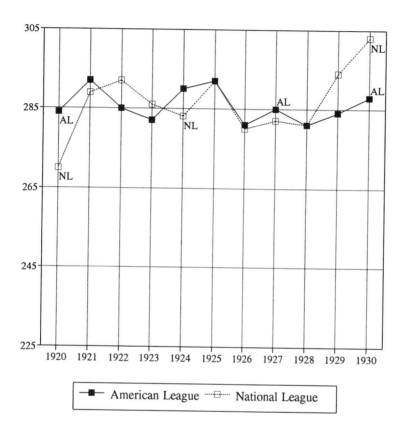

Year	AL Batting Avg	AL Leader	NL Batting Avg	NL Leader
1920	284	**Browns**	270	Cards
1921	292	**Tigers**	289	Cards
1922	285	**Browns**	292	Pirates
1923	282	**Indians**	286	Giants
1924	290	Tigers	283	**Giants**
1925	292	A's	292	**Pirates**
1926	281	**Senators**	280	Reds
1927	285	**Yankees**	282	Pirates
1928	281	Yankees	281	**Pirates**
1929	284	Tigers	294	**Phillies**
1930	288	Yankees	303	**Giants**

Figure 2-14 shows batting average by year for the American and National leagues from 1930 through 1940. The scale of the graph includes the highest and lowest values of batting average in the century. The same scale is used for all decades so it is possible to see at a glance how batting averages in one decade compare to the highs and lows for the century. The exact values of batting average for each year are shown below the graph together with the teams that led each league. Teams that led the majors are shown in bold.

The NL adopted a new ball for 1931 in an attempt to reduce home runs. The ball had raised seams and a new cover. The new ball resulted in reduced runs and batting averages as well as reduced home runs. The AL accepted the raised seams, but it did not accept the new cover. Batting averages declined a little for the AL, but not nearly as much as in the NL. In a good example of the decoupling of batting averages and runs, the NL and AL had nearly the same averages in 1931 and 1932, with the AL having an larger edge in 1933, the last year the NL used its new ball. But the AL greatly outscored the NL over the 1931-33 period (Figure 2-4) with 1933 marking an all-time high in the difference between the leagues in scoring runs. The AL also hit more home runs than the NL in the period, but the differences were modest (Figure 2-24).

When the NL decided to use the AL ball for the 1934 season (both leagues would always the same ball after that), batting averages were the same in both leagues (the NL was actually slightly above than the AL). Home runs were also nearly identical, but the AL continued to outscore the NL by a wide margin. As the decade progressed, NL batting averages slowly declined. After reaching a decade peak in 1936, when the AL set its all-time record for runs, AL batting averages also declined for the rest of the decade. But AL batting averages led NL batting averages from 1936 onward by the largest margins of the decade. By 1940 batting averages for both the AL and NL were at their lowest levels since 1919. Pitchers finally had regained a competitive balance with hitters.

Part of the reason the AL was far ahead of the NL in runs during the 1930s was the fact that the Yankees of the 1930s scored runs at a rate that has never been equalled in either league. They led the majors in runs 8 of the 10 years between 1930 and 1939 (the Tigers led the other 2 years). But the Yankees only led the AL in batting average in 1930 and 1931. The Tigers led 4 times and the Red Sox led in 1938 and 1939 (Ted Williams was a rookie in 1939), marking the emergence of the Red Sox as a great hitting team. The Red Sox and Tigers lead the Yankees at the top of the AL batting average leader's list (Table 4-3), although the Tigers have not led the AL since 1961.

The 1930s also marked the replacement of the Giants by the Cards in terms of leading the NL in batting average. The Cards edge out the Pirates in years leading the NL in batting average, with the Giants third. But the Giants have not been competitive with the Cards and Pirates in batting average since 1930.

Figure 2-14. AL/NL Batting Average 1930-40

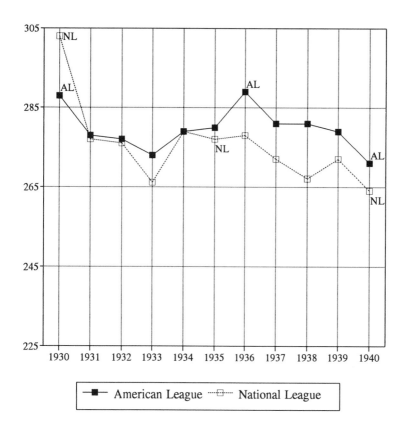

Year	AL Batting Avg	AL Leader	NL Batting Avg	NL Leader
1930	288	Yankees	303	**Giants**
1931	278	**Yankees**	277	Cubs
1932	277	A's	276	**Phillies**
1933	273	**Senators**	266	Pirates
1934	279	**Tigers**	279	Cards
1935	280	**Tigers**	277	Cubs
1936	289	**Indians**	278	Pirates
1937	281	**Tigers**	272	Cubs
1938	281	**Red Sox**	267	Cards
1939	279	Red Sox	272	**Cards**
1940	271	**Tigers**	264	Pirates

Figure 2-15 shows batting average by year for the American and National leagues from 1940 through 1950. The scale of the graph includes the highest and lowest values of batting average in the century. The same scale is used for all decades so it is possible to see at a glance how batting averages in one decade compare to the highs and lows for the century. The exact values of batting average for each year are shown below the graph together with the teams that led each league. Teams that led the majors are shown in bold.

Batting averages continued to fall at the beginning of the decade, and the combination of the WWII draft and the poorer materials available for use in the ball soon drove averages to their lowest levels in 25 years. The NL hit its low for the decade in 1942 and the AL followed in 1943. But the leagues behaved differently after that. The NL rose to its decade peak in 1945 as "replacement" players took over, and it could not exceed the 1945 level for batting average even as players returned from WWII and runs began to rise (Figure 2-5). The AL rebounded from its 1943 low in 1944, but averages fell again in 1945 and stayed nearly constant through 1947. Then AL batting averages began to rise as runs increased, and by 1950 the AL was back to where it had been in 1940.

Part of the reason batting averages did not increase substantially after WWII while runs began to increase was that home runs were rising sharply in the late 1940s (Figure 2-25). This produced an increase in runs without a corresponding increase in batting averages. This was a trend that would continue for the rest of the century. Walks were also reaching record levels in both leagues at the end of the 1940s (Figure 3-15), and this also helped runs to increase.

There were, however, some outstanding team and individual batting averages recorded in the period. The Red Sox led the AL in batting average 6 times in the 11 seasons from 1940 through 1950, and they led the majors 5 times. This launched the Red Sox towards their position at the top of the AL leader list for batting average (Table 4-3). Through 1998 the Red Sox have led the AL 21 times in batting average, and they have led the majors 16 times. The Red Sox peaked in 1950 with a team average of .302. They remain the last team in the majors to exceed .300 for a season. The Red Sox were led by Ted Williams who won the league batting title 4 times, including an average of .406 in 1941. This is the last year the .400 mark was topped in the majors.

The Cards led the NL 5 times in the period, leading the majors twice. This also launched the Cards toward their position at the top of the NL leaders list. The Cards have 22 batting titles through 1998, but they have only led the majors 8 times compared to 16 for the Red Sox. The Cards were led by Stan Musial, who matched the four league batting titles of Ted Williams.

The Braves led the league (and the majors) in 1947 for the first time in their history. They won another league title (and a pennant) in 1948, but they have been able to win only 4 more titles in the ensuing 50 years.

Figure 2-15. AL/NL Batting Average 1940-50

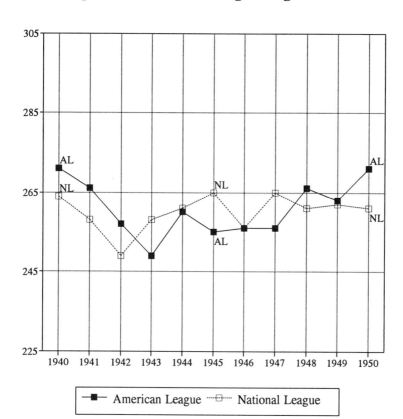

Year	AL Batting Avg	AL Leader	NL Batting Avg	NL Leader
1940	271	**Tigers**	264	Pirates
1941	266	**Red Sox**	258	Dodgers
1942	257	**Red Sox**	249	Cards
1943	249	Tigers	258	**Cards**
1944	260	Red Sox	261	**Cards**
1945	255	White Sox	265	**Cubs**
1946	256	**Red Sox**	256	Cards
1947	256	Yankees	265	**Braves**
1948	266	**Indians**	261	Braves
1949	263	**Red Sox**	262	Cards
1950	271	**Red Sox**	261	Dodgers

Figure 2-16 shows batting average by year for the American and National leagues from 1950 through 1960. The scale of the graph includes the highest and lowest values of batting average in the century. The same scale is used for all decades so it is possible to see at a glance how batting averages in one decade compare to the highs and lows for the century. The exact values of batting average for each year are shown below the graph together with the teams that led each league. Teams that led the majors are shown in bold.

The leagues were relatively close in batting average in the 1950s. The AL fell from its 1950 lead to nearly match the NL in 1951, and the leagues tracked each other after that with the NL generally having the advantage. They were tied entering the 1960s (the AL actually led by a small amount). Runs generally followed a similar pattern (Figure 2-6), but the NL took a commanding lead in home runs and set its all-time record in 1955 (Figure 2-26).

The Yankees led the AL in batting average 5 times from 1950 through 1960 as they won 9 pennants during the period. But the Yankees would lead the league again only in 1962 before getting back to the top in the 1990s. The White Sox, surprisingly, led the AL 3 times in the period, but their last batting title in 1960 is so far the last in their history. At present it's the longest period without a batting title in the AL, although the Angels, who were born in 1961, have never won a batting title.

In a similar pattern in the NL, the Dodgers won the batting title 4 times in the period and led the majors 3 times. But their 1955 title was the last one the franchise has won. At present this is the longest drought for a batting title in the majors. But the Braves, as noted in the text accompanying Figure 2-15, did not win their first title until 1947, and the Astros, born in 1962, have never won a batting title.

Familiar names such as Stan Musial (4 times) and Ted Willams (twice) appeared again at the top of the batting title lists in the period. But some new names bound for the Hall of Fame also appeared on the lists in the 1950s. Making it twice were Hank Aaron and Richie Ashburn, while Al Kaline, Mickey Mantle, and Willie Mays made their first (and only) appearances.

The surge of home runs in the 1950s (and the increasing strikeouts as hitters swung for the fences) established a new "standard" for league batting average. Except for the AL in 1950 and the NL in 1953, neither league got above the .265 line during the 1950s. From 1951 through 1992, the AL was able to pass the .265 line only 4 times in spite of adopting the designated hitter in 1973. But the DH and the new offensive surge starting in 1993 has kept the AL above .265 since 1993 (Figure 2-30). In the NL, 1953 marked its last appearance above the .265 line until 1994. The offensive surge of the 1993-97 period and "Arcade Baseball" in Denver got it to .267 in 1994, but the NL has not been above .265 since. The game of the 1990s is the long ball game, not the high average game.

Figure 2-16. AL/NL Batting Average 1950-60

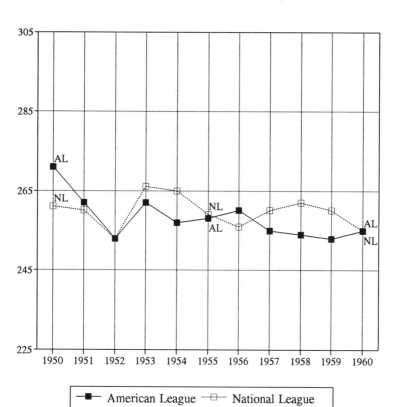

Year	AL Batting Avg	AL Leader	NL Batting Avg	NL Leader
1950	271	**Red Sox**	261	Dodgers
1951	262	White Sox	260	**Dodgers**
1952	253	Yankees	253	**Cards**
1953	262	Yankees	266	**Dodgers**
1954	257	Yankees	265	**Cards**
1955	258	White Sox	259	**Dodgers**
1956	260	**Tigers**	256	Cards
1957	255	Yankees	260	**Cards**
1958	254	**Yankees**	262	Braves
1959	253	Indians	260	**Reds**
1960	255	White Sox	255	**Pirates**

Figure 2-17 shows batting average by year for the American and National leagues from 1960 through 1970. The scale of the graph includes the highest and lowest values of batting average in the century. The same scale is used for all decades so it is possible to see at a glance how batting averages in one decade compare to the highs and lows for the century. The exact values of batting average for each year are shown below the graph together with the teams that led each league. Teams that led the majors are shown in bold.

The leagues had dramatically different results in batting average in the 1960s. The strike zone change from 1963 through 1968 produced a severe reduction in runs (Figure 2-7) and a decrease in home runs (Figure 2-27). Both leagues fell in a nearly identical manner (and at nearly identical levels) in runs, while the AL had a sometimes strong advantage in home runs. But the NL had a substantial advantage over the AL in batting average. This continued the edge the NL had built up in the 1950s. In the 21 seasons from 1952 through 1972, the NL led the AL in batting average 18 times while the AL led only 3 times. The leagues had been evenly split before that except for the domination of the AL in the 1930s.

After being nearly tied in 1963, the AL trailed the NL by a huge 16 percentage points in 1966, and the AL hit its all-time low for batting average in 1968 (still trailing the NL by 13 percentage points). Both leagues rebounded and were much closer together after the strike zone was changed back and the mound lowered for the 1969 season, but the AL still trailed. The AL would not lead the NL again until the AL adopted the designated hitter in 1973.

The difference between the leagues meant that NL teams led the majors in batting average every year between 1960 and 1970. The Pirates led 5 times during the period, and the Reds, who would become the constant competitors of the Pirates in the playoffs, led 3 times. The Twins led the AL 4 times but they were never able to lead the majors. The Orioles led the AL in 1966, the first time the franchise had led the league in batting since their predecessors, the St. Louis Browns, did so 44 years earlier in 1922.

One reason the Pirates led the NL in batting 5 times was that Roberto Clemente won the NL batting title 4 times. Other double winners in the NL during the period were Tommy Davis of the Dodgers and newcomer Pete Rose of the Reds. In the AL, Red Sox players won 5 titles with Pete Runnels doing it twice and Carl Yastrzemski doing it 3 times. Yastrzemski won his first title in 1963 and his second in 1967 when he also led the AL in runs, hits, home runs, total bases, runs batted in, on base percentage, and slugging average. His third title came in 1968 and was also notable but in a much different way. His average of .3005 was the lowest ever to win a batting title.

The Twins were led to their 4 titles in the period by Tony Oliva, who won the batting championship in 1964 and 1965, and by Rod Carew, who won the first of 7 titles in his career in 1969.

Figure 2-17. AL/NL Batting Average 1960-70

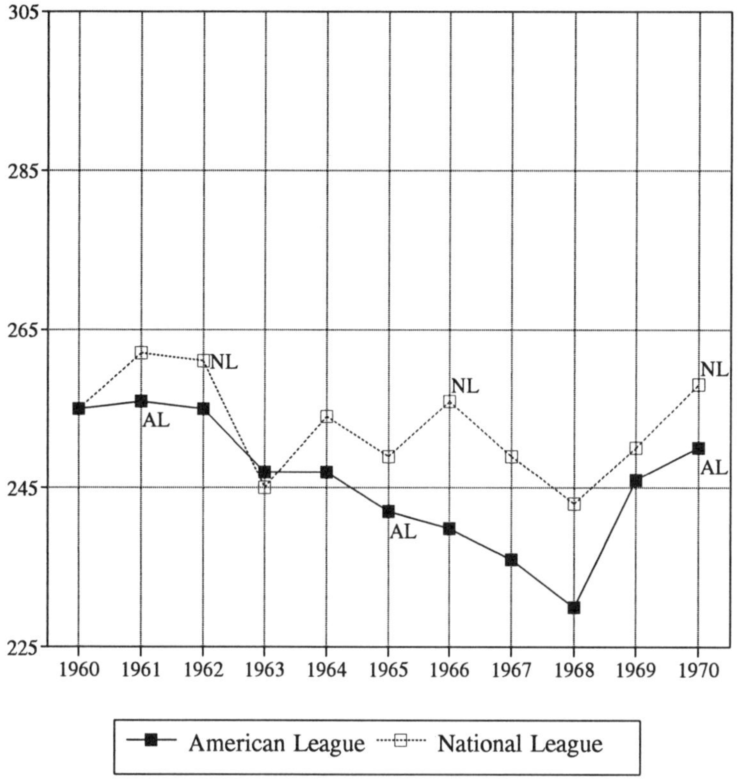

Year	AL Batting Avg	AL Leader	NL Batting Avg	NL Leader
1960	255	White Sox	255	**Pirates**
1961	256	Tigers	262	**Pirates**
1962	255	Yankees	261	**Giants**
1963	247	Twins	245	**Cards**
1964	247	Red Sox	254	**Braves**
1965	242	Twins	249	**Reds**
1966	240	Orioles	256	**Pirates**
1967	236	Red Sox	249	**Pirates**
1968	230	A's	243	**Reds**
1969	246	Twins	250	**Pirates**
1970	250	Twins	258	**Reds**

Figure 2-18 shows batting average by year for the American and National leagues from 1970 through 1980. The scale of the graph includes the highest and lowest values of batting average in the century. The same scale is used for all decades so it is possible to see at a glance how batting averages in one decade compare to the highs and lows for the century. The exact values of batting average for each year are shown below the graph together with the teams that led each league. Teams that led the majors are shown in bold.

The AL rebound from the all-time low of 1968 lasted only two seasons after the strike zone change of 1963 was reversed and the mound lowered in 1969. The league batting average fell to .239 in 1972, a mark that tied 1908 as the third lowest ever in the league. Runs also fell close to the all-time lows reached in 1968 (Figure 2-8). That was enough for the AL. They adopted the designated hitter rule as an experiment for the 1973 season and they made it a permanent change in 1975. The NL was invited to change as well, but they declined to do so. The result was that the AL took over the batting average lead in 1973, and the AL has led in every season since. Through 1998 the AL has led the NL in batting average for 26 consecutive seasons.

The Reds of the Big Red Machine managed to lead the majors in batting average in 1976, and that was the last time a team from the NL led the majors in batting average until 1998 when the Rockies made it to the top. The Twins led the AL four times in the 1960-70 period, but more notable was the fact that for the first time expansion teams made it to the top of the league. The Royals did it twice and the Rangers and Brewers each did it once. In the NL the Cards led the league four times on their way to leading the NL more times than any other team both from 1901 through 1972 and from 1973 through 1998 (Table 4-3). The Cards are the only team in either league to lead any of the measure categories used in this book both for the 1901-72 and 1973-98 periods.

The use of the DH permitted the AL to reach a league batting average of .270 in 1979. This was the highest average in the league since 1950 when the AL hit .271 as the Red Sox became the last team to exceed .300 for a season. The AL would not top the .270 mark again until 1994 (Figure 2-20). The NL has not exceeded the .270 level since 1939 (its closest approach was .267 in 1994).

Rod Carew of the Twins won six AL batting titles between 1970 and 1980, but the best performance in a single year was that of George Brett of the Royals. Brett won his second batting title of the period in 1980 with an average of .390. This was the highest average in the majors since Ted Williams hit .406 in 1941. Other players who won two batting titles in the period were Bill Madlock of the Cubs and Dave Parker of the Pirates.

The AL led the NL in batting average by 10 percentage points in 1980. The last year the AL had such a big lead was 1950, and the last year before 1950 was 1938. But with the DH such leads would become routine in the years ahead.

Figure 2-18. AL/NL Batting Average 1970-80

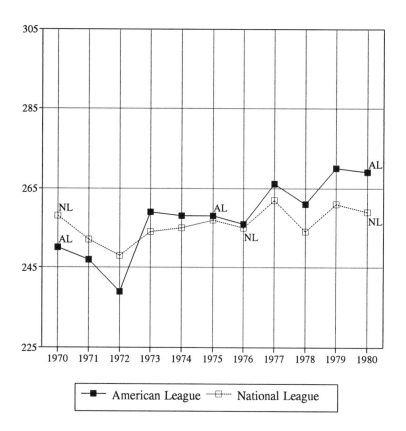

Year	AL Batting Avg	AL Leader	NL Batting Avg	NL Leader
1970	250	Twins	258	**Reds**
1971	247	Orioles	252	**Cards**
1972	239	Royals	248	**Pirates**
1973	259	**Twins**	254	Braves
1974	258	Rangers	255	**Pirates**
1975	258	**Red Sox**	257	Cards
1976	256	Twins	255	**Reds**
1977	266	**Twins**	262	Phillies
1978	261	**Brewers**	254	Cubs
1979	270	**Red Sox**	261	Cards
1980	269	**Royals**	259	Cards

Figure 2-19 shows batting average by year for the American and National leagues from 1980 through 1990. The scale of the graph includes the highest and lowest values of batting average in the century. The same scale is used for all decades so it is possible to see at a glance how batting averages in one decade compare to the highs and lows for the century. The exact values of batting average for each year are shown below the graph together with the teams that led each league. Teams that led the majors are shown in bold.

The AL led the NL in batting average every year in the 1980-90 period as it had since the DH was adopted in 1973, and as it will indefinitely. The NL almost matched the AL in batting average in the split season of 1981 when the player's strike caused a dip in all offensive measures. The NL has never since been as close to the AL as it was in 1981. The 15 percentage point lead the AL held over the NL in 1989 was the biggest edge for the AL since 1902.

The Red Sox led the AL (and the majors) in batting average 7 times in the 11 seasons between 1980 and 1990. Since 1973 the Red Sox have led the majors in batting average 10 times (Table 4-3). This increased their total years leading the league in the century to 21, the best in the AL (the Cards have led the NL 22 times). The best any other team has done since 1973 in leading in batting average is 5 times by the Twins and the Cards. The Red Sox are clearly the batting average kings of the majors since the DH was introduced in 1973. At the other extreme the Blue Jays won their one and only batting title in 1983 (but the Angels and Mariners have never won a batting title).

Wade Boggs of the Red Sox led the AL in batting 5 times in the period, making the biggest contribution to the 7 titles won by his team. Tony Gwynn of the Padres almost matched Boggs by winning 4 NL titles in the period, even thought the Padres did not win any titles as a team (the Padres have never won a batting title in the 30 years they have existed in spite of the fact that Tony Gwynn has spent his entire career with the Padres). Bill Madlock of the Pirates and Willie McGee of the Cards also won two batting titles each in the period.

The highest batting average for the NL in the period was .261 in 1987, when there was a huge offensive surge in both leagues in both runs (Figure 2-9) and home runs (Figure 2-29). But an average of .261 marks the lowest high in any decade in the century for the NL. Even in "dead ball" decades the NL had at least one year that exceeded .261. The lowest average in the period for the NL was .246 in 1989. Except for 1963 and 1968, when the strike zone was changed in favor of the pitcher, the average of .246 for the NL in 1989 was its lowest since 1909. Considering the improvements in the ball and the lowering of the pitcher's mound that had taken place since 1909, the .246 average for the NL in 1989 was its worst performance in the century, probably even outstripping the record low of .239 the NL posted in 1908 (Figure 2-11). It took expansion to the mile high city of Denver to bring NL batting averages back above .260 again.

Figure 2-19. AL/NL Batting Average 1980-90

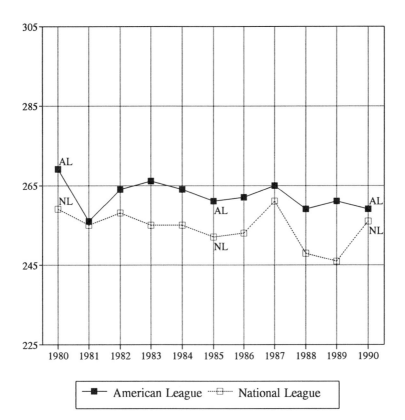

Year	AL Batting Avg	AL Leader	NL Batting Avg	NL Leader
1980	269	**Royals**	259	Cards
1981	256	**Red Sox**	255	Phillies
1982	264	**Royals**	258	Pirates
1983	266	**Blue Jays**	255	Braves
1984	264	**Red Sox**	255	Phillies
1985	261	**Red Sox**	252	Cards
1986	262	**Indians**	253	Mets
1987	265	**Red Sox**	261	Mets
1988	259	**Red Sox**	248	Cubs
1989	261	**Red Sox**	246	Cubs
1990	259	**Red Sox**	256	Reds

Figure 2-20 shows batting average by year for the American and National leagues from 1988 through 1998. The scale of the graph includes the highest and lowest values of batting average in the century. The same scale is used for all decades so it is possible to see at a glance how batting averages in one decade compare to the highs and lows for the century. The exact values of batting average for each year are shown below the graph together with the teams that led each league. Teams that led the majors are shown in bold.

The most dramatic even of the period was the NL expansion of 1993. This expansion included the Rockies who began play in Mile High Stadium in Denver. It had been forecast that offense would greatly increase in the thin air of Denver and that's exactly what happened. The Rockies helped by deciding to stock their team with hitters rather than pitchers and what would have been a team oriented towards offense at sea level became a team that would lead the league in hitting (and in giving up runs) by a wide margin in Denver. My book *Crossing the Plate* explains other events that came to fruition in 1993, and that would have produced a surge in offense in both leagues regardless of the added attraction of the thin air in Denver. The combination of these two factors caused an explosion in runs (Figure 2-10) that has been topped only by the 1920s and 1930s, and an explosion in home runs that has never been topped in the AL and is near record levels in the NL (Figure 2-30).

Batting averages also surged in 1993, but with an emphasis on the big swing and hitting it out, averages did not approach prior highs. Batting averages were ignored in favor of extra-base hits. The result was new records in strikeouts (Figure 3-10) rather than batting average. The AL remained well ahead of the NL in batting average thanks to the DH, and the AL peaked at .277 in 1996, its highest batting average since 1939. The NL peaked a little earlier at .267 in 1994, also its highest batting average since 1939. In spite of the emphasis on home runs, batting averages have consistently stayed well ahead of prior decades since the expansion of 1993. It is likely they will remain at these relatively high levels, even if they do not challenge the prior league records.

In the 1991-98 period, the Twins, Yankees, and Indians each led the AL twice in batting average. The Rockies are the only NL team to lead the league more than once in the period, and their fourth straight title in 1998 ties them with the Giants (1910 through 1913) and Red Sox (1987 through 1990) as the only major league teams to win four in a row. In addition, the 1998 Rockies were the first NL team to lead the majors in batting average since the 1976 Reds.

The top individual performance in the period was that of Tony Gwynn. He hit .394 in 1994, the highest average in the majors since Ted Williams hit .406 in 1941 (Gwynn also topped the .390 of George Brett in 1980). Gwynn led the NL in batting average 4 straight years from 1994 through 1997. Edgar Martinez had the best performance in the AL with batting titles in 1992 and 1995.

Figure 2-20. AL/NL Batting Average 1988-98

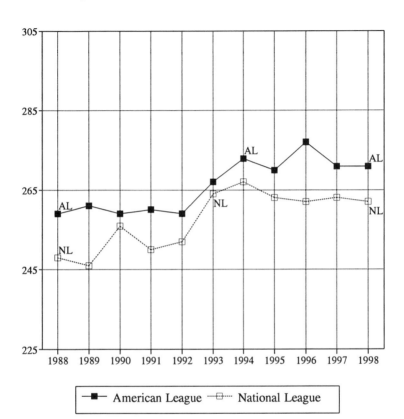

Year	AL Batting Avg	AL Leader	NL Batting Avg	NL Leader
1988	259	**Red Sox**	248	Cubs
1989	261	**Red Sox**	246	Cubs
1990	259	**Red Sox**	256	Reds
1991	260	**Twins**	250	Pirates
1992	259	**Twins**	252	Cards
1993	267	**Yankees**	264	Giants
1994	273	**Yankees**	267	Reds
1995	270	**Indians**	263	Rockies
1996	277	**Indians**	262	Rockies
1997	271	**Red Sox**	263	Rockies
1998	271	Rangers	262	**Rockies**

Figure 2-21 shows home runs per game by year for the American and National leagues from 1900 through 1910. The scale of the graph includes the highest and lowest values of home runs per game in the century. The same scale is used for all decades so it is possible to see at a glance how home runs in one decade compare to the highs and lows for the century. The exact values of home runs per game for each year are shown below the graph together with the teams that led each league. Teams that led the majors are shown in bold.

Until Babe Ruth started his home run revolution in 1919, home runs were not part of baseball strategy. They were essentially accidents. Further, except in very small stadiums, many home runs were inside-the-park home runs. For example, Ty Cobb won the triple crown in 1909 by leading the AL in batting average, home runs, and runs batted in (for that matter he also led the league in hits, runs, total bases, slugging average, on base percentage and stolen bases). But every one of his home runs (his total of 9 led the league and the majors by 2) were inside-the-park home runs.

Not surprisingly, the period from 1900 through 1910 had the lowest level of home runs in the century. The next decade would be a little higher because of the designation of the cork-center ball as the official ball in 1911, and because of the stadium building boom from 1909 onward that reduced the distance to the stands in many parks. In the 10 seasons from 1901 through 1910 the NL led the AL in home runs 6 times and the AL led the NL 4 times. This is what would be expected in a situation in which home runs were essentially being hit at random.

The NL recorded its all-time low in home runs in 1903 at 0.09 home runs per game, while the AL reached its all-time low in 1907 at 0.08 home runs per game. The AL mark is also the major league low. In today's terms, an average of 0.08 home runs per team per game means the AL, with its 14 teams, would hit a total of 181 home runs in one year for an average of 13 per team. In the AL's record year of 1996, the average *team* hit a total of 196 home runs for the season. As a league, the AL hit 15 times more home runs per game in 1996 than it did in 1908. No other measure has increased by as large a ratio during the century as have home runs. It truly is a different game today.

The A's led the AL 5 times in the period and the Red Sox led 4 times. The Giants led the NL 4 times and the Dodgers 3 times. Not much connection between home runs and winning would be expected in a situation in which home runs were random acts, but except perhaps for the Dodgers, these teams did have some of the best teams in their respective leagues during the period.

Consistent with the fact that the A's led in home runs most often, Harry Davis of the A's had the most league home run titles (4) during the period. Except for Davis, only Sam Crawford of the Reds and later the Tigers won more than one title. Crawford won 2 home runs titles and tied Socks Seybold of the A's for the highest yearly total at 16.

Figure 2-21. AL/NL Home Runs Per Game 1900-10

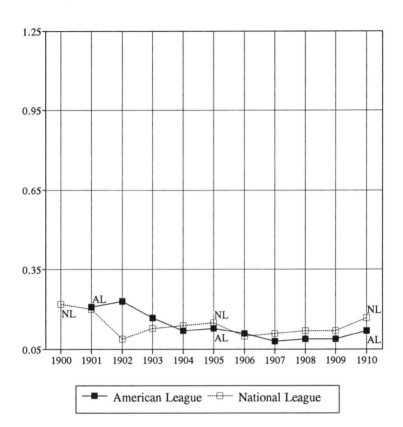

Year	AL HR/Game	AL Leader	NL HR/Game	NL Leader
1900	--	--	0.22	**Braves**
1901	0.21	Red Sox	0.20	**Cards**
1902	0.23	**Senators**	0.09	Dodgers
1903	0.17	**Red Sox**	0.13	Pirates
1904	0.12	**A's**	0.14	Giants
1905	0.13	Red Sox	0.15	**Giants**
1906	0.11	**A's**	0.10	Dodgers
1907	0.08	A's	0.11	**Giants**
1908	0.09	A's	0.12	**Dodgers**
1909	0.09	A's	0.12	**Giants**
1910	0.12	**Red Sox**	0.17	Cubs

Figure 2-22 shows home runs per game by year for the American and National leagues from 1910 through 1920. The scale of the graph includes the highest and lowest values of home runs per game in the century. The same scale is used for all decades so it is possible to see at a glance how home runs in one decade compare to the highs and lows for the century. The exact values of home runs per game for each year are shown below the graph together with the teams that led each league. Teams that led the majors are shown in bold.

Home runs increased in each league in 1911 when the cork-center ball became the official ball. Until 1919 the increase compared to the prior decade was about 15 percent in the AL (home runs per game more than doubled in the AL between 1918 and 1919 when Babe Ruth broke all existing major league records), but in the NL home runs on average increased by almost exactly 50 percent compared to the prior decade. The increase in both leagues was much influenced by stadium factors now that the cork-center ball permitted hitters to more readily hit home runs over the wall as well as inside the park.

The Phillies, in tiny Baker Bowl, led the NL in home runs 6 times between 1910 and 1920. They led the majors the first four times, but their last two titles came in 1919 and 1920 when the Yankees took over the major league lead. The Yankees led the AL in home runs 5 times in the period, partly because they began to share the Polo Grounds, which had short foul lines, with the Giants in 1913. The A's, in brand new Shibe Park, led the AL 4 times in the period. The Giants were often close behind the Phillies, and the Giants exploited the Polo Grounds for home runs to a much larger extent in the 1920s. As a result, teams from New York and Philadelphia would be the prime home run teams in each league until the late 1930s. In the 36 seasons from 1901 through 1936, the Yankees led the AL 16 times, and the A's, Giants, and Phillies each led their respective leagues 13 times. These same four teams top the AL and NL home run leaders list from 1901 through 1972 (Table 4-4).

Because of the home runs being hit in Baker Bowl and the Polo Grounds, the NL led the AL in home runs every year until 1919 when Babe Ruth hit more home runs by himself than 11 of the 16 teams in the majors. Gavvy Cravath of the Phillies was the leading home run hitter in the decade from 1910 through 1919, in spite of Babe Ruth's heroics in 1919. Cravath led the NL in home runs 5 times, while not far away in Shibe Park, Frank "Home Run" Baker of the A's led the AL 3 times. Of the 20 leaders from each league between 1911 and 1920, 14 were teams from New York and Philadelphia.

Babe Ruth made 1919 a turning point, but 1920 marked the first year that hitting home runs became part of the strategy of the game. Although Ruth's total of 54 in 1920 was more than all teams except the Phillies (64), 11 teams hit over 30 home runs, the most ever (the best prior year was 8 in 1911). In 1921, 14 of the 16 teams did so. The home run had arrived in the majors to stay.

Figure 2-22. AL/NL Home Runs Per Game 1910-20

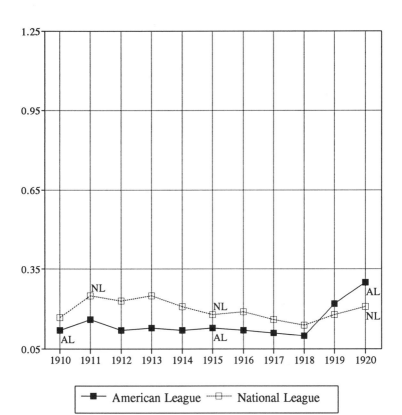

Year	AL HR/Game	AL Leader	NL HR/Game	NL Leader
1910	0.12	**Red Sox**	0.17	Cubs
1911	0.16	A's	0.25	**Phillies**
1912	0.12	Red Sox	0.23	**Giants**
1913	0.13	A's	0.25	**Phillies**
1914	0.12	A's	0.21	**Phillies**
1915	0.13	Yankees	0.18	**Phillies**
1916	0.12	Yankees	0.19	**Cubs**
1917	0.11	Yankees	0.16	**Giants**
1918	0.10	A's	0.14	**Cards**
1919	0.22	**Yankees**	0.18	Phillies
1920	0.30	**Yankees**	0.21	Phillies

Figure 2-23 shows home runs per game by year for the American and National leagues from 1920 through 1930. The scale of the graph includes the highest and lowest values of home runs per game in the century. The same scale is used for all decades so it is possible to see at a glance how home runs in one decade compare to the highs and lows for the century. The exact values of home runs per game for each year are shown below the graph together with the teams that led each league. Teams that led the majors are shown in bold.

Between 1920 and 1921, home runs increased by 30 percent in the AL and 80 percent in the NL. As the NL caught on to the big swing style established by Babe Ruth, it began to hit more home runs than the AL. This was partly because the Yankees moved out of the Polo Grounds and into Yankee Stadium in 1923. Yankee Stadium was a good place to hit home runs for left-handed pull hitters (like Babe Ruth and Lou Gehrig), but the power alleys were huge compared to the Polo Grounds, Baker Bowl, and even Wrigley Field in Chicago. The Yankees as a team could (and did) hit home runs anywhere, but the rest of the league did not get the advantage of hitting in the small NL parks. With the good pitching that the Yankees had, the rest of the league did not hit many home runs in Yankee Stadium either.

As a result the NL led the AL in home runs nine straight years from 1922 through 1930. The Phillies led the NL in home runs 6 times in the 1920-30 period, and the Phillies also made a major contribution to home runs in the NL by offering up the worst pitching staff in the league in tiny Baker Bowl. The Giants led the NL in home runs 3 times in the period, and although the Giants had good pitching in the same vein as the Yankees, other teams still found the small power alleys in the Polo Grounds an inviting home run target.

The Yankees led the AL in home runs 9 of the 11 years in the period, and they led the majors 6 of those years. No team could hit home runs like the Yankees, even if the NL was the dominant league. Babe Ruth led the AL in home runs 9 of the 11 years in the period, and he led the majors 7 times, tying for the major league lead in 1923 and being beaten by Hack Wilson of the Cubs in 1930 when Wilson hit what was then the all-time NL record of 56 home runs.

Wilson led the NL in home runs twice in the period, and also tied for the lead twice. Similarly, Cy Williams of the Phillies led twice and tied with Wilson in 1927. Rogers Hornsby of the Cards was the only other double winner.

Both leagues set home run records in 1925, declined for three years, and then set successive new records in 1929 and 1930. But after the explosion of 1930, the NL would not hit a new peak until 1949. The AL also declined from its 1930 peak in 1931, but first the A's and then the Yankees drove the AL record steadily higher into the 1940s. However, the AL still would not top the 1930 mark of the NL until 1950 (by which time the NL had already set a new record). The NL 1930 peak was a seminal event for its time.

Figure 2-23. AL/NL Home Runs Per Game 1920-30

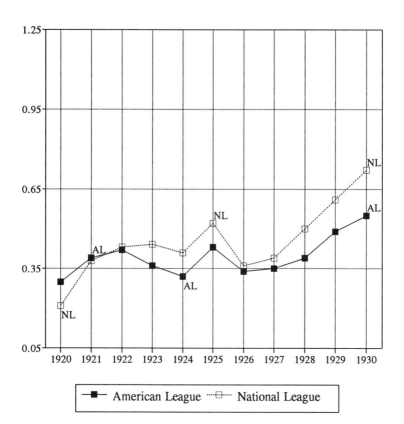

Year	AL HR/Game	AL Leader	NL HR/Game	NL Leader
1920	0.30	**Yankees**	0.21	Phillies
1921	0.39	**Yankees**	0.38	Phillies
1922	0.42	A's	0.43	**Phillies**
1923	0.36	Yankees	0.44	**Phillies**
1924	0.32	**Yankees**	0.41	Phillies
1925	0.43	Browns	0.52	**Giants**
1926	0.34	**Yankees**	0.36	Cards
1927	0.35	**Yankees**	0.39	Giants
1928	0.39	**Yankees**	0.50	Giants
1929	0.49	Yankees	0.61	**Phillies**
1930	0.55	Yankees	0.72	**Cubs**

Figure 2-24 shows home runs per game by year for the American and National leagues from 1930 through 1940. The scale of the graph includes the highest and lowest values of home runs per game in the century. The same scale is used for all decades so it is possible to see at a glance how home runs in one decade compare to the highs and lows for the century. The exact values of home runs per game for each year are shown below the graph together with the teams that led each league. Teams that led the majors are shown in bold.

The NL fell dramatically from its 1930 peak when it elected to use a new ball with raised stitches and a new cover from 1931 through 1933. The NL wanted to reduce the number of home runs and it definitely succeeded. Home runs in the NL decreased by 45 percent from 1930 in 1931, and by 1933 they were down 50 percent. The AL adopted the raised stitches but not the new cover, and AL home runs changed little from the 1930 peak in the next five years.

In 1932, led by Jimmie Foxx with 58 home runs, the A's hit 172 home runs to set what was then the all-time major league record for team home runs. That drove the AL to a new league record of 0.58 home runs per game. But the 1936 Yankees hit 182 home runs to break the team record of the 1932 A's, and they drove the AL to a new league record of 0.61 home runs per game. The AL set new league records through 1940, but the record of the 1936 Yankees was not topped in the league until the Yankees did so in 1956 (the Giants set a new major league record with 221 home runs in 1947). The A's and Yankees kept the AL ahead of the NL in home runs for 11 straight years from 1931 through 1941.

The Yankees led the AL in home runs 8 times and the A's led 3 times in the 11 years from 1930 through 1940 (the Yankees led the AL in home runs 12 straight years from 1936 through 1947, leading the majors 9 times). The NL changed to the AL ball from 1934 onward, and the 1935 Giants managed to lead the majors in home runs. It was the only year between 1931 and 1942 that a team from the NL led the majors in home runs. The Giants led the NL 7 times from 1930 through 1940 with the Phillies leading twice, the last time in 1936. The Phillies moved to Shibe Park in 1938 when Baker Bowl literally collapsed, and the Phillies did not lead the NL in home runs again until 1984, a gap of 48 years (they have not led since 1984). This emphasizes the importance of Baker Bowl on the home run performance of the Phillies before 1938.

Jimmie Foxx led the AL 3 times between 1930 and 1940 with a Triple Crown in 1933. He also tied Hank Greenberg in 1935, and Greenberg won 2 other titles. Babe Ruth and Lou Gehrig also won twice. Mel Ott led the NL 4 times and tied "Ducky" Medwick in 1937 when Medwick won the Triple Crown. Chuck Klein of the Phillies led twice with a Triple Crown in 1933, the same year Foxx won one for the A's. Johnny Mize also led twice, but except for Hack Wilson's 56 home runs in 1930 (the NL record until 1998), the top AL home run hitter always hit more home runs than his NL counterpart during the period.

Figure 2-24. AL/NL Home Runs Per Game 1930-40

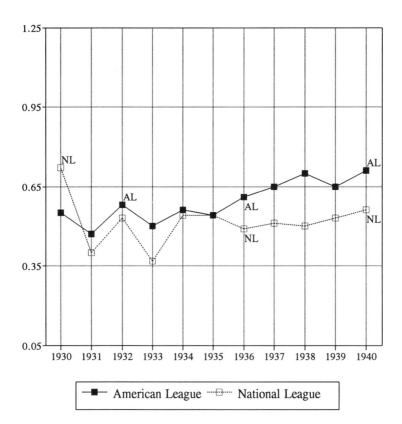

Year	AL HR/Game	AL Leader	NL HR/Game	NL Leader
1930	0.55	Yankees	0.72	**Cubs**
1931	0.47	**Yankees**	0.40	Giants
1932	0.58	**A's**	0.53	Phillies
1933	0.50	**Yankees**	0.37	Giants
1934	0.56	**A's**	0.54	Giants
1935	0.54	A's	0.54	**Giants**
1936	0.61	**Yankees**	0.49	Phillies
1937	0.65	**Yankees**	0.51	Giants
1938	0.70	**Yankees**	0.50	Giants
1939	0.65	**Yankees**	0.53	Giants
1940	0.71	**Yankees**	0.56	Cards

Figure 2-25 shows home runs per game by year for the American and National leagues from 1940 through 1950. The scale of the graph includes the highest and lowest values of home runs per game in the century. The same scale is used for all decades so it is possible to see at a glance how home runs in one decade compare to the highs and lows for the century. The exact values of home runs per game for each year are shown below the graph together with the teams that led each league. Teams that led the majors are shown in bold.

Home runs declined in both leagues as the impact of WWII, in terms of poorer material in the ball and the drafting of top players, was reflected in lower offense. But home runs in the first of the 1940s were not much different than in the first half of the 1920s when the home run explosion began (Figure 2-23). What had changed dramatically was the expected level of home runs.

As soon as the top players returned from WWII, home runs began another upward surge. Helped by the greater influx of black players into the NL after the signing of Jackie Robinson, the NL regained its leadership in home runs. The AL led the NL in home runs only 3 times in the period, and, after Robinson arrived in the majors in 1947, the NL led the AL 14 straight years from 1947 through 1959. The 1947 Giants set what was then a major league record with 221 home runs (1.43 per game). The 1961 Yankees (and subsequent AL teams) set new major league records, but the 1947 Giants (and 1956 Reds) held the NL record until the 1997 Rockies, in the thin air of Denver, hit 239 (1.48 per game).

The Giants led the NL in home runs 6 times between 1940 and 1950, but the Dodgers, who led a total of 3 times, led the NL and the majors in 1949 and 1950 when home runs reached what were then record levels. The Dodgers would lead the majors 7 straight years from 1949 through 1955, becoming a new home run power. The Yankees continued their reign in the AL, leading in home runs 8 times in the period, but 1948 marked the beginning of the end of the domination of the Yankees in both the AL and the majors. By 1947 the Yankees had led the AL in home runs 27 times in the 33 seasons since 1915. They led the majors 17 of those years. But the Yankees would lead only 6 more times in the 14 years from 1948 through 1961, and after 1961 they would not lead again. Although the Yankees top the leader list for home runs (Table 4-4), since 1961 no team, old or new, has gone longer without a home run title than the Yankees.

As both leagues reached new home run peaks in 1950, the Dodgers led the NL and the Indians the AL. Ted Williams was the home run leader in the AL, winning 4 titles in the period. In spite of his time in the Air Force, he hit 234 home runs between 1940 and 1949 to be the major league leader for the decade. But since Babe Ruth's home run revolution in 1919, this was (and is) the lowest total to lead a decade. Hank Greenberg won 2 titles, and in the NL Ralph Kiner won 3 titles and tied twice with Johnny Mize, winner of another title outright. Bill "Swish" Nicholson of the Cubs won 2 wartime titles in 1943 and 1944.

Figure 2-25. AL/NL Home Runs Per Game 1940-50

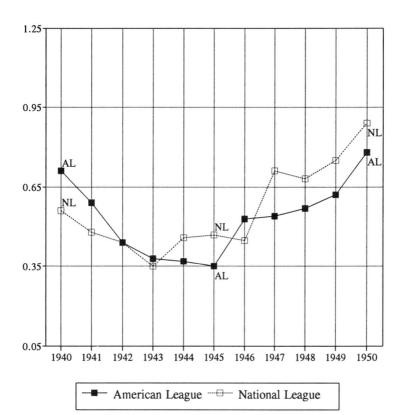

Year	AL HR/Game	AL Leader	NL HR/Game	NL Leader
1940	0.71	**Yankees**	0.56	Cards
1941	0.59	**Yankees**	0.48	Dodgers
1942	0.44	Yankees	0.44	**Giants**
1943	0.38	**Yankees**	0.35	Giants
1944	0.37	Yankees	0.46	**Cards**
1945	0.35	Yankees	0.47	**Giants**
1946	0.53	**Yankees**	0.45	Giants
1947	0.54	Yankees	0.71	**Giants**
1948	0.57	Indians	0.68	**Giants**
1949	0.62	Red Sox	0.75	**Dodgers**
1950	0.78	Indians	0.89	**Dodgers**

Figure 2-26 shows home runs per game by year for the American and National leagues from 1950 through 1960. The scale of the graph includes the highest and lowest values of home runs per game in the century. The same scale is used for all decades so it is possible to see at a glance how home runs in one decade compare to the highs and lows for the century. The exact values of home runs per game for each year are shown below the graph together with the teams that led each league. Teams that led the majors are shown in bold.

The NL established its superiority over the AL in the 1950s in nearly every way, and its edge in home runs was especially notable. The NL set its all-time home run record in 1955 at 1.03 home runs per game. The NL was the first league to average above 1.00 home runs per team per game, and it has never been able to get above that level since, even in the offensive outburst of the 1990s. The AL was not able to top 1.00 until 1986 when it averaged 1.01. The AL broke the NL mark in 1987, and then broke all previous records in the 1990s, but it took the DH to do it.

Once again stadiums had a lot to do with home run records. In addition to the Polo Grounds, Ebbets Field in Brooklyn became a great home run target for the new home run hitters in the league. The Reds modified Crosley Field, once on the most difficult parks in which to hit home runs, so that it became a home run haven. This was a big help to the 1956 Reds when they hit 221 home runs to tie the record of the 1947 Giants. It also helped the Milwaukee Braves, with their home run tandem of Hank Aaron and Eddie Mathews, set an all-time record for home runs on the road in the decade. Milwaukee County Stadium was not a good home run park, but the Braves hit home runs by the ton in the Polo Grounds, Ebbets Field, and the now friendly confines of Crosley Field.

From 1953 through 1955, the NL averaged 0.96 home runs per game while the AL averaged 0.72. That put the NL 33 percent above the AL for that period. The AL closed the gap starting in 1956, when the Yankees broke the AL record for team home runs (set by the 1936 Yankees), and by 1960 the AL had pulled ahead of the NL. In the 13 years from 1961 through 1972, the NL led only 3 more times. After 1973, when the DH started in the AL, the NL never led again. 1955 marked the high water mark for NL home runs in more ways than one.

The Dodgers led the NL 6 times in the period (including one tie with the Giants), and the Braves led 3 times. The Yankees and Indians each led the AL 5 times. Individually, Duke Snider of the Dodgers hit the most home runs in the 1950-59 decade, although he led the NL only in 1956. Ralph Kiner, Eddie Mathews, and Ernie Banks were double winners in the NL during the period. Mickey Mantle led the AL 4 times, including a Triple Crown in 1956, while Al Rosen and Larry Doby of the Indians each led the AL twice. Hank Aaron only led the NL once in its biggest home run decade. Aaron, the most famous home run hitter since Babe Ruth, led the NL only 4 times in his long career.

Figure 2-26. AL/NL Home Runs Per Game 1950-60

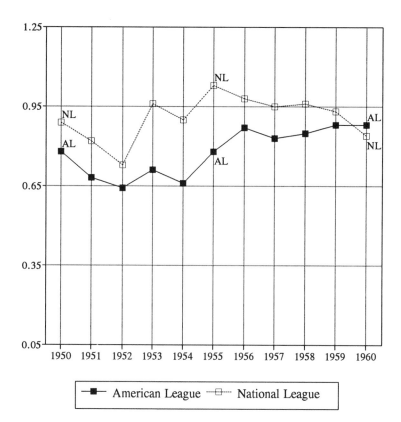

Year	AL HR/Game	AL Leader	NL HR/Game	NL Leader
1950	0.78	Indians	0.89	Dodgers
1951	0.68	Yankees	0.82	Dodgers
1952	0.64	Indians	0.73	Dodgers
1953	0.71	Indians	0.96	Dodgers
1954	0.66	Indians	0.90	Dod/Gnts
1955	0.78	Yankees	1.03	Dodgers
1956	0.87	Yankees	0.98	Reds
1957	0.83	A's	0.95	Braves
1958	0.85	Yankees	0.96	Cubs
1959	0.88	Indians	0.93	Braves
1960	0.88	**Yankees**	0.84	Braves

Figure 2-27 shows home runs per game by year for the American and National leagues from 1960 through 1970. The scale of the graph includes the highest and lowest values of home runs per game in the century. The same scale is used for all decades so it is possible to see at a glance how home runs in one decade compare to the highs and lows for the century. The exact values of home runs per game for each year are shown below the graph together with the teams that led each league. Teams that led the majors are shown in bold.

At the beginning of the 1960s, AL home runs rose to what were then league records in 1961 and 1962. The Yankees set a new major league record for team home runs (240) in the AL expansion year of 1961, a record that was not broken until 1996 when the Orioles hit 257. But 1961 was the last gasp for the Yankees as a home run leader. They have not led the AL in home runs since 1961, the longest drought for any AL team. Home runs in the league continued at a high level even after the strike zone was enlarged in 1963, but as pitchers took control home runs fell. By 1968 AL home runs were at their lowest level since 1954.

The NL trailed the AL during the period, and by 1968 NL home runs were at their lowest level since 1946. The replacement of the Polo Grounds and Ebbets Field by Candlestick Park and Dodger Stadium respectively contributed to the decline in NL home runs, and the change in the strike zone in 1963 made the downturn even more severe. NL home runs rebounded after the strike zone change was reversed and the mound lowered for the 1969 season, but NL home runs were still well below their peaks of the 1950s as the 1960s ended.

The Red Sox and Tigers replaced the Yankees as home run leaders in the AL, with the Red Sox winning 4 titles and the Tigers 3 during the period. The Twins led the AL in 1963 and 1964 thanks primarily to the exploits of Harmon Killebrew. It was the first time the franchise led the league in home runs since 1902 when the Washington Senators led for the only time. The Twins have not led the league in home runs since 1964. The Tigers led the AL for the first time in franchise history in 1962, but after 1962 the Tigers have led the AL in home runs more times than any other team (Table 4-4).

The Braves led the NL 5 times in the period, and the Giants, in spite of now playing in Candlestick Park, led 3 times. The Giants of the 1960s also led in home runs on the road, something the Polo Grounds Giants were unable to do. Thus, the Candlestick Park Giants of the 1960s were the best home run teams in franchise history, but after 1972 they never led the NL in home runs again.

Harmon Killebrew led the AL 5 times (including one tie). Roger Maris led in 1961 when he hit 61 home runs to break Babe Ruth's record, but the Yankees have had only one leader since (Graig Nettles in 1976). Frank Howard of the new Washington Senators led twice at the end of the period. The Giants dominated the NL list with Willie Mays leading 3 times and Willie McCovey winning twice and tying Hank Aaron once (Aaron won another title on his own).

Figure 2-27. AL/NL Home Runs Per Game 1960-70

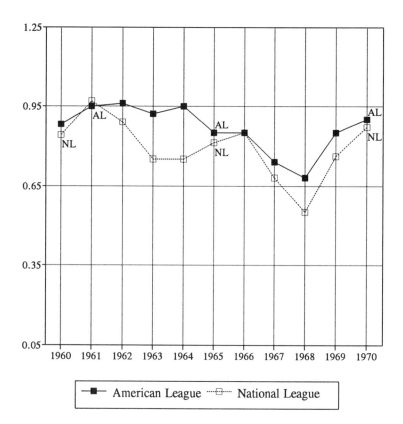

Year	AL HR/Game	AL Leader	NL HR/Game	NL Leader
1960	0.88	**Yankees**	0.84	Braves
1961	0.95	**Yankees**	0.97	Braves
1962	0.96	**Tigers**	0.89	Giants
1963	0.92	**Twins**	0.75	Giants
1964	0.95	**Twins**	0.75	Giants
1965	0.85	Red Sox	0.81	**Braves**
1966	0.85	Tigers	0.85	**Braves**
1967	0.74	**Red Sox**	0.68	**Braves**
1968	0.68	**Tigers**	0.55	Cubs
1969	0.85	**Red Sox**	0.76	Reds
1970	0.90	**Red Sox**	0.87	Reds

Figure 2-28 shows home runs per game by year for the American and National leagues from 1970 through 1980. The scale of the graph includes the highest and lowest values of home runs per game in the century. The same scale is used for all decades so it is possible to see at a glance how home runs in one decade compare to the highs and lows for the century. The exact values of home runs per game for each year are shown below the graph together with the teams that led each league. Teams that led the majors are shown in bold.

In spite of the favorable (for hitters) strike zone change and the lowering of the mound in 1969, AL home runs fell early in the 1970s, hitting their lowest level since 1949 in 1972. This matched the league's big decline in runs (Figure 2-8), and as a result the AL adopted the designated hitter rule for the 1973 season. Home runs rebounded in the AL in 1973, but, after declining a little after 1973, they hit their lowest level since 1948 in 1976. The NL also declined in home runs in 1976, hitting its lowest level since 1968, which in turn was its lowest since 1946. But there was a recovery in both leagues in 1977, and as the AL began to master the use of the DH the home run gap between the AL and the NL increased steadily after 1977.

The AL has led the NL in home runs every year since 1973, and since 1977 the 1989 Mets are the only NL team to lead the majors in home runs (the 1990 Mets also tied the Tigers). The Dodgers led the NL in home runs 5 times in the period, making them the team leading the NL in home runs the most times since 1973 (Table 4-4). But after leading in 1980 and 1983, the Dodgers have not led the NL since. The AL has a similar pattern. The Red Sox led the AL 4 times in home runs in the 1970-80 period. They led for the last time in the period in 1979, and the Red Sox have not led the AL in home runs since. The Brewers led the AL in home runs in 1978 for the first time in franchise history, but after leading again in 1980 and 1982, the Brewers have not been back on top since. The White Sox led for the first and only time in franchise history in 1974.

Mike Schmidt led the NL 4 times in home runs in the period, while Johnny Bench, Willie Stargell (who led the decade in home runs), and George Foster (then with the Reds) had 2 titles each. In the AL, only Dick Allen (then with the White Sox), and Jim Rice were able to win as many as 2 titles each, although Reggie Jackson won one title and tied for another. Perhaps the most notable winner of only one title in the AL was Graig Nettles. He won in 1976, the league's lowest year for home runs in the period. Through 1998, Nettles is the last player from the Yankees to lead the AL in home runs.

The Yankees are the AL's top team in wins both before and after the DH, but in the DH era the Yankees have not relied on home runs to win in spite of the fact that they were the leading home run team before the DH. This is exactly the right strategy. In the DH era, nearly all AL teams can hit the long ball. Thus, to stand apart, a team needs to excel in the other phases of the game.

Figure 2-28. AL/NL Home Runs Per Game 1970-80

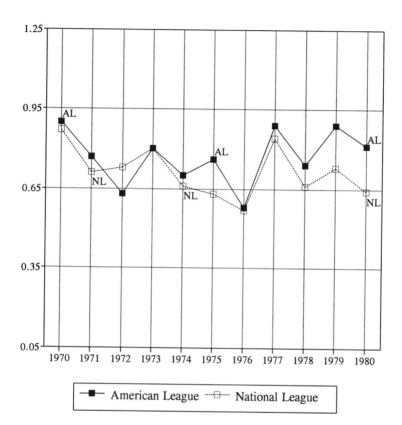

Year	AL HR/Game	AL Leader	NL HR/Game	NL Leader
1970	0.90	**Red Sox**	0.87	Reds
1971	0.77	**Tigers**	0.71	Pirates
1972	0.63	A's	0.73	**Giants**
1973	0.80	Indians	0.80	**Braves**
1974	0.70	White Sox	0.66	**Dodgers**
1975	0.76	**Indians**	0.63	Pirates
1976	0.58	Red Sox	0.57	**Reds**
1977	0.89	**Red Sox**	0.84	Dodgers
1978	0.74	**Brewers**	0.66	Dodgers
1979	0.89	**Red Sox**	0.73	Dodgers
1980	0.81	**Brewers**	0.64	Dodgers

Figure 2-29 shows home runs per game by year for the American and National leagues from 1980 through 1990. The scale of the graph includes the highest and lowest values of home runs per game in the century. The same scale is used for all decades so it is possible to see at a glance how home runs in one decade compare to the highs and lows for the century. The exact values of home runs per game for each year are shown below the graph together with the teams that led each league. Teams that led the majors are shown in bold.

The AL remained substantially ahead of the NL in home runs in the period as the DH became an established aid to offense in the AL. There was a surge upward in home runs in both leagues from 1985 through 1987, with the AL going over 1.00 home runs per game for the first time in 1986, and then setting what was then the all-time major league record of 1.16 home runs per game in 1987. This broke the NL record of 1.03 set in 1955 (Figure 2-26). The NL surge to 0.94 home runs per game in 1987 was the highest level in the NL since 1961. There were outcries of a "juiced ball" in 1987, but no one made claims about a "deadened ball" when home runs fell off sharply in 1988.

There was a dip in 1981 due to the strike near the middle of that year, but home runs rebounded in 1982, climbed to their peak in 1987, fell sharply after the 1987 peak, and then declined farther in the AL while rebounding in the NL. In fact, AL home runs declined to the point that the NL almost tied the AL in 1990 for the first time since 1976. The leagues have not been that close since.

The Mets led the NL in home runs 3 straight years at the end of the period just after the Cubs had led the NL 3 straight years. The Mets also led the majors in home runs in 1989 and tied the Tigers for the major league lead in 1990. This made the Mets the only NL team to lead the majors in home runs since the Reds did so in 1976. The Phillies led the NL in home runs in 1984 for the first time since 1936, a gap of 48 years. The Phillies have not been back on top since.

The Tigers led the AL 4 times in the period, becoming the AL team leading the league most often since the DH was born in 1973 (Table 4-4). The A's led in 1981 for the last time in franchise history while the Brewers did the same in 1982. On the other side of the coin, the Blue Jays and Angels each led for the first and only time in franchise history in 1988 and 1989 respectively. The Orioles led in 1983 for the first time since 1925, when the Browns led for their only time (the Orioles set a short lived all-time record in 1996).

Mike Schmidt led the NL in home runs 4 times in the period and in 1984 he also tied with Dale Murphy (who later won a title on his own). In the AL, Reggie Jackson tied for the home run title in 1980 and 1982. But he was not among the 4 players who tied for first in the split year of 1981. Tony Armas of the A's was, however, one of the 4, and he later won a title on his own with the Red Sox in 1984. With home runs commonplace in the AL due to the DH, there was no one dominant individual leader in the period.

Figure 2-29. AL/NL Home Runs Per Game 1980-90

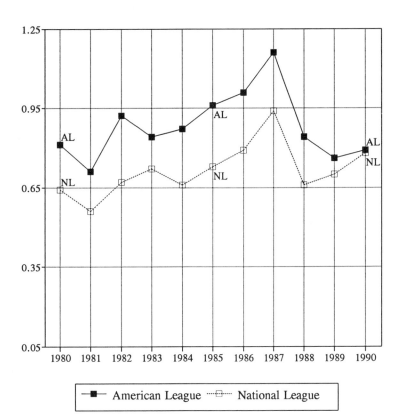

Year	AL HR/Game	AL Leader	NL HR/Game	NL Leader
1980	0.81	**Brewers**	0.64	Dodgers
1981	0.71	**A's**	0.56	Expos
1982	0.92	**Brewers**	0.67	Braves
1983	0.84	**Orioles**	0.72	Dodgers
1984	0.87	**Tigers**	0.66	Phillies
1985	0.96	**Orioles**	0.73	Cubs
1986	1.01	**Tigers**	0.79	Cubs
1987	1.16	**Tigers**	0.94	Cubs
1988	0.84	**Blue Jays**	0.66	Mets
1989	0.76	Angels	0.70	**Mets**
1990	0.79	**Tigers**	0.78	**Mets**

Figure 2-30 shows home runs per game by year for the American and National leagues from 1988 through 1998. The scale of the graph includes the highest and lowest values of home runs per game in the century. The same scale is used for all decades so it is possible to see at a glance how home runs in one decade compare to the highs and lows for the century. The exact values of home runs per game for each year are shown below the graph together with the teams that led each league. Teams that led the majors are shown in bold.

The AL stayed near the 0.80 level in home runs from 1988 through 1992, but the NL fell to its lowest level in 1992 since the strike year of 1981. That low level was quickly erased in 1993, which was the beginning of a sharp increase in home runs in both leagues. As I describe in *Crossing the Plate*, a critical mass of hitters who had grown up with the DH, aluminum bats, serious weight training, and a focus on the long ball combined with a new round of expansion to return AL runs to near-record levels and to push AL home runs to new highs in the 1993-97 period. Offense also increased sharply in the NL, but without the DH the NL still remained far from its runs records although arcade baseball in Denver did help the league approach its home run records of the 1950s.

The offensive surge starting in 1993 produced a home run peak in 1996. The AL set the all-time major league record for home runs in 1996 at 1.21 per game, while the NL mark of 0.98 was enough to set a new combined league record as well in 1996. But 1996 was only the 4th best year for the NL behind 1955, 1998, and 1956 (Figure 2-26). The AL hit 23 percent more home runs than the NL in 1996, demonstrating that having the DH on every team in the league was far superior to having only one team (the Colorado Rockies) come close to the AL leaders in the mile high home run haven of Denver.

The resurgent Braves led the NL in home runs 4 times during the period on their way to being the best team in baseball in the decade of the 1990s. The newborn Rockies and the Mets led 3 times each at opposite ends of the decade. The Tigers led the AL 3 times while the Indians and Mariners each led twice. In 1997, the Mariners led the AL for the first time and set a new AL and major league record for home runs by a team in one season (264) while the Rockies set a new NL record for team home runs in one season (239).

Ken Griffey, Jr., led the AL 3 times in the period (hitting 56 in 1997 and 1998), while Cecil Fielder and Juan Gonzalez each led twice. Mark McGwire led the AL with 52 home runs for the A's in 1996, hit 58 in 1997 for the A's and Cards, and set the all-time major league record in 1998 with 70 for the Cards. In the great home run chase of 1998, Sammy Sosa also broke the prior major league record of 61 while setting the NL record with 66. Although no one led the NL more than once, the Rockies had 3 straight leaders with Dante Bichette in 1995, Andres Galarraga in 1996, and Larry Walker in 1997. Fred McGriff led the AL in 1989 for the Blue Jays and the NL in 1992 for the Padres.

Figure 2-30. AL/NL Home Runs Per Game 1988-98

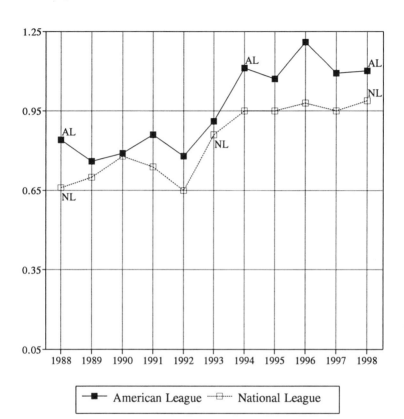

Year	AL HR/Game	AL Leader	NL HR/Game	NL Leader
1988	0.84	**Blue Jays**	0.66	Mets
1989	0.76	Angels	0.70	**Mets**
1990	0.79	**Tigers**	0.78	**Mets**
1991	0.86	**Tigers**	0.74	Reds
1992	0.78	**Tigers**	0.65	Braves
1993	0.91	**Rangers**	0.86	Braves
1994	1.11	**Indians**	0.95	Braves
1995	1.07	**Indians**	0.95	Rockies
1996	1.21	**Orioles**	0.98	Rockies
1997	1.09	**Mariners**	0.95	Rockies
1998	1.10	**Mariners**	0.99	Cards

Figure 2-31 shows stolen bases per game by year for the American and National leagues from 1900 through 1910. The scale of the graph includes the highest and lowest values of stolen bases per game in the century. The same scale is used for all decades so it is possible to see at a glance how stolen bases in one decade compare to the highs and lows for the century. The exact values of stolen bases per game for each year are shown below the graph together with the teams that led each league. Teams that led the majors are shown in bold.

Stolen bases are a good indicator of the style of play in each decade. When it is difficult to score runs, stolen bases tend to increase because the chance of being thrown out is an acceptable risk for putting a runner in scoring position. When runs come more readily, stolen bases decline because it is not worthwhile to risk giving up an out just to advance one base. However, this effect must be balanced against the fact that the distance between the bases is fixed and as the average runner becomes faster and faster, a stolen base becomes a more attractive option because the probability of being caught is reduced.

Stolen bases reached their highest levels early in the century because runs were hard to score and the basic strategy was to advance the runner into a more likely scoring position. Also, the skills of catching and throwing the ball were near minimum levels when the century started. Taking 1901 as the starting point, the AL set the all-time record in 1912 at 1.46 while the NL set its record at 1.39 in 1903. But the NL recorded a mark of 1.48 in 1900 before the AL began play.

The White Sox led the AL 4 straight times after the league was born. The White Sox went on to lead the majors more times than any other team during the century (Table 4-5). During the period the Yankees led the AL 3 times and the Senators twice. The Giants and Cubs each led the NL 3 times with the Giants leading the majors every year they led the NL.

The AL quickly fell behind the NL in stolen bases after 1901, but by 1906 the leagues were very close and they stayed that way for the rest of the decade. It is not clear what caused the AL dip early in the period, but adopting the foul strike rule for the first time in 1903 may have been a major factor. Offense fell sharply after the rule was adopted (Figure 2-1), and even if the strategy is to move into scoring position there must be runners on base for bases to be stolen. This is why stolen bases increased at the end of the decade as offense increased after the cork-center ball was introduced. At this early point in the century the strategy was still to advance one base at a time, and with more runners reaching base the number of stolen bases increased.

Honus Wagner led the NL in stolen bases 5 times in the period, while Bob Bescher of the Reds led twice, his titles in 1909 and 1910 being the first of 4 straight he won over two decades. The only players to win more than one title in the AL were Ty Cobb, who won in 1907 and 1909 (his rookie season was 1905), and Elmer Flick of the Indians who won in 1904 and 1906.

Figure 2-31. AL/NL Stolen Bases Per Game 1900-10

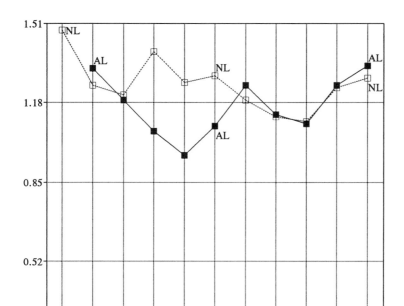

Year	AL SB/Game	AL Leader	NL SB/Game	NL Leader
1900	--	--	1.48	**Dodgers**
1901	1.32	**White Sox**	1.25	Cubs
1902	1.19	**White Sox**	1.21	Cubs
1903	1.06	White Sox	1.39	**Dodgers**
1904	0.96	White Sox	1.26	**Giants**
1905	1.08	Yankees	1.29	**Giants**
1906	1.25	Senators	1.19	**Giants**
1907	1.13	Senators	1.12	**Pirates**
1908	1.09	**Yankees**	1.10	Cubs
1909	1.25	Tigers	1.24	**Reds**
1910	1.33	Yankees	1.28	**Reds**

Figure 2-32 shows stolen bases per game by year for the American and National leagues from 1910 through 1920. The scale of the graph includes the highest and lowest values of stolen bases per game in the century. The same scale is used for all decades so it is possible to see at a glance how stolen bases in one decade compare to the highs and lows for the century. The exact values of stolen bases per game for each year are shown below the graph together with the teams that led each league. Teams that led the majors are shown in bold.

In the AL, stolen bases increased as offense increased from 1910 through 1912 due to the use of the cork-center ball. The AL reached its all-time high in 1912, but then began a steady decline when offense declined as described in the text accompanying Figure 2-2. For the same reasons, the NL tracked the decline in the AL, but from 1915 onward the NL remained relatively constant while the AL continued its decline. This brought the NL above the AL in stolen bases in 1918 for the first time since 1908.

The home run revolution started by Babe Ruth in 1919 caused AL stolen bases to drop sharply at the end of the period because it no longer made sense to risk being thrown out to advance one base when extra-base hits suddenly started to become commonplace. The NL also dropped sharply in 1920 when the hitters in the NL started to copy the Babe Ruth style in earnest. Stolen bases would not begin to increase again in either league until the 1960s, when pitchers regained the upper hand and runs once again were at a premium.

The Senators led the AL 3 times in stolen bases during the period, while the Yankees, Tigers, and White Sox all led twice. There was no dominant team in the league during the period, but stadiums once again helped determine the style of play. As Babe Ruth led the way to the long ball game, teams like the White Sox and Senators, who played in stadiums where home runs were hard to hit, stole bases at a higher rate than other teams. As a result, the White Sox and Senators led the AL in stolen bases for much of the next 3 decades. The Senators led for the last time in 1948 as their teams began to decline in all areas. The White Sox continued to lead for 2 more decades (they were know as the Go Go Sox in the 1950s). But the White Sox led for the last time in 1966 (Table 4-5).

The Giants led the NL 6 times in the period with the Pirates leading 4 times. Under John McGraw the Giants used the stolen base as a key offensive weapon, and they set the all-time team record for stolen bases at 2.25 per game for a total of 347 in 1911. The Pirates, who led the NL late in the period, were like the Senators and White Sox in stealing more than average due to their huge stadium.

Ty Cobb led the AL in stolen bases 5 times in the period (doing it in the 8 seasons from 1910 through 1917), and Clyde Milan of the Senators led twice. In the NL, Max Carey of the Pirates led 6 times (in the 8 seasons from 1913 through 1920), Bob Beschler of the Reds led 3 times (from 1910 through 1912), and George Burns of the Giants led twice.

Figure 2-32. AL/NL Stolen Bases Per Game 1910-20

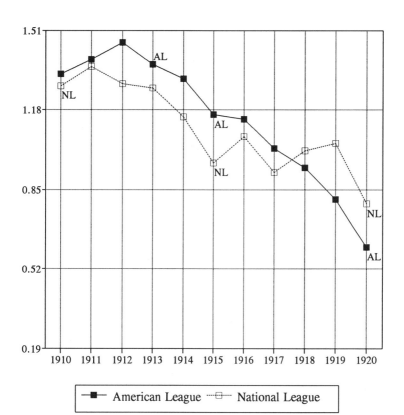

Year	AL SB/Game	AL Leader	NL SB/Game	NL Leader
1910	1.33	Yankees	1.28	**Reds**
1911	1.39	Tigers	1.36	**Giants**
1912	1.46	Senators	1.29	**Giants**
1913	1.37	Senators	1.27	**Giants**
1914	1.31	**Yankees**	1.15	Giants
1915	1.16	**Tigers**	0.96	Pirates
1916	1.14	**Browns**	1.07	Giants
1917	1.02	**White Sox**	0.92	Giants
1918	0.94	Indians	1.01	**Pirates**
1919	0.81	White Sox	1.04	**Pirates**
1920	0.61	Senators	0.79	**Pirates**

Figure 2-33 shows stolen bases per game by year for the American and National leagues from 1920 through 1930. The scale of the graph includes the highest and lowest values of stolen bases per game in the century. The same scale is used for all decades so it is possible to see at a glance how stolen bases in one decade compare to the highs and lows for the century. The exact values of stolen bases per game for each year are shown below the graph together with the teams that led each league. Teams that led the majors are shown in bold.

AL stolen bases were relatively constant during the period, but what were then all-time lows were reached in 1922 and 1926 followed by a rebound each time. New lows were reached again in 1929 and 1930, and the following decades would demonstrate the same pattern until a true all-time low was reached in 1950 (Figure 2-36). The NL followed a similar cycle as stealing bases became a neglected strategy in the long-ball game. However, for some reason the AL regularly had more stolen bases than the NL after 1925. Both leagues were dedicated to the long-ball game in the 1920s, and the AL had by far the higher offense in the 1930s, but the AL led the NL in stolen bases 15 straight years from 1930 through 1944 after the NL popped ahead briefly in 1929.

As discussed in the text accompanying Figure 2-32, the White Sox and Senators became the AL stolen base leaders because they played in huge stadiums not well suited to the long ball game. The White Sox led the AL 5 times in the period and the Senators led 4 times. In the NL the Pirates also played in a huge park and led the league 4 times in stolen bases. The Giants, who practically invented the game built around stolen bases in the prior decades, only led twice in the 1920s as they adapted to the long ball game in the Polo Grounds with its extremely short foul lines. After 1926 the Giants did not lead the league in stolen bases again until 1956 when Willie Mays was on the scene. But even with Mays, the Giants last led the league in stolen bases in 1957 (Table 4-5).

The Cards replaced the Giants as the NL leader in 1927. It was the first time the Cards had led in stolen bases, and they went on to lead the majors in the 1930s with the "Gashouse Gang". Fifty years later they would lead the majors in the 1980s, and ultimately move to the top of the NL list and tie the Dodgers in leading the NL in stolen bases most often during the century (Table 4-5).

Although he was best know for his hitting, George Sisler led the AL in stolen bases 3 times in the period. Matching the emphasis the White Sox put on the stolen base as part of their strategy, Eddie Collins and Johnny Mostil of the White Sox each led twice. Similarly, with the Forbes Field Pirates putting an emphasis on the stolen base, Max Carey led the NL 5 times in stolen bases in the 1920s, giving him a total of 10 titles in his career with the Pirates. Kiki Cuyler won for the Pirates in 1926, and then led 3 times for the Cubs at the end of the decade. Frankie Frisch won for the Giants in 1921, and then led the league for the Cards in 1927 when they won their first title in franchise history.

Figure 2-33. AL/NL Stolen Bases Per Game 1920-30

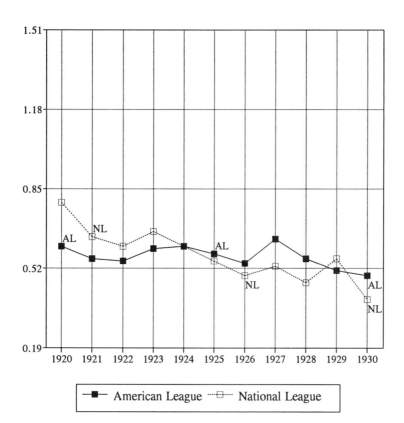

Year	AL SB/Game	AL Leader	NL SB/Game	NL Leader
1920	0.61	Senators	0.79	**Pirates**
1921	0.56	Senators	0.65	**Giants**
1922	0.55	Browns	0.61	**Pirates**
1923	0.60	**White Sox**	0.67	Cubs
1924	0.61	White Sox	0.61	**Pirates**
1925	0.58	Senators	0.55	**Pirates**
1926	0.54	**White Sox**	0.49	Giants
1927	0.64	**Tigers**	0.53	Cards
1928	0.56	**White Sox**	0.46	Reds
1929	0.51	White Sox	0.56	**Reds**
1930	0.49	**Senators**	0.39	Pirates

Figure 2-34 shows stolen bases per game by year for the American and National leagues from 1930 through 1940. The scale of the graph includes the highest and lowest values of stolen bases per game in the century. The same scale is used for all decades so it is possible to see at a glance how stolen bases in one decade compare to the highs and lows for the century. The exact values of stolen bases per game for each year are shown below the graph together with the teams that led each league. Teams that led the majors are shown in bold.

Average stolen bases continued to decline in both leagues during the 1930s, even though NL runs declined from the all-time highs reached in the 1920s. The AL, however, set its all-time high in runs in 1936 and scored at a high level during most of the 1930s. By the end of the 1930s stolen bases took place only when a steal situation was obvious and not as a regular part of game strategy. The AL led the NL in stolen bases throughout the decade, but this was probably more a result of the fact that the AL was the superior offensive league in every category rather than a result of a fundamental difference in strategy in the two leagues. The difference between the AL and NL was especially high in 1939, but by 1940 the leagues were close together again.

The Senators and the Yankees each led the AL 3 times in the period, but the reasons were much different. The Senators were continuing with the stolen base as a part of their strategy to score runs while the Yankees were simply superior to all teams in nearly every phase of the game. A notable event came in 1935 when the Red Sox led the AL in stolen bases for the first and only time in the history of the franchise.

The Cards led the NL in stolen bases 7 times in the period, and they were the only team in the league to lead more than once. The Pepper Martin version of the Gashouse Gang got started when the Cards upset the A's in the 1931 World Series, and if the Cards had not been edged by the Reds by one stolen base in 1935, the Cards would have won 7 straight titles from 1931 through 1937. A notable title was won by the Cubs in 1939. It was their fifth title, but also their last. The Cubs have not led the league in stolen bases since, and they have never led the majors in stolen bases. When the Red Sox produced their one and only stolen base title in 1935, they at least also led the majors that year.

Ben Chapman led the AL in stolen bases 3 times for the Yankees. Chapman then tied Billy Werber of the A's for the lead in 1937 while splitting time with the Senators and the Red Sox (the Red Sox had sent Werber to the A's even though he had won 2 previous titles for them). At the end of the decade in 1939 and 1940, George Case of the Senators won the first 2 of what would be 5 straight titles. In the NL, Pepper Martin won 3 titles for the Cards and Augie Galan of the Cubs won 2 during the period. Perhaps the most notable title was that won by slugger Chuck Klein of the Phillies in 1932, the year before he won the Triple Crown. Combined speed and power also existed back in the 1930s.

Figure 2-34. AL/NL Stolen Bases Per Game 1930-40

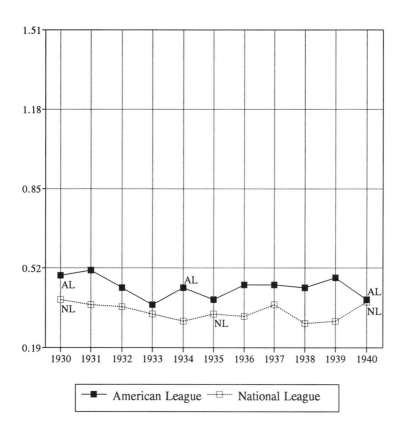

Year	AL SB/Game	AL Leader	NL SB/Game	NL Leader
1930	0.49	**Senators**	0.39	Pirates
1931	0.51	**Yankees**	0.37	Cards
1932	0.44	**Tigers**	0.36	Cards
1933	0.37	Yankees	0.33	**Cards**
1934	0.44	**Tigers**	0.30	Cards
1935	0.39	**Red Sox**	0.33	Reds
1936	0.45	**Senators**	0.32	Cards
1937	0.45	**A's**	0.37	Cards
1938	0.44	**Yankees**	0.29	Dodgers
1939	0.48	**White Sox**	0.30	Cubs
1940	0.39	Senators	0.38	**Cards**

Figure 2-35 shows stolen bases per game by year for the American and National leagues from 1940 through 1950. The scale of the graph includes the highest and lowest values of stolen bases per game in the century. The same scale is used for all decades so it is possible to see at a glance how stolen bases in one decade compare to the highs and lows for the century. The exact values of stolen bases per game for each year are shown below the graph together with the teams that led each league. Teams that led the majors are shown in bold.

AL stolen bases increased during WWII when offense fell and runs became harder to score. But NL stolen bases remained near all-time lows from 1941 through 1944. When the players began to return from WWII in 1945, the NL led the AL in stolen bases for the first time since 1929. The league leader varied after that, but by 1950, when the AL set its all-time low for stolen bases, the AL had led the NL 33 times in stolen bases while the NL had led 17 times. 1950 marked the turning point in this competition. Since 1950 the AL has led the NL only 7 times in stolen bases while the NL has led the AL 42 times. The more rapid influx of black players into the NL as compared to the AL put the NL in the lead in the 1950s, and the DH cemented the change in 1973 (Figure 2-37).

The White Sox focused even stronger on a stolen base strategy with speed throughout the team in the 1940s, and they led the AL in stolen bases 6 times in the period. The Senators continued their stolen base strategy of prior decades and led the AL in stolen bases 4 times. Between them the White Sox and Senators led the majors 6 times in the period. But the Senators had entered a period of decline that would mark their last decade in Washington. They led the league in stolen bases for the last time in franchise history in 1948 (Table 4-5). Their successors, the Minneapolis Twins, have never led the league in stolen bases.

With the signing of Jackie Robinson, the Dodgers embarked on a potent combination of great power and great speed. They led the NL 6 times in stolen bases in the period, winning the last 5 years in a row from 1946 through 1950, and they stretched that to 8 titles in a row by 1953. With the coming of Maury Wills in the 1960s to build on their success in the 1940s and 1950s, the Dodgers climbed to the top of the list in leading the NL in stolen bases the most times. But that all changed after Wills was gone. The Dodgers have not led the NL in stolen bases since 1970, although they are still tied with the Cards at the top of the list (Table 4-5). Another notable event was the stolen base title won by the Braves in 1945. It is the one and only title in franchise history.

George Case of the Senators led the AL 5 times in stolen bases in the period, while Bob Dillinger of the Browns led 3 times and Snuffy Stirnweiss of the Yankees led twice. In the NL the Dodgers dominated the individual titles as well as the team titles. Jackie Robinson led twice as did Pete Reiser, and Arky Vaughan won in 1943 after coming over to the Dodgers from the Pirates in 1942 to wind up his great career in Brooklyn.

Figure 2-35. AL/NL Stolen Bases Per Game 1940-50

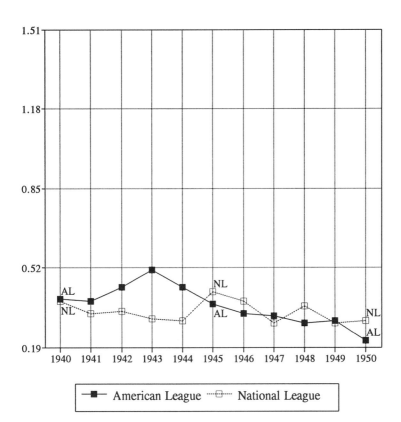

Year	AL SB/Game	AL Leader	NL SB/Game	NL Leader
1940	0.39	Senators	0.38	**Cards**
1941	0.38	**White Sox**	0.33	Reds
1942	0.44	**White Sox**	0.34	Dodgers
1943	0.51	**White Sox**	0.31	Pirates
1944	0.44	**Senators**	0.30	Pirates
1945	0.37	**Senators**	0.42	Braves
1946	0.33	White Sox	0.38	**Dodgers**
1947	0.32	**White Sox**	0.29	Dodgers
1948	0.29	Senators	0.36	**Dodgers**
1949	0.30	White Sox	0.29	**Dodgers**
1950	0.22	A's	0.30	**Dodgers**

Figure 2-36 shows stolen bases per game by year for the American and National leagues from 1950 through 1960. The scale of the graph includes the highest and lowest values of stolen bases per game in the century. The same scale is used for all decades so it is possible to see at a glance how stolen bases in one decade compare to the highs and lows for the century. The exact values of stolen bases per game for each year are shown below the graph together with the teams that led each league. Teams that led the majors are shown in bold.

Stolen bases hit their lowest levels of the century during the 1950s. Home runs were at record levels and no one was interested in moving up just one base unless it was a sure thing. The AL had its record low in 1950 at 0.22 stolen bases per game. This means the average team stole only 34 bases for the entire season. Dom DiMaggio of the Red Sox led the league with 15 stolen bases, and only 4 players in the league stole more than 10 bases. The NL reached its low point for the century in 1954, with an average team stealing 42 bases during the year. But Bill Bruton of the Braves led the league with 34, and the top five players all stole at least 11 bases. The NL low was definitely higher than the AL low, and during the period the NL led the AL in stolen bases every year but 1954 when the NL recorded its all-time low.

The White Sox led the AL in stolen bases every year but 1950, winning 11 titles in a row from 1951 through 1961. They also led the majors 8 times, winning 6 major league titles in a row from 1956 through 1961. The Go Go Sox used the stolen base as a key strategy in the period, winning the pennant in 1959 and having a winning season every year they led in stolen bases (the White Sox had 17 winning seasons in a row from 1951 through 1967). They led the league in stolen bases 30 times in the century, far more often than the Senators/Twins who rank second with 13 (Table 4-5). The White Sox are also far ahead of the Dodgers and Cards who tie for the NL lead at 21. But the White Sox led the AL for the last time in 1966, and they had 10 losing seasons in the 14 years after 1966 before becoming regular winners again in the early 1980s.

The Dodgers led the NL in stolen bases 8 of the 11 years in the period, but they were a powerful high-scoring team that did everything well. The Giants led in 1956 and 1957, with 1956 being the first time they led since 1926, and 1957 being the last time they led in franchise history. Willie Mays was the primary reason the Giants reappeared on the leader list.

Mays led the NL in stolen bases 4 years in a row from 1956 through 1959. Before Mays took over, Sam Jethro of the old Boston Braves won 2 titles in his first 2 years in the league and Bill Bruton of the new Milwaukee Braves won 3 titles in his first 3 years in the league. White Sox players dominated the AL leaders. Luis Aparicio won 5 titles in a row from 1956 through 1960 (he made it 9 in a row with the White Sox and Orioles through 1964). Minnie Minoso won 3 titles from 1951 through 1953, and Jim Rivera led the league in 1955.

Figure 2-36. AL/NL Stolen Bases Per Game 1950-60

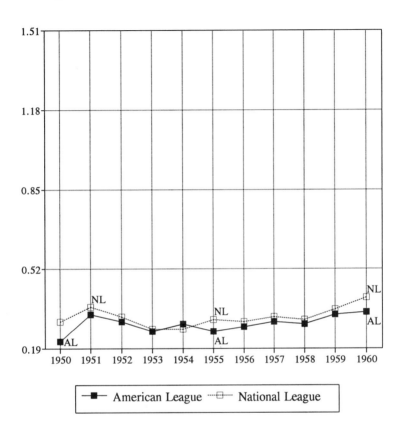

Year	AL SB/Game	AL Leader	NL SB/Game	NL Leader
1950	0.22	A's	0.30	**Dodgers**
1951	0.33	**White Sox**	0.36	Dodgers
1952	0.30	White Sox	0.32	**Dodgers**
1953	0.26	White Sox	0.27	**Dodgers**
1954	0.29	**White Sox**	0.27	Cards
1955	0.26	White Sox	0.31	**Dodgers**
1956	0.28	**White Sox**	0.30	Giants
1957	0.30	**White Sox**	0.32	Giants
1958	0.29	**White Sox**	0.31	Dodgers
1959	0.33	**White Sox**	0.35	Dodgers
1960	0.34	**White Sox**	0.40	Dodgers

Figure 2-37 shows stolen bases per game by year for the American and National leagues from 1960 through 1970. The scale of the graph includes the highest and lowest values of stolen bases per game in the century. The same scale is used for all decades so it is possible to see at a glance how stolen bases in one decade compare to the highs and lows for the century. The exact values of stolen bases per game for each year are shown below the graph together with the teams that led each league. Teams that led the majors are shown in bold.

The strike zone change in 1963 that put pitchers back in charge was responsible for bringing the stolen base back into the strategy of the game. Runs became hard to score and the balance between advancing a base compared to the risk of being thrown out started to move back in favor of the stolen base. The fact that the average runner was faster than before supported this move. The AL had a 30 percent increase in stolen bases between 1964 and 1965, and the level of stolen bases moved up consistently until there was a drop in 1970 (the strike zone change was reversed in 1969). But the 1970 level was still higher than the increased level that occurred in 1965. The NL did not show a significant change, but the NL started the decade ahead of the AL, and the NL stayed ahead every year in the period except 1968 and 1969 (1968 was the first year the AL led the NL in stolen bases since 1954).

The Kansas City/Oakland A's took over from the White Sox as the new AL leader. The A's led 4 times and the White Sox 3 times in the period. No other team led more than once. The A's were starting to build the kind of team that would set the all-time AL record for stolen bases in 1976 (Figure 2-38), and the version of the A's that left Kansas City for Oakland in 1968 was far superior to the version that left Philadelphia for Kansas City in 1955.

The Los Angeles Dodgers picked up where the Brooklyn Dodgers left off in leading the NL in stolen bases, and, with Maury Wills as the key, the Dodgers led the NL in stolen bases 7 times in the period. The Dodgers won 8 titles in a row from 1958 (the year they moved to Los Angeles) through 1965 (1966 was the last year Wills was with the Dodgers). The Dodgers won another title in 1970, but it was their last. From 1901 through 1972, the Dodgers led the NL in stolen bases 21 times, well ahead of the Giants who were in second place with 13. But through 1998 both the Dodgers and Giants remain frozen in time, and the Cards have moved into a first place tie with the Dodgers (Table 4-5).

Luis Aparicio led the AL 5 times from 1960 through 1964, playing for the White Sox through 1962 and for the Orioles in 1963 and 1964. Bert Campaneris of the A's led 5 of the next 6 years, including 4 in a row from 1965 through 1968. In the NL, Maury Wills led for 6 straight years from 1960 through 1965, setting what was then the major league record with 104 steals in 1962. Lou Brock (who eventually set both the single year and all-time career record in the NL), then led the next 4 years in a row from 1966 through 1969.

Figure 2-37. AL/NL Stolen Bases Per Game 1960-70

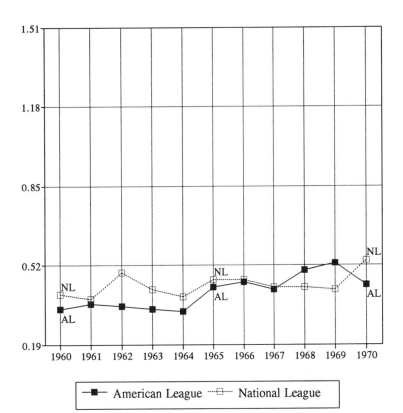

Year	AL SB/Game	AL Leader	NL SB/Game	NL Leader
1960	0.34	**White Sox**	0.40	Dodgers
1961	0.36	**White Sox**	0.38	Dodgers
1962	0.35	Rangers	0.49	**Dodgers**
1963	0.34	Orioles	0.42	**Dodgers**
1964	0.33	Indians	0.39	**Dodgers**
1965	0.43	A's	0.46	**Dodgers**
1966	0.45	**White Sox**	0.46	Cards
1967	0.42	**A's**	0.43	Cards
1968	0.50	**A's**	0.43	Pirates
1969	0.53	**Brewers**	0.42	Astros
1970	0.44	**A's**	0.54	**Dodgers**

Figure 2-38 shows stolen bases per game by year for the American and National leagues from 1970 through 1980. The scale of the graph includes the highest and lowest values of stolen bases per game in the century. The same scale is used for all decades so it is possible to see at a glance how stolen bases in one decade compare to the highs and lows for the century. The exact values of stolen bases per game for each year are shown below the graph together with the teams that led each league. Teams that led the majors are shown in bold.

The two leagues stayed close together in stolen bases from 1970 through 1974, and the level of stolen bases was slightly above the already increased level at which the 1960s ended. The AL surged ahead in 1975 and 1976 as the A's, winners of the World Series 3 straight years from 1972 through 1974, set the all-time AL record in 1976. But 1976 was the last year the AL led the NL until 1998. The designated hitter rule was adopted by the AL in 1973, and with the leagues playing under different rules for the first time since 1902, the strategy was also different. Runs were easier to come by in the AL with the DH, and the stolen base lost some of its value. Runs were harder to come by in the NL, and the stolen base was much more viable. Thus, the NL moved well ahead of the AL in stolen bases after the unique performance of the A's in 1976.

The A's led the AL 4 times in the period, and the new Kansas City Royals, who replaced the A's in Kansas City, also led 4 times. The A's had balanced teams with good speed, good pitching, good defense, and good offense. This is why they matched the Yankees as they only teams to win the World Series 3 or more times in a row. In 1976 the A's had 341 steals (2.12 per game). The only team to top that mark is the 1911 Giants who had 347 (2.25 per game). But the 1976 A's were 144 percent above the league average while the 1911 Giants were only 65 percent above. The 1976 A's were unique for their time. The brand new Royals were very good for an expansion team, but they had limited power and used speed and stolen bases to manufacture runs.

In 1980 the NL reached its highest level in stolen bases since 1919. NL leaders were more widely spread than in the AL, but the Reds won 4 titles because the Big Red Machine matched the A's as a well balanced team that excelled in all phases of the game. The Reds won the World Series in 1975 and 1976, the first NL team to win back-to-back titles since the Giants did it in 1921 and 1922. The Cards and Pirates each led the league twice in the period, but no other team led more than once.

Bert Campaneris and Bill North of the A's each led the AL twice. No other AL player led more than once, but Ron LeFlore won with the Tigers in 1978 and with the Expos in 1980. In a passing of the baton, Rickey Henderson won the first of his 12 AL titles with 100 steals in 1980 while Lou Brock won 4 of his 8 NL titles, setting the all-time NL record at 118 with his last title in 1974. Davey Lopes of the Dodgers and Omar Moreno of the Pirates each won twice.

Figure 2-38. AL/NL Stolen Bases Per Game 1970-80

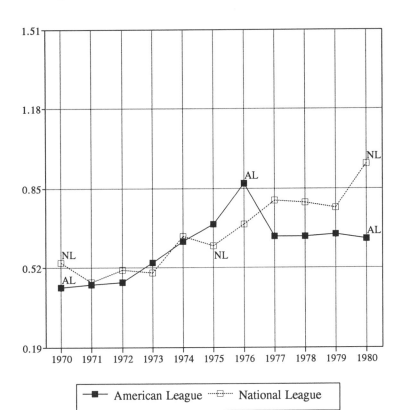

Year	AL SB/Game	AL Leader	NL SB/Game	NL Leader
1970	0.44	A's	0.54	**Dodgers**
1971	0.45	**Royals**	0.46	Cards
1972	0.46	Rangers	0.51	**Reds**
1973	0.54	Orioles	0.50	**Reds**
1974	0.63	A's	0.65	**Cards**
1975	0.70	**Angels**	0.61	Reds
1976	0.87	**A's**	0.70	Reds
1977	0.65	**A's**	0.80	**Pirates**
1978	0.65	**Royals**	0.79	Pirates
1979	0.66	**Royals**	0.77	Astros
1980	0.64	Royals	0.95	**Padres**

Figure 2-39 shows stolen bases per game by year for the American and National leagues from 1980 through 1990. The scale of the graph includes the highest and lowest values of stolen bases per game in the century. The same scale is used for all decades so it is possible to see at a glance how stolen bases in one decade compare to the highs and lows for the century. The exact values of stolen bases per game for each year are shown below the graph together with the teams that led each league. Teams that led the majors are shown in bold.

Stolen bases increased on average in both leagues in the 1980s as players with both speed and power became commonplace. The NL stayed well ahead of the AL throughout the decade since stolen bases were still more valuable in the NL without the DH, but the average level of stolen bases in the majors was higher than at any time since 1919. In a demonstration of how power and speed were being combined in an unprecedented way, the AL had its highest level of stolen bases in the period in 1987 when the AL set what was then the all-time major league record for home runs.

The Brewers led the AL 4 times in the period and the A's and Indians led twice. The Brewers led 4 times in a row late in the decade because they ranked near the bottom of the home of the league in home runs and they were using team speed to manufacture runs. No individual Brewer won a stolen base title during the period. On the other hand, the A's were leaders because Rickey Henderson was setting individual stolen base records. In 1982, when Henderson set the major league single season record for steals at 130, he stole more bases than 9 of the other 13 teams in the league. If he had stolen 7 more bases he would have outrun 12 of the other 13 teams. The Indians would have been the only team to beat him.

In the NL the Cards led the NL 7 times in a row from 1982 through 1988, and the Expos led 3 times. The Cards adopted team speed as a major strategy in the 1980s. No team in the majors hit fewer home runs both at home and on the road than the Cards, but they scored a lot of runs by moving runners around the bases (they led the league in runs in 1982 and 1985). The Cards had 314 stolen bases in 1985, the most in the NL since the 1912 Giants had 319. Accordingly, the Cards are the only one of the 8 NL teams in existence in 1901 to set their team record in stolen bases after 1913.

Rickey Henderson led the AL in stolen bases every year in the period except 1987. Henderson had spent all of his career with the A's when he moved to the Yankees in 1985. But he moved back to the A's in 1989, and in the 1990s he became the major league career leader in stolen bases still playing primarily for the A's. The Expos led the NL early in the decade with Ron LeFlore winning the title in 1980 and Tim Raines winning the next 4 titles from 1981 through 1984. But Vince Coleman of the Cards took over in 1985 and won the title every year from 1985 through 1990 for a total of 6 titles in the period.

Figure 2-39. AL/NL Stolen Bases Per Game 1980-90

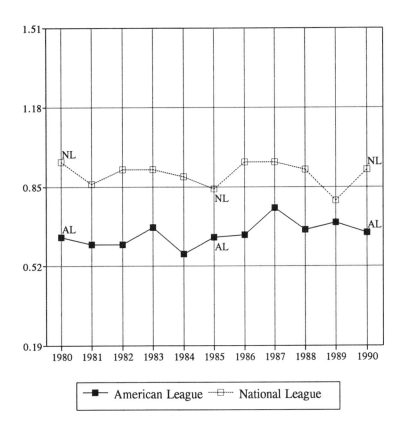

Year	AL SB/Game	AL Leader	NL SB/Game	NL Leader
1980	0.64	Royals	0.95	**Padres**
1981	0.61	Indians	0.86	**Expos**
1982	0.61	**A's**	0.92	Cards
1983	0.68	**A's**	0.92	Cards
1984	0.57	Blue Jays	0.89	**Cards**
1985	0.64	Yankees	0.84	**Cards**
1986	0.65	Indians	0.95	**Cards**
1987	0.76	Brewers	0.95	**Cards**
1988	0.67	Brewers	0.92	**Cards**
1989	0.70	**Brewers**	0.79	Expos
1990	0.66	Brewers	0.92	**Expos**

Figure 2-40 shows stolen bases per game by year for the American and National leagues from 1988 through 1998. The scale of the graph includes the highest and lowest values of stolen bases per game in the century. The same scale is used for all decades so it is possible to see at a glance how stolen bases in one decade compare to the highs and lows for the century. The exact values of stolen bases per game for each year are shown below the graph together with the teams that led each league. Teams that led the majors are shown in bold.

In the AL stolen bases were relatively constant during the period, maintaining the nearly stable level they reached in the late 1970s after the league learned how to use the designated hitter. The strategy of how often to try to steal a base has not changed in any significant way in the AL over the last 20 years. Stolen bases declined, however, in the NL during the period. 1990 marked the NL high point for the decade, and the decline continued as the expansion of 1993 produced an increase in NL runs and home runs.

After nearly falling below AL levels in 1994, NL stolen bases rebounded a little for three years and then took a sharp drop in 1998. The NL averaged only 0.62 stolen bases per game in 1998, the lowest level in the league since 1975 when the Big Red Machine was on the march. Perhaps NL runners and managers were mesmerized by the sight of Mark McGwire and Sammy Sosa hitting those home runs. The NL decrease was so sharp that the AL led the NL in stolen bases in 1998 for the first time since the A's set the all-time AL team record in 1976. This broke a winning streak of 21 straight years for the NL.

From 1991 onward the Blue Jays and Royals each won 2 AL titles and were the only teams to lead the league more than once. But when the Tigers led in 1997, it was the first time the Tigers led the league since 1934, a gap of 63 years. When the Blue Jays led both the AL and the majors in 1998, it not only helped the AL to its first lead over the NL in 21 years, it marked the first time in franchise history that the Blue Jays led the majors.

In the NL, the Expos led 3 times from 1991 onward with the Reds leading twice. This put the Expos just ahead of the Reds in second place behind the Cards for the team leading the NL most often since 1973 (Table 4-5). The Rockies made a nice parlay of speed and power when they led the NL in stolen bases in 1996 while tying the all-time NL team record for home runs. When the Pirates won in 1998, it was the first time the franchise had led since 1978.

Rickey Henderson won his 12th AL stolen base title in 1998, a gap of 7 years since his titles in 1990 and 1991. Kenny Lofton of the Indians led the AL in stolen bases from 1992 through 1996, then was traded to the Braves in 1997. He finished far down the NL list after being injured. He came back to the Indians in 1998 and finished behind Henderson. In the NL, Marquis Grissom won 2 titles for the Expos in 1991 and 1992, and newcomer Tony Womack of the Pirates won titles in 1997 and 1998. No one else won more than once.

Figure 2-40. AL/NL Stolen Bases Per Game 1988-98

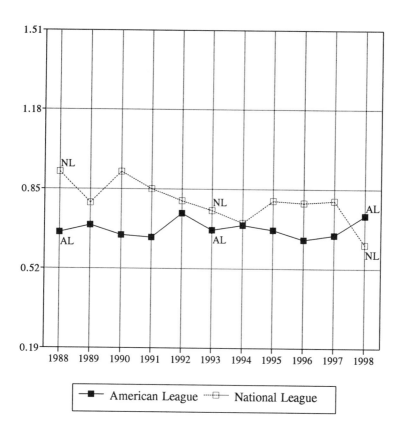

Year	AL SB/Game	AL Leader	NL SB/Game	NL Leader
1988	0.67	Brewers	0.92	**Cards**
1989	0.70	**Brewers**	0.79	Expos
1990	0.66	Brewers	0.92	**Expos**
1991	0.65	A's	0.85	**Expos**
1992	0.75	**Brewers**	0.80	Cards
1993	0.68	Blue Jays	0.76	**Expos**
1994	0.70	**Royals**	0.71	Expos
1995	0.66	Indians	0.80	**Reds**
1996	0.64	Royals	0.79	**Rockies**
1997	0.66	Tigers	0.80	**Reds**
1998	0.74	**Blue Jays**	0.62	Pirates

Part III
Defensive Measures

Strikeouts by Year

Figure 3-1 shows strikeouts per game by year for the American and National leagues from 1900 through 1910. The scale of the graph includes the highest and lowest values of strikeouts per game in the century. The same scale is used for all decades so it is possible to see at a glance how strikeouts in one decade compare to the highs and lows for the century. The exact values of strikeouts per game for each year are shown below the graph together with the teams that led each league. Teams that led the majors are shown in bold.

NL strikeouts increased by almost 60 percent between 1900 and 1901 because the foul strike rule was first adopted by the NL in 1901. The same effect took place in the AL between 1902 and 1903 when the adoption of the foul strike rule in 1903 increased AL strikeouts by 53 percent. The new higher level of strikeouts would be maintained in both leagues until the effects of WWI late in the next decade and the rule changes in 1920 forbidding "doctored" pitches would drive strikeouts down to levels not seen since the foul strike rule was enacted. The AL had higher strikeouts than the NL for 13 straight years from 1903 through 1915. During the 1900-10 period, the AL lead was primarily due to Connie Mack's great strikeout teams in Philadelphia led by Rube Waddell. The Washington Senators would take over in the next decade behind Walter Johnson.

The A's led the AL in strikeouts for 9 straight seasons from 1902 through 1910 (they led the majors every year after 1902). The A's were one of the dominant teams in baseball in the period, and it's easy to see why Connie Mack came to the conclusion that pitching is "75 percent" of the game because he always had great pitching when he had winning teams. The Giants led the NL in strikeouts 6 times in the period, and they also were one of the dominant teams in the game. Both the A's and Giants had one great strikeout pitcher on their staff, but Rube Waddell had the edge on Christy Mathewson and that edge translated into the lead that the AL had over the NL.

Waddell led the AL in strikeouts 6 straight years from 1902 through 1907 (the eccentric pitcher went to the Browns in 1908). He struck out 349 batters in 1904, a mark that was not topped until Sandy Koufax struck out 384 in 1965. Waddell still has the 4th highest major league total in the century behind Nolan Ryan and Koufax. Mathewson also led the NL 6 times in the period, but his peak was "only" 267 strikeouts in 1903. This was the high for the NL until Koufax recorded 269 strikeouts in 1961.

Figure 3-1. AL/NL Strikeouts Per Game 1900-10

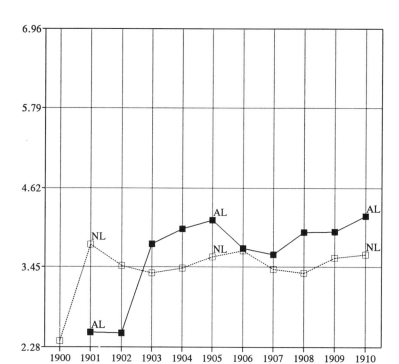

Year	AL SO/Game	AL Leader	NL SO/Game	NL Leader
1900	--	--	2.37	**Pirates**
1901	2.49	White Sox	3.78	**Dodgers**
1902	2.48	A's	3.47	**Pirates**
1903	3.79	A's	3.36	Giants
1904	4.01	A's	3.43	Giants
1905	4.14	A's	3.60	Giants
1906	3.72	A's	3.69	Cubs
1907	3.63	A's	3.42	Giants
1908	3.96	A's	3.36	Cubs
1909	3.97	A's	3.58	Giants
1910	4.20	A's	3.63	Giants

Figure 3-2 shows strikeouts per game by year for the American and National leagues from 1910 through 1920. The scale of the graph includes the highest and lowest values of strikeouts per game in the century. The same scale is used for all decades so it is possible to see at a glance how strikeouts in one decade compare to the highs and lows for the century. The exact values of strikeouts per game for each year are shown below the graph together with the teams that led each league. Teams that led the majors are shown in bold.

The AL continued its lead over the NL through 1915, with Walter Johnson of the Senators making the prime difference between the leagues. The arrival of the cork-center ball in 1910 and 1911 made very little difference in strikeouts even though offense soared (Figure 2-2). This was because there was essentially no change in the swing of most hitters. They still concentrated on hitting line drives and kept the bat under control. Thus, strikeouts stayed nearly the same even after offense fell sharply as pitchers redoubled their efforts to "doctor" the ball after the cork-center ball appeared. The dilution of talent due to the Federal League in 1914 and 1915 produced only small changes, but the effects of WWI produced a major decline. That's why it appears that the changes of 1920 had little effect on strikeouts. But considering that strikeouts should have soared as the "big swing" era arrived, the fact that they stayed nearly the same (and then declined) shows that the loss of "doctored" pitchers cut strikeouts substantially.

Behind Walter Johnson, the Senators led the AL in strikeouts 8 straight years from 1912 through 1919. During that streak they led the majors every year except 1917. The franchise led the AL in strikeouts for the first time in 1912, but after 1919 it led the AL only one more time as the 1962 Minneapolis Twins (Table 4-6). The Phillies led the NL 3 times during the period with a great strikeout staff headed by Grover Cleveland Alexander. The Giants and Cubs also led 3 times each, with Alexander contributing to the Cubs at the end of the decade after coming over from the Phillies. After leading in 1916, the Phillies did not lead the NL again until 1983. Similarly, after 1919 the Cubs did not lead again until 1938 and then not again until 1977. Completing the pattern, the Giants did not lead again until 1937 after they led in 1916, and the Giants never led the league again after 1937. The Dodgers were a main contributor to all of these gaps because, from 1920 onward, the Dodgers led the NL in strikeouts 34 times, by far the most times in either league (Table 4-6).

Walter Johnson led the AL in strikeouts 9 times in the period, including 8 straight times from 1912 through 1919. He was the dominant strikeout pitcher of the decade. But Grover Cleveland Alexander led the NL 6 times in the period, 5 times with the Phillies and once with the Cubs in 1920. That gave the Cubs 3 straight leaders after Jim "Hippo" Vaughn led for the Cubs in 1918 and 1919. In a similar way, Alexander led the Phillies to 7 titles in the period because Earl Moore and Tom Seaton of the Phillies won titles in 1910 and 1913 respectively.

Figure 3-2. AL/NL Strikeouts Per Game 1910-20

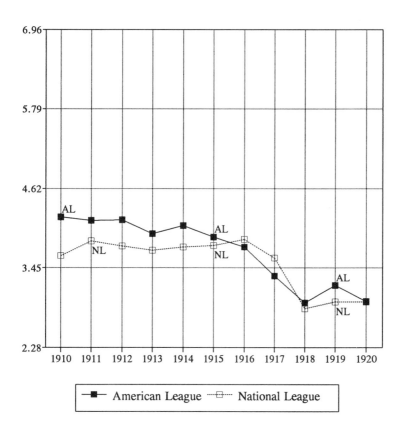

Year	AL SO/Game	AL Leader	NL SO/Game	NL Leader
1910	4.20	A's	3.63	Giants
1911	4.15	White Sox	3.85	**Giants**
1912	4.16	**Senators**	3.78	Pirates
1913	3.96	**Senators**	3.71	Phillies
1914	4.07	**Senators**	3.76	Phillies
1915	3.91	**Senators**	3.79	Phillies
1916	3.76	**Senators**	3.88	Giants
1917	3.33	Senators	3.60	**Cubs**
1918	2.93	**Senators**	2.85	Cubs
1919	3.19	**Senators**	2.95	Cubs
1920	2.96	Red Sox	2.95	**Dodgers**

Figure 3-3 shows strikeouts per game by year for the American and National leagues from 1920 through 1930. The scale of the graph includes the highest and lowest values of strikeouts per game in the century. The same scale is used for all decades so it is possible to see at a glance how strikeouts in one decade compare to the highs and lows for the century. The exact values of strikeouts per game for each year are shown below the graph together with the teams that led each league. Teams that led the majors are shown in bold.

Hitters began in earnest to copy the big swing of Babe Ruth after 1920, and at any other time in the century this would have meant increased strikeouts. But not in the 1920s. The rule changes outlawing "doctored" pitchers in 1920 left pitchers suddenly without their tools, and hitters took command. Offense soared but strikeouts did not. Strikeout-to-walk ratios were substantially less than 1.00 (the 1926 Browns walked nearly twice as many batters as they struck out for a ratio of 0.52). The effect was the same for pitchers everywhere and there was little difference between the leagues in strikeouts. Only the fact that the foul strike rule was not in effect until 1901 in the NL and 1903 in the AL kept both leagues from setting all-time lows in strikeouts. Overall, strikeouts before 1920 were 30 percent higher than they were in the 1920s, in spite of the fact that before 1920 batters made controlled swings at the ball to hit line drives while after 1920 they were generally swinging from the heels to hit it out. By the end of the decade pitchers were beginning to adjust and strikeouts began to increase.

Returning to the top of the AL, the A's led the league in strikeouts 6 straight years from 1925 through 1930. The teams that won the pennant in the 1929-31 period are remembered for their hitters (Jimmie Foxx, Al Simmons, and Mickey Cochrane). But what set the A's apart in those years of high offense everywhere was their great pitching (led by Lefty Grove). Once again Connie Mack proved to himself that pitching was 75 percent of the game. The Yankees led the AL 3 times in strikeouts early in the decade, but the A's pushed them aside after 1924. The A's tie the Yankees at the top of the list for leading the AL most often in strikeouts (Table 4-6), but after 1930 the A's did not lead the AL in strikeouts again until 1971, and they have not led since. In the NL, the Dodgers began to climb to the top in leading the majors the most times in strikeouts (Table 4-6). They led the NL 9 times in the period, including 8 times in a row from 1922 through 1929. The Dodgers have led the league in strikeouts at least once in every decade since (and usually much more often than once).

Walter Johnson won the last of his 12 AL strikeout titles in 1924, giving him 3 titles in the period. Lefty Grove took over as the AL strikeout king and won the title 6 years in a row from 1925 through 1930. In the NL, Dazzy Vance of the Dodgers went Grove one better by winning 7 titles in a row from 1922 through 1928. Burleigh Grimes, one of the last legal spitballers in the league, gave the Dodgers another strikeout title in 1921.

Figure 3-3. AL/NL Strikeouts Per Game 1920-30

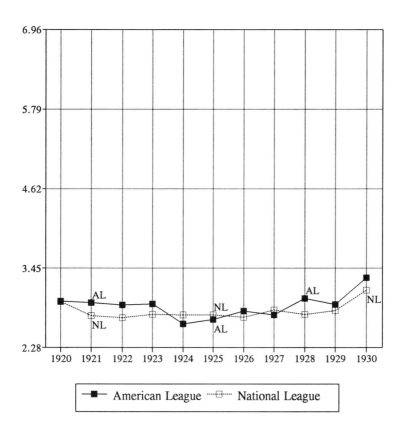

Year	AL SO/Game	AL Leader	NL SO/Game	NL Leader
1920	2.96	Red Sox	2.95	**Dodgers**
1921	2.93	Yankees	2.74	**Pirates**
1922	2.90	**Browns**	2.71	Dodgers
1923	2.92	Yankees	2.76	**Dodgers**
1924	2.62	Yankees	2.75	**Dodgers**
1925	2.69	A's	2.75	**Dodgers**
1926	2.81	A's	2.72	Dodgers
1927	2.75	A's	2.83	**Dodgers**
1928	3.00	A's	2.76	Dodgers
1929	2.91	A's	2.82	Dodgers
1930	3.31	A's	3.12	Cards

Figure 3-4 shows strikeouts per game by year for the American and National leagues from 1930 through 1940. The scale of the graph includes the highest and lowest values of strikeouts per game in the century. The same scale is used for all decades so it is possible to see at a glance how strikeouts in one decade compare to the highs and lows for the century. The exact values of strikeouts per game for each year are shown below the graph together with the teams that led each league. Teams that led the majors are shown in bold.

Strikeouts in the 1920s never climbed above 3.00, but, as described in the text accompanying Figure 3-3, during the decade pitchers began to adjust to the loss of their tools in 1920. By 1930 strikeouts climbed above 3.00 for the first time since 1919 in the AL and 1917 in the NL. Except for 1933 in the NL, which was the last year the league used the new ball it adopted with disastrous results in 1931, strikeouts stayed well above 3.00 in the period from 1930 through 1940. By 1940 strikeouts moved solidly above the 3.45 line in both leagues. Pitchers were beginning to gain the edge that would lead to sharp increases in strikeouts after WWII when the big swing got even bigger. Once again the leagues were relatively close in strikeouts, but as usual the AL led the NL most often. From 1901 through 1940 the AL led the NL 30 times in strikeouts while the NL led only 10 times. This would also change after WWII.

The Yankees led the majors in nearly every favorable statistic in the 1930s and strikeouts were no exception. They led the AL in strikeouts 6 times in the period, leading the majors 4 times. The Tigers developed a good strikeout staff at the end of the decade, leading the AL and the majors in 1939 and 1940. The Tigers led the AL for the first time in franchise history in 1939, and they became the dominant strikeout team in baseball through the next 10 years. But they only led 3 other times in the following 50 years. The Cards followed a similar pattern in the NL. The Cards led the NL for the first time in franchise history in 1930, and they led the NL 6 times in a row from 1930 through 1935. The Cards became leaders once more starting in 1941 when their pitching staff dominated the war years. But after 1947 the Cards never led again.

After Lefty Grove won the last 2 of his 7 AL strikeout titles in 1930 and 1931, Lefty Gomez won 3 titles for the Yankees in the middle years of the decade. Bob Feller then won the first 3 of his 7 AL strikeout titles from 1938 through 1940. Tommy Bridges of the Tigers also won 2 titles in 1935 and 1936.

Pitchers for the Cards led the NL in strikeouts every year the Cards as a team led the NL in strikeouts. Bill Hallahan led the league in 1930 and 1931, and Dizzy Dean led 4 years in a row from 1932 through 1935. Dean was amazingly consistent, leading the NL with consecutive totals of 191, 199, 195, and 190 strikeouts in the 4 years. Dean also had 195 strikeouts in 1936, but he was topped by Van Lingle Mungo of the Dodgers who had 238. Mungo drove the 1936 Dodgers to their only team strikeout title of the 1930s.

Figure 3-4. AL/NL Strikeouts Per Game 1930-40

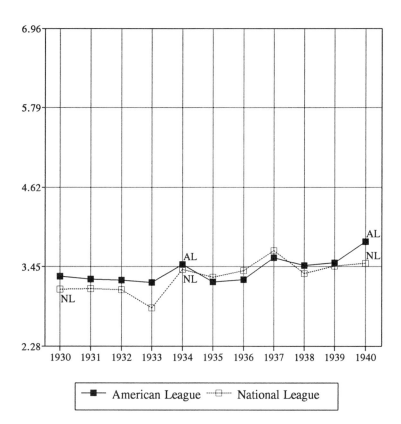

Year	AL SO/Game	AL Leader	NL SO/Game	NL Leader
1930	3.31	A's	3.12	Cards
1931	3.27	Yankees	3.13	Cards
1932	3.25	Yankees	3.11	Cards
1933	3.22	Yankees	2.85	Cards
1934	3.48	Yankees	3.41	Cards
1935	3.23	Yankees	3.29	Cards
1936	3.26	Yankees	3.39	Dodgers
1937	3.58	Red Sox	3.69	Giants
1938	3.47	Indians	3.35	Cubs
1939	3.51	Tigers	3.46	Reds
1940	3.82	Tigers	3.50	Dodgers

Figure 3-5 shows strikeouts per game by year for the American and National leagues from 1940 through 1950. The scale of the graph includes the highest and lowest values of strikeouts per game in the century. The same scale is used for all decades so it is possible to see at a glance how strikeouts in one decade compare to the highs and lows for the century. The exact values of strikeouts per game for each year are shown below the graph together with the teams that led each league. Teams that led the majors are shown in bold.

Strikeouts declined as players were drafted for WWII, and by 1945 strikeouts were down nearly 11 percent in both leagues compared to 1940. But there was a sharp increase in 1946 when the players returned in force. This was the start of an increase in strikeouts that continued steadily for the next two decades. The AL set what was then a major league record in 1946, averaging 4.21 strikeouts per game, the first time either league exceeded 4.00 per game. There was a decline and then a rebound in the AL after 1946, but NL strikeouts continued steadily upward and the NL went over the 4.00 mark with an average of 4.05 strikeouts per game in 1950. It took nearly 50 years to exceed 4.00 strikeouts per game, but it took less than 10 years to push the level above 5.00 (Figure 3-6).

The Tigers led the AL in strikeouts 7 times in the period, and they also led the majors each time. But after 1948 the Tigers led only in 1958, 1960, and 1969. Still, the 1940s outburst was good enough to leave the Tigers tied for third in leading the AL the most times in strikeouts (Table 4-6). The Yankees led 3 times in the period, and the 1944 Browns were the only other AL team to lead in the 1940s. It was the first time the Browns led in strikeouts since 1922; it was the only time the franchise won a pennant while they were in St. Louis; and it was the last time the franchise led the AL in strikeouts. After the franchise moved to Baltimore the Orioles had many great pitching teams, while the St. Louis version of the franchise was infamous for its terrible pitching teams. But the Orioles have never led the AL in strikeouts.

The Dodgers led the NL 6 times in strikeouts during the period and the Cards led 5 times. The Dodgers went on to lead the NL many more times, but 1947 was the last year the Cards were NL strikeout leaders. In spite of the long gap since the Cards led, they still tie the Mets for second place in leading the NL in strikeouts most often (Table 4-6). Both teams are far behind the Dodgers.

Bob Feller led the AL in strikeouts in 1940 and 1941, and then in 1946 through 1948 when he returned from WWII. In 1946 he had 348 strikeouts, the most in baseball since Rube Waddell had 349 in 1904. That was the major contribution to the AL surge above 4.00 per game in 1946. Hal Newhouser of the Tigers was the only other AL pitcher to lead more than once. He won titles in 1944 and 1945. Johnny "Double No-Hit" VanderMeer of the Reds won 3 NL strikeout titles from 1941 through 1943, and then there was a new leader in the NL every year until Warren Spahn won in 1949 and 1950.

Figure 3-5. AL/NL Strikeouts Per Game 1940-50

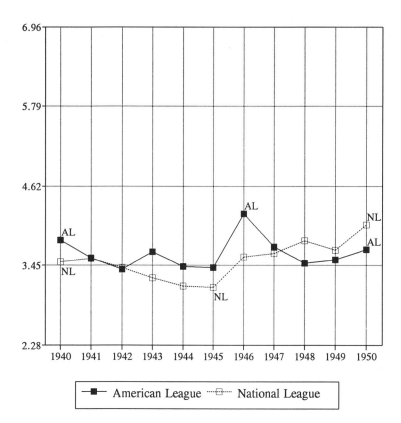

Year	AL SO/Game	AL Leader	NL SO/Game	NL Leader
1940	3.82	**Tigers**	3.50	Dodgers
1941	3.56	**Tigers**	3.55	Cards
1942	3.39	**Tigers**	3.42	Cards
1943	3.65	**Tigers**	3.27	Cards
1944	3.43	Browns	3.15	**Cards**
1945	3.42	**Tigers**	3.13	Dodgers
1946	4.21	**Tigers**	3.57	Dodgers
1947	3.72	**Yankees**	3.62	Cards
1948	3.48	**Tigers**	3.81	Dodgers
1949	3.53	Yankees	3.67	**Dodgers**
1950	3.68	Yankees	4.05	**Dodgers**

Figure 3-6 shows strikeouts per game by year for the American and National leagues from 1950 through 1960. The scale of the graph includes the highest and lowest values of strikeouts per game in the century. The same scale is used for all decades so it is possible to see at a glance how strikeouts in one decade compare to the highs and lows for the century. The exact values of strikeouts per game for each year are shown below the graph together with the teams that led each league. Teams that led the majors are shown in bold.

The NL set its all-time home run records in the 1950s (Figure 2-26), and the AL also set home run records they would break in later years. The big swing was bigger than ever and pitchers continued to hone their tools to deal with such hitters. The result was a steady increase in strikeouts. Records were broken nearly every year, and the NL ended the period with its highest mark ever while the AL was down just slightly from the record it set the year before. Mickey Mantle was probably the best model for the new kind of hitter. Strikeouts were considered meaningless if the hitter had enough power to drive the ball every time he did connect. Measuring the distance Mantle's home runs travelled was of much more interest than measuring his strikeouts. It was a trend that would not be reversed, and it would be taken to new heights in the 1990s. Strikeouts were nearly identical in each league in the period until the NL pulled away a little at the end of the decade, but the NL led 9 times and the AL only twice.

The Yankees and Indians led the AL in strikeouts 3 times in the period, and the White Sox and Tigers each led twice. There was no dominant strikeout team in the AL in the 1950s. The story was completely different in the NL. The Dodgers led the NL every year in the period. They were in the middle of a streak that ran from 1948 through 1963 as the Dodgers led the NL in strikeouts 16 years in a row (they led the majors in 13 of those years). No team has dominated any measure the way the Dodgers have dominated strikeouts. No team can match the consecutive years streak of the Dodgers, nor can any team match the 34 times the Dodgers led in strikeouts (Table 4-6). The closest similar domination of a measure is that of the Yankees in home runs (Table 4-4), but although the Yankees led 33 times, the last year they led was 1961. The Dodgers are still among the top strikeout leaders today.

A different pitcher led the AL in strikeouts every year until Herb Score of the Indians led in 1955 and 1956. Score made a sensational debut in 1955, but early in 1957 he was hit in the eye by a line drive off the bat of Gil McDougald of the Yankees. Score's season ended at that moment and for all practical purposes so did his career. Early Wynn won 2 titles for the Indians and White Sox, and Jim Bunning won the last 2 of the period for the Tigers. In the NL, Warren Spahn won 3 titles as did Sam Jones for the Cubs and Cards, and Robin Roberts of the Phillies won twice. In spite of their team domination, no pitcher for the Dodgers led in strikeouts until Don Drysdale did it in 1959 and 1960.

Figure 3-6. AL/NL Strikeouts Per Game 1950-60

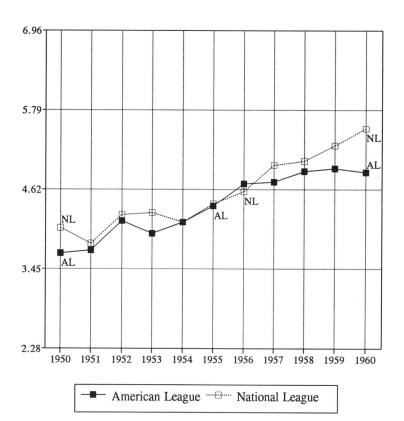

Year	AL SO/Game	AL Leader	NL SO/Game	NL Leader
1950	3.68	Yankees	4.05	**Dodgers**
1951	3.72	Yankees	3.82	**Dodgers**
1952	4.15	White Sox	4.24	**Dodgers**
1953	3.97	White Sox	4.27	**Dodgers**
1954	4.13	Red Sox	4.13	**Dodgers**
1955	4.37	**Indians**	4.40	Dodgers
1956	4.70	**Indians**	4.58	Dodgers
1957	4.72	Indians	4.97	**Dodgers**
1958	4.88	Tigers	5.03	**Dodgers**
1959	4.92	Yankees	5.26	**Dodgers**
1960	4.86	Tigers	5.51	**Dodgers**

Figure 3-7 shows strikeouts per game by year for the American and National leagues from 1960 through 1970. The scale of the graph includes the highest and lowest values of strikeouts per game in the century. The same scale is used for all decades so it is possible to see at a glance how strikeouts in one decade compare to the highs and lows for the century. The exact values of strikeouts per game for each year are shown below the graph together with the teams that led each league. Teams that led the majors are shown in bold.

Strikeouts were at record levels in both leagues when the strike zone was changed in favor of pitchers in 1963. As expected, strikeouts rose to new records in the 1963-68 period. AL strikeouts declined when the strike zone was changed back and the mound lowered in 1969, but the NL continued at record levels until 1970. The AL went ahead of the NL in 1964 for the first time since 1957. The AL remained ahead until the strike zone change was reversed, making 1968 the last year the AL led the NL in strikeouts. For 68 seasons through 1968, the AL led 43 times and the NL 25 times. The NL led from 1969 through 1972, and since the designated hitter rule was adopted by the AL in 1973, the AL has never led the NL in strikeouts. This is the expected result of stopping thoroughly overmatched pitchers from being sent to the plate. As long as the NL continues this practice, the NL will always lead the AL in strikeouts. Through 1998 the NL has led the AL in strikeouts for 30 straight seasons.

The Indians led the AL in strikeouts 7 times in the period, including all 6 years when the strike zone was changed in the 1963-68 period. The Indians also led the majors in strikeouts 5 straight years. In 1967 the Indians set an all-time AL team record for strikeouts per game that wasn't broken until 1995 (by the Mariners) when the strikeout frenzy of the 1990s was underway. Since 1995 was a strike year, the total strikeout record of the 1967 Indians wasn't broken until 1997 (again by the Mariners). The Indians set records because they just happened to have assembled a staff of strikeout pitchers when the strike zone was changed in their favor. The Indians never led in strikeouts again after 1970 (Table 4-6). The Dodgers led the NL in strikeouts 5 times in the period and the Reds led 3 times. The Astros led twice including an all-time major league team record in 1969. On a per game basis the record of the 1969 Astros stood until 1994, and on a total year basis it stood until 1996. The Braves broke it each time.

Sam McDowell of the Indians led the AL in strikeouts 5 times in the 6 years between 1965 and 1970. Earlier, Camilo Pascual celebrated the move of the (now) Twins to Minneapolis by leading in strikeouts from 1961 through 1963. Sandy Koufax led the NL in strikeouts 4 times, including 1965 when he struck out 382 batters. It was the highest total in the century at the time, and only Nolan Ryan, who fanned 383 in 1973, has topped it since. Don Drysdale led in 1960 and 1962 as the only other pitcher to lead his league at least twice, but Jim Bunning led the AL for the Tigers in 1960 and the NL in 1967 for the Phillies.

Figure 3-7. AL/NL Strikeouts Per Game 1960-70

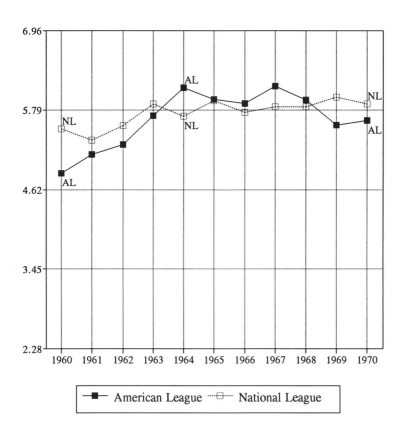

Year	AL SO/Game	AL Leader	NL SO/Game	NL Leader
1960	4.86	Tigers	5.51	**Dodgers**
1961	5.14	Angels	5.35	**Dodgers**
1962	5.28	Twins	5.56	**Dodgers**
1963	5.71	Indians	5.88	**Dodgers**
1964	6.12	**Indians**	5.70	Reds
1965	5.95	**Indians**	5.93	Reds
1966	5.89	**Indians**	5.76	Dodgers
1967	6.14	**Indians**	5.84	Reds
1968	5.94	**Indians**	5.84	Astros
1969	5.57	Tigers	5.98	**Astros**
1970	5.63	**Indians**	5.88	Mets

Figure 3-8 shows strikeouts per game by year for the American and National leagues from 1970 through 1980. The scale of the graph includes the highest and lowest values of strikeouts per game in the century. The same scale is used for all decades so it is possible to see at a glance how strikeouts in one decade compare to the highs and lows for the century. The exact values of strikeouts per game for each year are shown below the graph together with the teams that led each league. Teams that led the majors are shown in bold.

Strikeouts in the early 1970s declined a little from their highs in the 1960s after the strike zone change of 1963 was reversed in 1969 and the mound was lowered. But after the designated hitter rule was adopted by the AL in 1973, strikeouts in the AL declined steadily and reached their lowest levels since 1955 by the end of the decade. In a "sympathetic" reaction, strikeouts in the NL also declined after 1972, going below 5.00 strikeouts per game in 1976 for the first time since 1957. But strikeouts rebounded in the NL in 1977 and remained above the 5.00 level for the rest of the period. The NL led the AL in strikeouts every year in the period, continuing what would become a winning streak of 30 straight years by 1998.

A new strikeout team leader appeared in the AL in the 1970s. The Angels led the league in strikeouts 8 times in a row from 1972 through 1979. Before 1972 the Angels led the AL in strikeouts only once, and that was in the year of their birth in 1961. After the 1970s streak ended in 1979, the Angels never led the AL in strikeouts again. But there is no mystery about this sequence. Nolan Ryan joined the Angels in 1972 and immediately led the league in strikeouts (he also led the league in shutouts). To show that 1972 was no fluke, Ryan struck out 383 hitters in 1973, the highest one season total in the century and one that has yet to be topped. Ryan led the AL in strikeouts 7 of the 8 years the Angels led the league. He missed leading only in 1975 when he was injured, but teammate Frank Tanana took over to lead the league year. When Ryan left the Angels for the Astros as a free agent in 1980, the Angels left the strikeout leadership and never got it back again. The Astros, however, won the 1980 strikeout title in the NL with Ryan leading the staff in strikeouts.

The Mets become the new NL strikeout leader, winning the team title 6 times in the period while the Astros and Cubs each won twice. The Cubs won in 1977 for the first time since 1938, and they won in 1979 for the last time in franchise history (Table 4-6). But the Mets and Astros continued to win strikeout titles.

Nolan Ryan was the strikeout story in the AL in the period with his 7 strikeout titles. Tom Seaver played the Nolan Ryan role for the Mets, and Seaver won the NL strikeout title 5 times in the period. Other multiple winners included Steve Carlton of the Phillies, who won 3 titles, and J. R. Richard of the Astros, who won in 1978 and 1979 before his career was tragically ended by a stroke in the middle of the 1980 season.

Figure 3-8. AL/NL Strikeouts Per Game 1970-80

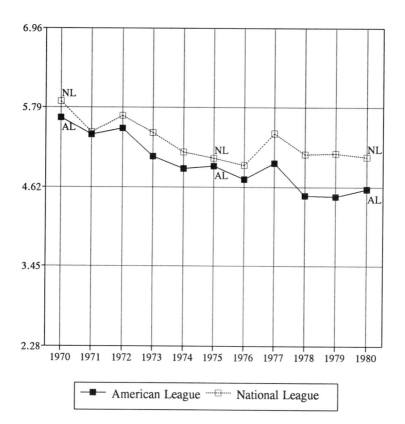

Year	AL SO/Game	AL Leader	NL SO/Game	NL Leader
1970	5.63	**Indians**	5.88	Mets
1971	5.39	A's	5.42	**Mets**
1972	5.48	Angels	5.67	**Mets**
1973	5.07	Angels	5.41	**Mets**
1974	4.89	**Angels**	5.13	Dodgers
1975	4.93	Angels	5.04	**Mets**
1976	4.73	Angels	4.94	**Mets**
1977	4.97	**Angels**	5.40	Cubs
1978	4.49	Angels	5.10	**Astros**
1979	4.48	Angels	5.11	**Cubs**
1980	4.58	Rangers	5.06	**Astros**

Figure 3-9 shows strikeouts per game by year for the American and National leagues from 1980 through 1990. The scale of the graph includes the highest and lowest values of strikeouts per game in the century. The same scale is used for all decades so it is possible to see at a glance how strikeouts in one decade compare to the highs and lows for the century. The exact values of strikeouts per game for each year are shown below the graph together with the teams that led each league. Teams that led the majors are shown in bold.

After sliding in the 1970s, strikeouts began climbing again in the 1980s. They marked time during the strike year of 1981, then marched steadily up to a peak in the big home run (and big swing) year of 1987 (Figure 2-29). The AL set what was then its all-time home run record in 1987, and it had its highest strikeout level since 1968 when the strike zone change in favor of pitchers was still in effect and the DH was not. The NL had its highest level of home runs in 1987 since 1961, and the NL averaged 6.00 strikeouts per game in 1987, just below the record of 6.01 it recorded in 1986. Both years marked the only time in the century to that time that strikeouts had exceeded 6.00 in either league. The connection between swinging for home runs and recording high strikeouts in 1987 was an indication of the strikeout frenzy to come in the 1990s. The other notable fact about 1987 was that the AL nearly matched the NL in strikeouts. They have not been that close since.

The Rangers led the AL in strikeouts in 1980 for the first time in franchise history, and they led a total of 4 times during the period. The Rangers led the majors only in 1989, the year Nolan Ryan joined the staff. The Mariners also had a first in franchise history when they led the AL in strikeouts in 1982, and they led a total of 3 times in the period. The Yankees, on the other hand, led twice in the period to give them a total of 16 AL strikeout titles to tie the A's for first place in this category (Table 4-6). But 1984 is the last year the Yankees led the league in strikeouts. In the NL, the Astros and Mets each led 4 times, and the Phillies led twice. The 1982 title for the Phillies was their first since 1915, a gap of 67 years. The Astros won 7 titles between 1968 and 1987, but 1987 marks their last year at the top.

Nolan Ryan was once again the top strikeout story in the majors. He won NL strikeout titles in 1987 and 1988 with the Astros, and then moved on to the Rangers and won AL strikeout titles in 1989 and 1900. That gave Ryan a total of 11 strikeout titles, 9 in the AL and 2 in the NL. He ended his career in 1993 with 5,714 strikeouts, a record that seems truly unreachable. The only other multiple winners in the AL were Mark Langston of the Mariners who won 3 titles in the middle of the decade, and Len Barker of the Indians who won 2 at the start of the decade. The other multiple winners in the NL reversed the sequence. Steve Carlton of the Phillies won 3 times at the beginning of the decade, and Doc Gooden of the Mets won twice in the middle of the decade.

Figure 3-9. AL/NL Strikeouts Per Game 1980-90

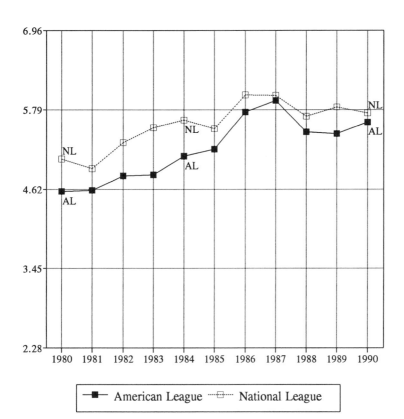

Year	AL SO/Game	AL Leader	NL SO/Game	NL Leader
1980	4.58	Rangers	5.06	**Astros**
1981	4.60	**Yankees**	4.92	Astros
1982	4.81	Mariners	5.30	**Phillies**
1983	4.83	Mariners	5.52	**Phillies**
1984	5.10	Yankees	5.63	**Dodgers**
1985	5.20	White Sox	5.50	**Mets**
1986	5.76	Rangers	6.01	**Astros**
1987	5.93	Rangers	6.00	**Astros**
1988	5.45	Red Sox	5.69	**Mets**
1989	5.43	**Rangers**	5.83	Mets
1990	5.60	Mariners	5.74	**Mets**

Figure 3-10 shows strikeouts per game by year for the American and National leagues from 1988 through 1998. The scale of the graph includes the highest and lowest values of strikeouts per game in the century. The same scale is used for all decades so it is possible to see at a glance how strikeouts in one decade compare to the highs and lows for the century. The exact values of strikeouts per game for each year are shown below the graph together with the teams that led each league. Teams that led the majors are shown in bold.

Strikeouts in both leagues reached all-time highs in the 1990s. AL strikeouts dipped in 1992 and then rose steadily to an all-time high in 1997 before declining a little in 1998, although 1998 was still the second highest level ever. The expansion of 1993 triggered the increase, and the AL passed 6.00 strikeouts per game in 1994 for the first time before going on to set a new record in 1997. NL strikeouts were remarkably consistent through 1993, but then they shot up in 1994 to break the prior record set in 1986. The NL set a new record every year after 1994 before falling off a little in 1998. It's possible that interleague play helped strikeouts decline somewhat in the NL because in games held in AL parks NL pitchers no longer have to bat. That effect did not decrease NL strikeouts in 1997, but it may have played a part in the 1998 decrease. But interleague play should not cause a decrease in strikeouts overall because AL strikeouts should increase in games where the DH is lost.

It's not a coincidence that all-time highs in strikeouts accompanied the peak of the big swing game in the 1990s. There's no reason to believe the big swing game will not continue, and thus there's no reason to believe that strikeouts will not go on to set new records in both leagues in future years.

From 1991 onward, the Mariners were the leading strikeout team in the AL behind Randy Johnson. The Mariners led the AL 4 times in the 1991-98 period, with the Rangers leading twice. The Mariners set the all-time team record for the AL in 1997 with 7.45 strikeouts per game. They also became the first AL team to exceed 1,200 strikeouts in one season with a total of 1,207.

In the NL from 1991 onward, the Braves led in strikeouts 4 times. When the Braves led the NL in strikeouts in 1994, it was the first time the franchise led the league in the century. Because 1994 and 1995 were shortened by the player's strike, it was not until 1996 that the Braves set a major league record for total strikeouts in one season as well as having the highest level of strikeouts per game. The 1996 Braves had a total of 1,245 strikeouts which corresponded to 7.69 strikeouts per game.

Randy Johnson led the AL in strikeouts 4 times in the 1991-98 period, losing his chance to lead a 5th time when he was traded to the Astros during the 1998 season. Roger Clemens also led 4 times, twice for the Red Sox and twice for the Blue Jays (including the title in 1998). John Smoltz of the Braves and Curt Schilling of the Phillies each led the NL twice in the period.

Figure 3-10. AL/NL Strikeouts Per Game 1988-98

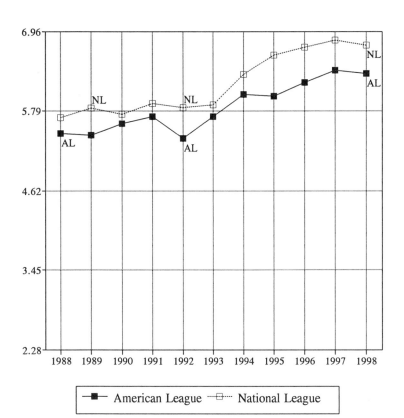

Year	AL SO/Game	AL Leader	NL SO/Game	NL Leader
1988	5.45	Red Sox	5.69	**Mets**
1989	5.43	**Rangers**	5.83	Mets
1990	5.60	Mariners	5.74	**Mets**
1991	5.71	Rangers	5.90	**Mets**
1992	5.38	Rangers	5.84	**Reds**
1993	5.71	Mariners	5.88	**Phillies**
1994	6.03	Blue Jays	6.32	**Braves**
1995	6.00	Mariners	6.61	**Braves**
1996	6.20	Red Sox	6.73	**Braves**
1997	6.38	Mariners	6.83	**Dodgers**
1998	6.32	Mariners	6.76	**Braves**

Figure 3-11 shows walks per game by year for the American and National leagues from 1900 through 1910. The scale of the graph includes the highest and lowest values of walks per game in the century. The same scale is used for all decades so it is possible to see at a glance how walks in one decade compare to the highs and lows for the century. The exact values of walks per game for each year are shown below the graph together with the teams that led each league. Teams that led the majors are shown in bold.

Walks in the AL fell 20 percent between 1902 and 1903 because the AL adopted the foul strike rule in 1903. It was the lowest level of walks in the century for the AL. A similar decline took place in the NL between 1900 and 1901 because the NL adopted the foul strike rule in 1901. But the decrease between 1900 and 1901 was only 10 percent in the NL, and it wasn't until 1902, when walks fell to 13 percent below the 1900 level, that the NL set its all-time low for walks in the century. The NL surged in walks between 1902 and 1903 when the AL stopped raiding NL players, and the NL stayed above the AL every year after 1903 as AL batters took longer to get used to the foul strike rule. This made the first decade the only decade in which the NL exceeded the AL in issuing walks by a large margin. The AL was better by a narrow margin in the 1970s, and the leagues essentially tied in the 1980s. But otherwise in the 98 seasons from 1901 through 1998, the NL had a lower level of walks than the AL by a margin of 73 years to 25 (through 1970 the NL led by 56 to 14).

The White Sox led the AL 4 times in the period in issuing the lowest number of walks, and the White Sox went on to lead the AL (and the majors) in the number of years issuing the fewest walks (Table 4-7). For most of the century the White Sox concentrated on pitching, speed, and defense because they played in huge Comiskey Park. The Senators and Red Sox also each led the AL twice in the period. In the NL, the Pirates led 6 times in the period. Like the White Sox, the Pirates tended to concentrate on pitching, speed, and defense because they played much of the century in huge Forbes Field. The result for the Pirates was similar to that for the White Sox in that the Pirates lead the NL in number of years issuing the fewest walks (Table 4-7). It is not a coincidence that both the White Sox and Pirates rank very low on the strikeout leaders list (Table 4-6). Issuing very few walks usually means recording very few strikeouts.

The best control pitcher in the AL in the period was Cy Young who joined the brand new league in 1901 at age 34 after 11 seasons in the NL. Young pitched for another 11 seasons in the AL, winning 225 games to go with his 286 wins in the NL for his record total of 511. Young led the league in fewest walks per game 5 times in 6 years through 1906 while pitching for the Red Sox. Addie Joss of the Indians led twice late in the decade. In the NL, Deacon Phillippe of the Pirates led the league 4 times before tying Christy Mathewson of the Giants in 1907. Mathewson went on to lead the league in 1908 and 1909.

Figure 3-11. AL/NL Walks Per Game 1900-10

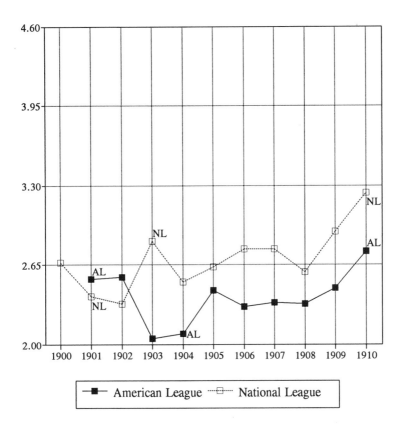

— American League ····⊟···· National League

Year	AL Walks/Game	AL Leader	NL Walks/Game	NL Leader
1900	--	--	2.67	**Cards**
1901	2.53	Senators	2.39	**Pirates**
1902	2.55	Senators	2.33	**Pirates**
1903	2.05	**Browns**	2.84	Cubs
1904	2.09	**Red Sox**	2.51	Cards
1905	2.44	**Red Sox**	2.63	Giants
1906	2.31	**White Sox**	2.78	Pirates
1907	2.34	**White Sox**	2.78	Pirates
1908	2.33	**White Sox**	2.59	Giants
1909	2.46	White Sox	2.92	**Pirates**
1910	2.76	**Yankees**	3.24	Pirates

Figure 3-12 shows walks per game by year for the American and National leagues from 1910 through 1920. The scale of the graph includes the highest and lowest values of walks per game in the century. The same scale is used for all decades so it is possible to see at a glance how walks in one decade compare to the highs and lows for the century. The exact values of walks per game for each year are shown below the graph together with the teams that led each league. Teams that led the majors are shown in bold.

Walks in both leagues increased sharply in 1910 and 1911 due to the introduction of the cork-center ball and a subsequent sharp increase in offense. Walks have always been a pitcher's decision (teams with big hitters nearly always draw the most walks), and pitchers decided to be much more careful with what was the only truly lively ball introduced in the century. Walks declined as expected in the NL as offense declined after peaking in 1911 because pitchers redoubled their efforts to "doctor" the new ball. But walks continued to increase in the AL, peaking in 1915 before declining only slightly afterwards. In the NL, walks declined by 32 percent between 1911 and 1919, and the NL almost matched its all-time low in walks in 1919. In the AL, walks actually increased slightly between 1911 and 1919. The fact that walks in the AL were 27 percent higher than in the NL in 1920 is reasonable because Babe Ruth started his home run revolution in earnest in 1920. But there is no explanation for the difference in the leagues between 1911 and 1920. This is typical of walks in this century. Nearly every decade has unexplainable differences between the leagues.

The White Sox led the AL 6 times in the period in issuing the fewest walks, and the Red Sox led 3 times. In the 14 seasons from 1906 through 1919, the White Sox led the AL 10 times in issuing the fewest walks. There was some irony in the fact that the Red Sox led 3 times between 1912 and 1917, because one of their best pitchers between 1915 and 1918 was Babe Ruth. When he became an outfielder, Ruth gave birth to the big swing game that would be the main reason for a huge upsurge in walks in the AL over the next two decades. The Giants were the masters of control pitching in the NL. They led the NL and the majors 7 times in the period. The Pirates led the NL 3 times and the majors twice. After the Yankees led the majors in fewest walks in 1910, no AL team led the majors in fewest walks until the Yankees did it again in 1942. In terms of control, the NL was the "pitcher's league" for 32 years rather than just in the decade of the 1930s when the term became commonplace.

Walter Johnson led the AL in fewest walks per game in 1913 and 1915 even though he also led the league in strikeouts. Reb Russell and Eddie Cicotte of the White Sox each led twice from 1916 through 1919, and with Ed Walsh and Ed White leading in 1910 and 1911, the White Sox had 6 leaders in the period. Christy Mathewson of the Giants was the best control pitcher on the best control staff, leading the NL 5 straight times from 1911 through 1915.

Figure 3-12. AL/NL Walks Per Game 1910-20

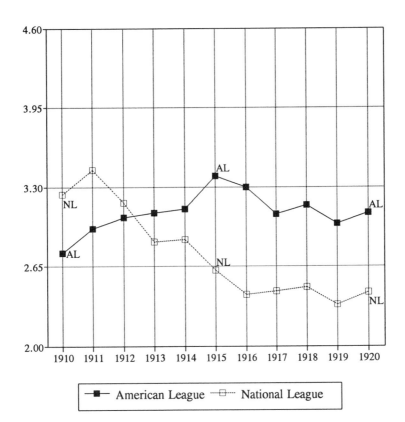

Year	AL Walks/Game	AL Leader	NL Walks/Game	NL Leader
1910	2.76	Yankees	3.24	Pirates
1911	2.96	White Sox	3.44	Giants
1912	3.05	Red Sox	3.17	Giants
1913	3.09	White Sox	2.85	Giants
1914	3.12	Red Sox	2.87	Giants
1915	3.39	White Sox	2.62	Giants
1916	3.30	White Sox	2.42	Phillies
1917	3.08	Red Sox	2.45	Giants
1918	3.15	White Sox	2.48	Giants
1919	3.00	White Sox	2.34	Pirates
1920	3.09	Indians	2.44	Pirates

Figure 3-13 shows walks per game by year for the American and National leagues from 1920 through 1930. The scale of the graph includes the highest and lowest values of walks per game in the century. The same scale is used for all decades so it is possible to see at a glance how walks in one decade compare to the highs and lows for the century. The exact values of walks per game for each year are shown below the graph together with the teams that led each league. Teams that led the majors are shown in bold.

In spite of the fact that the NL caught up to the AL in the big swing game in 1921, walks in the NL were near an all-time low that year and the AL issued 36 percent more walks than the NL. For the rest of the period, walks in the AL stayed reasonably consistent while walks in the NL slowly moved upward and then surged in 1928 to exceed the AL level for the first time since 1912. Walks in the NL moved lower once more after 1928, and the NL did not exceed the AL in walks again until 1958. It appeared that walks were becoming nearly equal in each league by the end of the period, but the leagues diverged wildly after 1930 (Figure 3-14). As is noted often in this book, there is no clear reason for the big difference in walks between the leagues in the first five decades.

There was no clear leader in issuing the fewest walks in the AL in the period. The Indians led the league 3 times, and the Browns, Tigers, and White Sox all led twice. One notable event is that the A's led in fewest walks in 1928. This was the first time in franchise history that the A's led, and they only led 3 more times the rest of the century (1944, 1952, and 1974). Of the 16 original teams, the A's are easily at the bottom of the list in issuing the fewest walks (Table 4-7).

In the NL, the Reds also led the league in issuing the fewest walks for the first time in the period. But the Reds led the NL and the majors 6 straight times from 1922 through 1927. The Reds did not have very good teams in the period, but they played in what became Crosley Field, and at that time Crosley Field had a configuration in which it was very hard to hit home runs. Pitchers for the Reds did not need to pitch around big hitters in their home park. The Giants, who were famous at the time for their control pitchers, led in 1921 and 1929. But in the 69 years after 1929 the Giants led only 4 more times, and they led for the last time in 1968 (Table 4-7).

Matching the team leaders, the individual leaders in the AL were widely distributed. Urban Shocker of the Browns, Sherry Smith of the Indians, Herb Pennock of the Yankees, and Jack Quinn of the Yankees and A's each led twice. In the NL, the leaders were elder citizens ending their careers. Grover Cleveland Alexander led 4 times, twice for the Cubs and twice for the Cards. Alexander was 41 years old and nearing the end of a 20 year career when he led in 1928. Babe Adams of the Pirates led 3 straight times from 1920 through 1922. Adams was 40 in 1922 and also nearing the end of his 19 years in baseball.

Figure 3-13. AL/NL Walks Per Game 1920-30

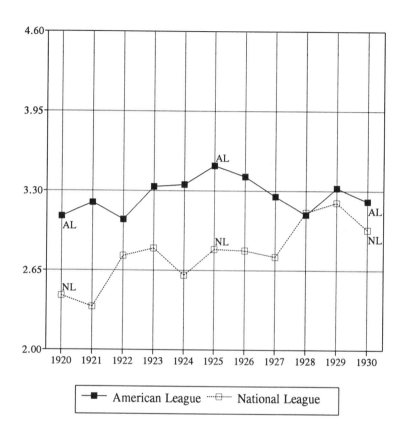

Year	AL Walks/Game	AL Leader	NL Walks/Game	NL Leader
1920	3.09	Indians	2.44	**Pirates**
1921	3.20	Indians	2.35	**Giants**
1922	3.06	Browns	2.77	**Reds**
1923	3.33	Tigers	2.83	**Reds**
1924	3.35	Tigers	2.61	**Reds**
1925	3.50	White Sox	2.82	**Reds**
1926	3.41	Indians	2.81	**Reds**
1927	3.25	Yankees	2.76	**Reds**
1928	3.10	A's	3.12	**Cards**
1929	3.32	Browns	3.20	**Giants**
1930	3.21	White Sox	2.98	**Dodgers**

Figure 3-14 shows walks per game by year for the American and National leagues from 1930 through 1940. The scale of the graph includes the highest and lowest values of walks per game in the century. The same scale is used for all decades so it is possible to see at a glance how walks in one decade compare to the highs and lows for the century. The exact values of walks per game for each year are shown below the graph together with the teams that led each league. Teams that led the majors are shown in bold.

Walks in the AL increased steadily in the 1930s as the Yankees drove a steadily increasing league offensive level up to an all-time AL record for runs in 1936 (Figure 2-4). Walks peaked for the period in 1938 and passed the 4.00 level for the first time in either league. They declined a little from the peak, but AL walks in 1940 were still 13 percent above the 1930 level. In the NL, the change in the ball in 1931 caused a big drop in walks (and home runs and runs and nearly everything else for that matter). By 1933 walks were at their lowest level in the NL since 1921, and AL walks were more than 49 percent higher than NL walks. This is the largest meaningful divergence between the leagues in any measure. The NL adopted the AL ball in 1934, but walks still stayed far below AL levels. This helped the NL to become known as the "pitcher's league" and the AL as the "hitter's league," but as usual there is no clear explanation for the huge difference in walks between the leagues. NL walks did increase after 1935 and by 1940 the AL was "only" 19 percent higher above the NL in walks.

AL team leaders in issuing the fewest walks again were well distributed. The White Sox led 3 times and the Indians and Red Sox each led twice. The Browns led in 1931, and this is the last year the franchise led while it was in St. Louis. The franchise would not lead again until 1958, and by then it had moved to Baltimore and become the Baltimore Orioles. Teams leading the NL continued to lead the majors in fewest walks because of the large difference between the leagues in total walks. The Dodgers led the NL 4 times, and the Reds, Giants, and Pirates all led twice. Contrary to their early and consistent lead in strikeouts, the Dodgers led in fewest walks for the first time in franchise history in 1930. The Braves also led for the first time in franchise history in 1937.

Ted Lyons of the White Sox led the AL in fewest walks per game in 1936, 1939, and 1940. Lyons was 40 years old in 1940 and near the end of a career of 21 years--all with the White Sox. As noted in the text accompanying Figure 3-13, Babe Adams and Grover Cleveland Alexander similarly led the NL in fewest walks per game when they were in their 40s near the end of very long careers. Perhaps the longer one pitches, the better one gets at keeping the ball over the plate. Herb Pennock of the Yankees led the AL the first two years of the decade and Clint Brown of the Indians led the next two. In the NL, Watty Clark of the Dodgers, Red Lucas of the Reds in 1933 and the Pirates in 1936, and Paul Derringer of the Reds each led the league twice in the period.

Figure 3-14. AL/NL Walks Per Game 1930-40

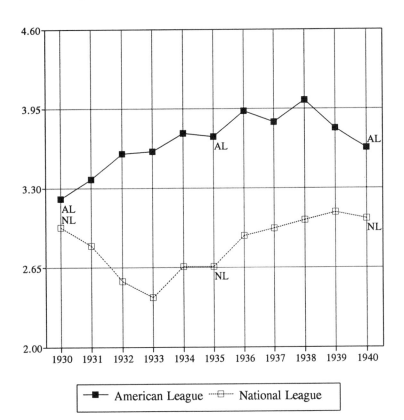

Year	AL Walks/Game	AL Leader	NL Walks/Game	NL Leader
1930	3.21	White Sox	2.98	Dodgers
1931	3.37	Browns	2.83	Dodgers
1932	3.58	Indians	2.54	Reds
1933	3.60	Senators	2.41	Reds
1934	3.75	Tigers	2.66	Giants
1935	3.72	Indians	2.66	Pirates
1936	3.93	Red Sox	2.91	Pirates
1937	3.84	Yankees	2.97	Braves
1938	4.02	Red Sox	3.04	Giants
1939	3.79	White Sox	3.10	Dodgers
1940	3.63	White Sox	3.05	Dodgers

Figure 3-15 shows walks per game by year for the American and National leagues from 1940 through 1950. The scale of the graph includes the highest and lowest values of walks per game in the century. The same scale is used for all decades so it is possible to see at a glance how walks in one decade compare to the highs and lows for the century. The exact values of walks per game for each year are shown below the graph together with the teams that led each league. Teams that led the majors are shown in bold.

In another unexplainable development regarding walks, all-time records in both leagues were set in the 1940-50 period. In the first half of the period, when the prime players were drafted into WWII, walks in the AL declined from their record levels of the 1930s, falling in 1944 to their lowest levels since 1928. But walks in the NL initially rose from their 1940 level, then remained nearly constant until dipping in 1944. The result was that walks were essentially identical in both leagues in 1944. It was the first time since 1928 that walks in the NL were not lower than walks in the AL. But the encyclopedias disagree on total walks in the NL in 1944, and it is possible that NL walks per game still might have been lower than in the AL in 1944. For sure, walks in 1944 were closer in the two leagues than at any time since 1928. They increased for the next two years but still stayed very close together.

But after 1946 walks soared in the AL and remained nearly constant in the NL. Walks in the AL increased by 43 percent between 1944 and 1949, when the AL set its all-time high in walks at 4.55 per game. There is no known reason for the increase, and walks actually fell in 1950 when the strike zone was changed in favor of hitters and an increase in walks was expected. The NL did have a small increase in 1950 and this put NL walks at an all-time high of 3.67 per game. But after 1950 walks fell in both leagues (Figure 3-16) in spite of the strike zone change encouraging more walks. The decrease in walks after 1950 in both leagues was almost as sharp as the increase before 1950. There is no explanation for the huge surge in walks around 1950, but the presence of so many runners on first base led to record levels of double plays in both leagues around 1950 (Figures 3-35 and 3-36).

In the period, the Tigers led the AL 3 times in fewest walks per game while the White Sox and Yankees each led twice. The Cubs led the NL 3 times, and the Reds and Braves each led twice. The Cubs led for the first time in 38 years in 1941, and the Phillies led for the first time in 34 years in 1950. Fred Hutchinson of the Tigers, who later complained loudly as a manager about pitchers who walked too many batters, led the AL 3 times in fewest walks per game from 1948 through 1950. Ted Lyons of the White Sox and Ernie Bonham of the Yankees each led twice earlier in the decade. In the NL, only Ken Raffensberger of the Phillies (1944) and Reds (1950) led as often as twice. But Schoolboy Rowe of the Phillies led in 1943 and tied for the lead in 1947.

Figure 3-15. AL/NL Walks Per Game 1940-50

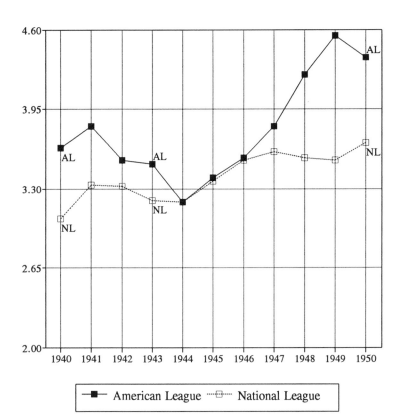

Year	AL Walks/Game	AL Leader	NL Walks/Game	NL Leader
1940	3.63	White Sox	3.05	**Dodgers**
1941	3.81	White Sox	3.33	**Cubs**
1942	3.53	**Yankees**	3.32	Pirates
1943	3.50	Yankees	3.20	**Cubs**
1944	3.19	A's	3.19	**Reds**
1945	3.39	Senators	3.36	**Cubs**
1946	3.55	Tigers	3.53	**Reds**
1947	3.81	Tigers	3.60	**Braves**
1948	4.23	Red Sox	3.55	**Braves**
1949	4.55	Indians	3.53	**Cards**
1950	4.37	Tigers	3.67	**Phillies**

Figure 3-16 shows walks per game by year for the American and National leagues from 1950 through 1960. The scale of the graph includes the highest and lowest values of walks per game in the century. The same scale is used for all decades so it is possible to see at a glance how walks in one decade compare to the highs and lows for the century. The exact values of walks per game for each year are shown below the graph together with the teams that led each league. Teams that led the majors are shown in bold.

As described in the text accompanying Figure 3-15, walks declined after the peaks in both leagues around 1950 even though the strike zone was changed in 1950 in favor of hitters. For the first part of the period NL walks remained well below AL walks, even though it was a period of high offense and the NL was hitting many more home runs and scoring more runs than the AL. The AL had a surge in walks from 1952 through 1956, and for only the fifth time in the century AL walks exceeded 4.00 in 1956. It is the last year AL walks were above the 4.00 level. NL walks had a small surge in 1954, but they remained well below their 1950 record of 3.67 and generally declined the rest of the decade. AL walks fell sharply from their 1956 rise, and by 1958 AL walks were 19 percent below their 1956 level and definitely lower than NL walks for the first time since 1928. But just as mysteriously as they fell, AL walks rose again and ended the period 13 percent above the NL.

The White Sox added to their lead for the century by leading the AL in fewest walks per game 4 times in the period. The Tigers led 3 times, but more notable was the fact that the Orioles led in 1958 for the first time in Baltimore, and the Orioles led the majors as well. It was the first time an AL team led the majors in fewest walks per game since the Yankees did it in 1942, and the 1942 Yankees were the first team to do it since the 1910 Yankees. The Phillies were the new control pitching team in the NL, and they led the league and the majors in fewest walks per game 6 times in the period. The Reds and Pirates each led twice (the Reds leading in 1958 for the last time in franchise history). The Phillies led in 1950 for the first time since 1916 (and they also won the pennant in 1950 for the first time since 1915).

Fred Hutchinson of the Tigers led the AL in fewest walks per game in 1950 and 1951 while Eddie Lopat of the Yankees led in 1953 and 1954. After 1954 there were new names every year until Hal Brown of the Orioles led in 1959 and 1960. Only 4 pitchers led the NL in the period. Robin Roberts of the Phillies led 4 times in the 5 seasons from 1952 through 1956. Roberts also led the league in wins, complete games, and innings pitched from 1952 through 1955, and he added the strikeout titles in 1953 and 1954 as well. Don Newcombe led in fewest walks per game for the Dodgers in 1955 and 1957 and for the Reds in 1959. Ken Raffensberger of the Reds led in 1950 and 1951, and Lew Burdette of the Braves led in 1958 and 1960.

Figure 3-16. AL/NL Walks Per Game 1950-60

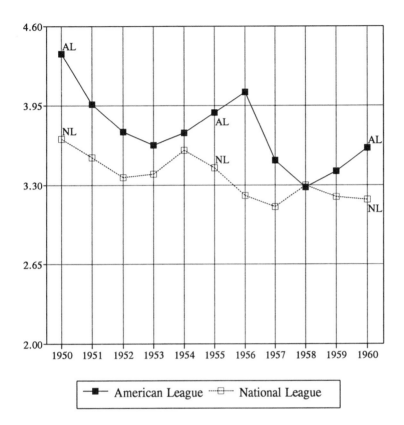

Year	AL Walks/Game	AL Leader	NL Walks/Game	NL Leader
1950	4.37	Tigers	3.67	**Phillies**
1951	3.96	White Sox	3.52	**Giants**
1952	3.73	A's	3.36	**Phillies**
1953	3.62	Senators	3.39	**Phillies**
1954	3.72	Indians	3.58	**Phillies**
1955	3.89	White Sox	3.44	**Reds**
1956	4.06	White Sox	3.21	**Phillies**
1957	3.50	White Sox	3.12	**Phillies**
1958	3.28	**Orioles**	3.30	Reds
1959	3.41	Tigers	3.20	**Pirates**
1960	3.60	Tigers	3.18	**Pirates**

Figure 3-17 shows walks per game by year for the American and National leagues from 1960 through 1970. The scale of the graph includes the highest and lowest values of walks per game in the century. The same scale is used for all decades so it is possible to see at a glance how walks in one decade compare to the highs and lows for the century. The exact values of walks per game for each year are shown below the graph together with the teams that led each league. Teams that led the majors are shown in bold.

From 1960 through 1962, walks in both leagues remained near their 1960 levels. But when the strike zone was changed in favor of pitchers in 1963, walks immediately fell. They remained near the reduced level through 1968, with the lowest level in each league in the period coming in 1968. When the strike zone change was reversed and the mound lowered for the 1969 season, walks rose sharply in both leagues. But a new phenomenon arose in 1970. NL walks definitely exceeded AL walks for the first time since 1958, and for only the second time since 1928. AL and NL walks were about to become nearly identical over a full decade (Figure 3-18) for the first time in the century. In addition, although NL walks per game fell to 2.63 in 1968, the lowest level since 1933, after 1968 NL walks would fall below 3.00 only one more time in the century (2.99 in 1988). But in the AL, although the level of walks in 1968 (3.01) was the lowest since 1919, AL walks in the future often would not be far above the 1968 level until they climbed substantially again in the 1990s. After 6 decades with NL walks much lower than AL walks, walk parity suddenly arrived in 1970.

During the same period that the Twins became a great home run team behind Harmon Killebrew, they also became the team with the best control pitchers in the AL. The Twins led the AL in fewest walks per game 4 times in the period, leading the majors in 1967. The usual team leader, the White Sox, led 3 times in the period and the Tigers led twice. But 1961 marked the last time the Tigers led the league in fewest walks per game (Table 4-7). In the NL, the Astros and Dodgers each led 3 times in fewest walks per game and the Pirates led twice. The Astros led for the first time in franchise history in 1963 and, after leading 3 years in a row, they led for the last time in franchise history in 1965. The Giants led in 1968, and although that put them on top of the NL list in leading the most times in the 1901-72 period (Table 4-7), the Giants never led again.

Fritz Peterson of the Yankees led the AL in fewest walks per game 3 years in a row from 1968 through 1970. Dick Donovan of the Indians was the only other multiple leader in the league in the period in 1962 and 1963. In the NL the two multiple leaders were much better known. Juan Marichal led the league 3 times in fewest walks per game in 1965, 1966, and 1969. This period was the peak of his career. He won 68 games in those 3 years with 1969 marking the last year he won more than 20 games. Lew Burdette of the Braves led the league in 1960 and 1961, the last two really good years of his 18 seasons in the majors.

Figure 3-17. AL/NL Walks Per Game 1960-70

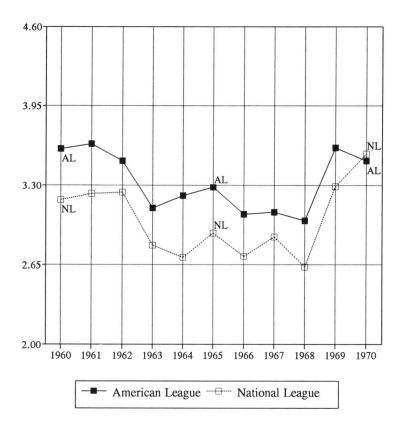

Year	AL Walks/Game	AL Leader	NL Walks/Game	NL Leader
1960	3.60	Tigers	3.18	**Pirates**
1961	3.64	Tigers	3.23	**Pirates**
1962	3.50	Twins	3.24	**Braves**
1963	3.11	White Sox	2.81	**Astros**
1964	3.21	White Sox	2.71	**Astros**
1965	3.28	White Sox	2.91	**Astros**
1966	3.06	Twins	2.72	**Dodgers**
1967	3.08	**Twins**	2.88	Dodgers
1968	3.01	Twins	2.63	**Giants**
1969	3.61	Orioles	3.29	**Dodgers**
1970	3.50	**Yankees**	3.56	Cubs

Figure 3-18 shows walks per game by year for the American and National leagues from 1970 through 1980. The scale of the graph includes the highest and lowest values of walks per game in the century. The same scale is used for all decades so it is possible to see at a glance how walks in one decade compare to the highs and lows for the century. The exact values of walks per game for each year are shown below the graph together with the teams that led each league. Teams that led the majors are shown in bold.

As described in the text accompanying Figure 3-17, the 1970s marked a new period of walk parity between the leagues. The AL had fewer walks than the NL 7 times in the period while the NL had fewer walks than the AL only 4 times. This is the only such period in the century that the AL had fewer walks than the NL. In the 69 years through 1969, the NL had fewer walks than the AL 56 times, or 81 percent. But in the 20 years after 1969 the NL had fewer walks than the AL only 8 times, or 40 percent. The change was due to the fact that NL walks increased from prior decades while AL walks decreased, and the two leagues met almost exactly in the middle.

Expansion was one cause of the increase in the NL. The Expos and Padres both were born in the 1969 expansion. On the list of the 11 highest years for walks by NL teams in the century, the Expos appear 3 times (1969, 1970, and 1973) while the Padres appear twice (1974 and 1977). But the AL decline is another walk mystery. With the DH coming into play in 1973, it would be assumed that walks would increase in the AL due to the presence of another big hitter in the lineup. In the same perverse behavior walks have exhibited during the century, walks in the AL instead declined from their prior averages.

The decline in walks in the AL and the increase in the NL resulted in AL teams leading the majors in fewest walks per game 6 times in the period. This was a huge change. In the 56 seasons from 1911 through 1966, AL teams led the majors only twice (1942 and 1958). The Yankees, Red Sox, and Brewers each led the AL in fewest walks per game 3 times in the period. The Yankees and Red Sox both led for the first time in 37 years, and 1973 is the last time the Yankees led in the century. The Dodgers led the NL 4 times while the Cubs led 3 times, but 1977 marked the last year the Dodgers led in fewest walks per game. This is not an unexpected result for a team constantly among the strikeout leaders. The 1979 Expos, however, did the unexpected by leading in fewest walks per game in the same decade the franchise was noted for most walks per game.

Ferguson Jenkins was the featured control pitcher of the period. He led the AL in fewest walks per game for the Rangers in 1974, 1975, and 1978, and also led the NL for the Cubs in 1970 and 1971. Other multiple leaders were Fritz Peterson of the Yankees, who led the AL 3 times at the start of the decade, Gary Nolan of the Reds, who led the NL in 1975 and 1976, and the Forsch brothers: Ken led with the Astros in 1979 and Bob led with the Cards in 1980.

Figure 3-18. AL/NL Walks Per Game 1970-80

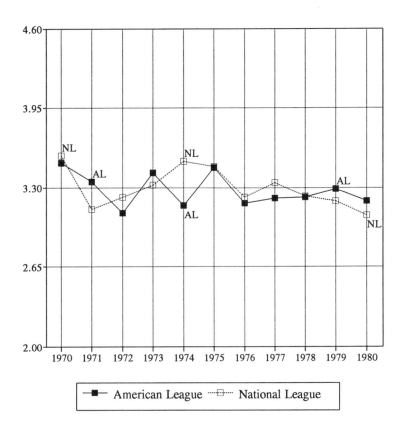

Year	AL Walks/Game	AL Leader	NL Walks/Game	NL Leader
1970	3.50	**Yankees**	3.56	Cubs
1971	3.35	Yankees	3.12	**Dodgers**
1972	3.09	**Orioles**	3.22	Cubs
1973	3.42	Yankees	3.32	**Cubs**
1974	3.15	**A's**	3.51	Dodgers
1975	3.46	Red Sox	3.47	**Dodgers**
1976	3.17	Red Sox	3.22	**Phillies**
1977	3.21	**Red Sox**	3.34	Dodgers
1978	3.22	Brewers	3.23	**Phillies**
1979	3.29	**Brewers**	3.19	Expos
1980	3.19	**Brewers**	3.07	Pirates

Figure 3-19 shows walks per game by year for the American and National leagues from 1980 through 1990. The scale of the graph includes the highest and lowest values of walks per game in the century. The same scale is used for all decades so it is possible to see at a glance how walks in one decade compare to the highs and lows for the century. The exact values of walks per game for each year are shown below the graph together with the teams that led each league. Teams that led the majors are shown in bold.

Walks in both leagues drew even closer together in the 1980s than they had in the turnaround decade of the 1970s (Figure 3-19). Both the difference between the leagues and the range over which walks varied remained unusually small. Walks slowly increased during the 1984 through 1987 increase in offense that culminated in the home run barrage of 1987, but the total increase was small. The NL had fewer walks than the AL 6 times in the period while the AL was lower 5 times. This simply reinforces the parity in walks between the leagues. AL walks would be expected to be higher than those in the NL due to the DH in the AL, but there was almost literally no difference between the leagues at all. Both leagues averaged 3.25 walks per game in the 1973-89 period (the DH was born in 1973). This was a decrease of 2 percent from the 3.32 average in the AL from 1901 through 1972, while for the NL it was an increase of 9 percent compared to the prior period. Whatever the reason, walks in the AL were lower than expected and NL walks were higher. The result was a dead heat.

The Brewers, Royals, and White Sox each led the AL twice in the period in fewest walks per game, and each led the majors once. The White Sox, who lead all teams in leading in fewest walks per game during the century (Table 4-7), led for the last time in 1983. The Blue Jays led for the first and only time in franchise history in 1990. The Expos, who made their mark in previous years by setting NL records for high walks, led the NL (and the majors) in fewest walks per game 3 times in the period. The Pirates led twice, and even the Padres, who were like the Expos in being known for high walk seasons, led the NL and the majors in fewest walks per game in 1985. This was also the first and last time in franchise history that the Padres led their league in this category.

There were only two multiple leaders in fewest walks per game in the majors in the period, and both won twice in the AL. LaMarr Hoyt led the AL for the White Sox in 1983 and 1984, and then led the NL after going to the Padres in 1985. Hoyt played the key role in leading the Padres to their one and only time leading the league in fewest walks per game in 1985. Allan Anderson of the Twins led the AL in fewest walks per game in 1988 and 1990. Anderson played only 6 years in the majors, coming up with the Twins in 1986 and leaving the Twins and the majors after the 1991 season. He had a great year in 1988, leading the league in ERA as well as in fewest walks per game. But his last winning season was 1989 in spite of leading in fewest walks per game again in 1990.

Figure 3-19. AL/NL Walks Per Game 1980-90

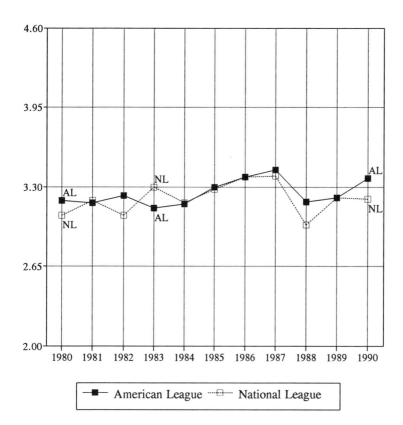

Year	AL Walks/Game	AL Leader	NL Walks/Game	NL Leader
1980	3.19	**Brewers**	3.07	Pirates
1981	3.17	Royals	3.19	**Expos**
1982	3.23	White Sox	3.07	**Expos**
1983	3.13	**White Sox**	3.30	Phillies
1984	3.16	**Royals**	3.17	Cubs
1985	3.30	Twins	3.28	**Padres**
1986	3.38	**Red Sox**	3.38	Cards
1987	3.44	Mariners	3.39	**Expos**
1988	3.18	Brewers	2.99	**Mets**
1989	3.21	**Indians**	3.21	Braves
1990	3.37	Blue Jays	3.20	**Pirates**

Figure 3-20 shows walks per game by year for the American and National leagues from 1988 through 1998. The scale of the graph includes the highest and lowest values of walks per game in the century. The same scale is used for all decades so it is possible to see at a glance how walks in one decade compare to the highs and lows for the century. The exact values of walks per game for each year are shown below the graph together with the teams that led each league. Teams that led the majors are shown in bold.

After 1989 walks resumed their "normal" pattern. AL walks climbed above the NL level and then increased sharply after the expansion of 1993 and the subsequent surge in offense. NL walks declined in 1992 and then increased after the 1993 expansion, but the increase was very slow and in 1994 AL walks were 15 percent higher than NL walks. This was the largest difference between the leagues in 30 years. The margin lasted through 1996, but in 1997 walks suddenly converged again. As had happened before, AL walks declined and NL walks increased and they came together. AL walks declined from 3.79 walks per game in 1996, the highest level in the AL since 1956, to 3.47 walks per game in 1997. By nearly matching the AL level in 1997, the NL recorded its highest level of walks since 1975. The leagues remained close together in 1998. It's possible interleague play contributed to the change in 1997 because AL walks would be expected to fall without the DH in NL parks, while NL walks would be expected to increase with the DH in AL parks. But walks have rarely shown the expected behavior during the century.

From 1991 through 1998, the Twins led the AL in fewest walks per game 3 times, while the Indians led twice. No other team led more than once. The Twins/Senators rank second behind the White Sox in leading the AL most often during the century in fewest walks per game (Table 4-7). In the NL during the same period, the Braves and Cards each led twice. In 1989 the Braves led the NL in fewest walks per game for the first time since 1962, and, although the Braves do not rank high in the number of times leading the NL, 1989 also marked the first time the Braves did not lead the majors when they led the NL. The Braves regained their touch in 1996 and 1997, leading both the NL and the majors before they just missed another title in 1998.

No pitcher led the AL more than once in fewest walks per game during the 1991-98 period. The only multiple leaders came in the NL. Greg Maddux of the Braves, perhaps the best pitcher in baseball during the period, led the NL 3 times in a row in fewest walks per game from 1995 through 1997. He was the prime contributor to the team titles the Braves won in 1996 and 1997. Bob Tewksbury, perhaps the only challenger to Maddux as the top control specialist in the period, led the NL in 1992 and 1993, driving the Cards to the team title both years. If Tewksbury had pitched a few more innings in 1998, he may well have been the AL leader as a member of the Twins, the winners of the AL team title in 1998.

Figure 3-20. AL/NL Walks Per Game 1988-98

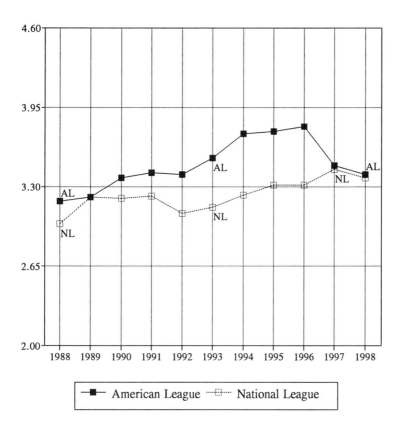

Year	AL Walks/Game	AL Leader	NL Walks/Game	NL Leader
1988	3.18	Brewers	2.99	Mets
1989	3.21	**Indians**	3.21	Braves
1990	3.37	Blue Jays	3.20	**Pirates**
1991	3.41	Indians	3.22	**Pirates**
1992	3.40	Brewers	3.08	**Cards**
1993	3.53	Twins	3.13	**Cards**
1994	3.73	Orioles	3.23	**Expos**
1995	3.75	Indians	3.31	**Mets**
1996	3.79	Royals	3.31	**Braves**
1997	3.47	Twins	3.44	**Braves**
1998	3.40	**Twins**	3.37	Astros

Figure 3-21 shows errors per game by year for the American and National leagues from 1900 through 1910. The scale of the graph includes the highest and lowest values of errors per game in the century. The same scale is used for all decades except that after 1950 a maximum scale value of 1.00 is used to facilitate league comparisons. Thus, it is possible to see at a glance how errors in one decade compare to the highs and lows for the century. The exact values of errors per game for each year are shown below the graph together with the teams that led each league. Teams that led the majors are shown in bold.

Both leagues had their highest level of errors per game in their first year in the century. The NL's highest year for errors is 1903 if the starting point is taken as 1901. Except for a brief increase in errors in the AL after the cork-center ball was introduced in 1910 (Figure 3-22), errors in both leagues decreased steadily throughout the full century. Errors are still declining today, and, in spite of temporary moves upward in some years, the overall average of errors per game has decreased in every decade since 1900.

It seems intuitive that errors would not differ much between leagues, and that both should exhibit the same general rate of decline as player skills improve and gloves and playing surfaces also improve. This was true up to WWII, but after 1946 errors began to decline more rapidly in the AL than in the NL. In the 52 seasons since 1946, errors per game in the AL were lower than those in the NL 46 times while the NL had lower values only 6 times. In the 46 seasons from 1901 through 1946, the NL had lower values 29 times and the AL 17. It is tempting to say that the DH aids the AL because players who fill the DH role often are poor fielders, but the AL edge over the NL started 26 years before the DH was born, and the edge for the AL over the NL in the 26 seasons both before and after the DH is exactly the same. There is no good explanation for the constantly lower level of errors in the AL. At any rate, from 1901 through 1910 the NL had the lowest level of errors per game 6 times while the AL was better 4 times. By 1906, AL errors were 33 percent lower than in 1901, and NL errors were 23 percent lower. They stayed relatively constant the rest of the decade.

The White Sox were the best fielding team in the AL in the period, leading the league in fewest errors per game 6 times while the A's led twice. In the NL, the Cubs led the NL 5 times while the Giants led twice. The White Sox and the Cubs each led their league most often in fewest errors per game from 1901 through 1972, but both teams finished second overall from 1901 through 1998 because they each led only once after 1972 (Table 4-8).

Individual fielding leaders are selected using the "Fielding Runs" measure in *Total Baseball*. Nap Lajoie led the AL 4 times at second base, once for the 1901 A's and 3 times for the Indians. Lee Tannehill led twice for the White Sox at third base. The only multiple leader in the NL was John Farrell of the Cards who led twice at second base even though he played only 5 years in the majors.

Figure 3-21. AL/NL Errors Per Game 1900-10

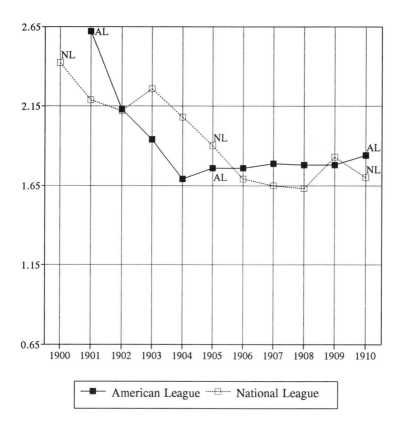

Year	AL Errors/Game	AL Leader	NL Errors/Game	NL Leader
1900	--	--	2.42	**Braves**
1901	2.62	Senators	2.19	**Phillies**
1902	2.13	White Sox	2.12	**Braves**
1903	1.94	**A's**	2.26	Giants
1904	1.69	**White Sox**	2.08	Giants
1905	1.76	**White Sox**	1.90	Cubs
1906	1.76	Indians	1.69	**Cubs**
1907	1.79	White Sox	1.65	**Cubs**
1908	1.78	White Sox	1.63	**Cubs**
1909	1.78	White Sox	1.83	**Pirates**
1910	1.84	**A's**	1.70	Cubs

Figure 3-22 shows errors per game by year for the American and National leagues from 1910 through 1920. The scale of the graph includes the highest and lowest values of errors per game in the century. The same scale is used for all decades except that after 1950 a maximum scale value of 1.00 is used to facilitate league comparisons. Thus, it is possible to see at a glance how errors in one decade compare to the highs and lows for the century. The exact values of errors per game for each year are shown below the graph together with the teams that led each league. Teams that led the majors are shown in bold.

The introduction of the cork-center ball in 1910 and the subsequent increase in offense may have been the cause of more errors in the AL from 1910 through 1912, but the NL showed no such effect. Errors were nearly the same in both leagues in 1913 as offense declined after pitchers redoubled their efforts to "doctor" the ball and negate the advantage the cork-center ball gave hitters. The NL had fewer errors per game than the AL in 8 of the 11 years in the period, but errors were nearly identical in both leagues from 1916 onward. In the 20 seasons from 1901 through 1920, the NL had fewer errors per game than the AL a total of 13 times. Errors per game in the AL declined by 24 percent between 1910 and 1920 (they declined by 30 percent between 1912 and 1920). In the NL, there was a decline of 15 percent between 1910 and 1920. Both leagues were at or near record lows at the end of the period. This was a common pattern during the century. Each league showed a decline in errors between the beginning and end of the period, and each league left the decade at or near a record low.

The A's were the best team in the AL between 1910 and 1914, winning the pennant 4 of the 5 years in the period. The Red Sox won the pennant the only year the A's did not (1912), and the Red Sox were big winners in the second half of the decade when Connie Mack broke up the A's after 1914. Confirming that the best teams are often good in every phase of the game, the A's had the fewest errors per game in the AL 5 straight times from 1910 through 1914, and the Red Sox did the same 5 straight times from 1916 through 1920. The Pirates were best in the NL 4 times during the period, while the Giants and Braves each led twice.

No player led the AL more than once in fielding runs in the period, but Lee Tannehill, who played third base for the White Sox, led the league in 1911 after previously leading in 1904 and 1906. Tannehill's 1911 rating was also the highest in the period in the AL. In the NL, Rabbit Maranville, playing shortstop for the Braves, led in 1914 and 1919. Maranville led the "Miracle Braves" of 1914 who came from last to first during the season and swept the world champion A's in the World Series. Maranville's rating in 1914 was the third highest in the century, trailing only Glenn Hubbard in 1985 and Bill Mazeroski in 1963. Art Fletcher of the Giants led in 1915 and 1918, and Dave Bancroft led for the Phillies in 1917 and for the Giants in 1920. Ironically, both players were also shortstops and were traded for each other in June of 1920.

Figure 3-22. AL/NL Errors Per Game 1910-20

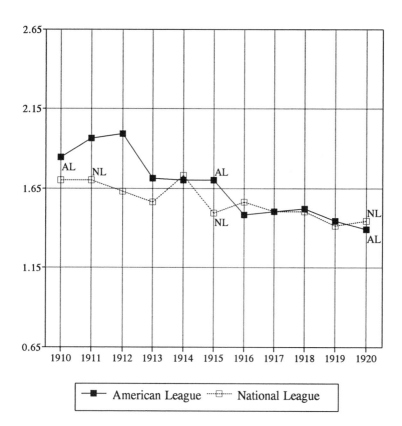

Year	AL Errors/Game	AL Leader	NL Errors/Game	NL Leader
1910	1.84	**A's**	1.70	Cubs
1911	1.96	**A's**	1.70	Pirates
1912	1.99	**A's**	1.63	**Pirates**
1913	1.71	**A's**	1.56	**Phillies**
1914	1.70	**A's**	1.73	Pirates
1915	1.70	Yankees	1.49	**Braves**
1916	1.48	**Red Sox**	1.56	Braves
1917	1.50	**Red Sox**	1.50	Giants
1918	1.52	**Red Sox**	1.50	Giants
1919	1.44	**Red Sox**	1.41	Reds
1920	1.39	**Red Sox**	1.44	Pirates

Figure 3-23 shows errors per game by year for the American and National leagues from 1920 through 1930. The scale of the graph includes the highest and lowest values of errors per game in the century. The same scale is used for all decades except that after 1950 a maximum scale value of 1.00 is used to facilitate league comparisons. Thus, it is possible to see at a glance how errors in one decade compare to the highs and lows for the century. The exact values of errors per game for each year are shown below the graph together with the teams that led each league. Teams that led the majors are shown in bold.

There was a huge offensive outburst in the 1920s due to the rule changes in 1920 outlawing "doctored" pitches and the change in procedure to put new balls into play much more often. Strikeouts and walks fell, and thus more balls than usual were put into play. But errors still slowly declined during the period. The cleaner balls that drove the high level of offense probably helped reduce errors as well. A wet spitball is often no easier to field than it is to hit. In addition, a new fielder's glove designed by pitcher Bill Doak of the Cards was put into production by Rawlings in 1920 and it led to a revolution in the design and manufacture of gloves. Errors per game in the AL declined by 9 percent between 1920 and 1930, and in the NL they declined by 17 percent during the same period. Each league recorded what were then all-time lows during the decade, but those records were broken in the next decade. The level of errors was nearly identical in both leagues, and the AL had fewer errors per game than the NL 6 times in the period while the NL was lower 5 times.

The Yankees and White Sox each led the AL in fewest errors per game 3 times in the period while the Red Sox and A's each did so twice. After leading the AL in 1930 for the 8th time in 30 seasons, the A's led once more in 1932 and then never led again (Table 4-8). This is the longest period any AL team has gone without leading the league in fewest errors per game. The Cubs led the NL in fewest errors per game 5 times in the period, and the Pirates led twice. The Pirates have an even more remarkable record than the A's. The Pirates led the NL for the 6th time in 22 seasons in 1922, but they never led again. This is the longest any NL team has gone without leading the league in fewest errors per game. But it just misses the record for the longest gap for any measure because the Pirates last led the league in strikeouts in 1921 (Table 4-6).

No player in the AL led the league in fielding runs more than once, but shortstop Everett Scott of the 1921 Red Sox had the highest rating in the league during the period. The only player in the NL to led the league more than once in fielding runs was Frankie Frisch, who led the Cards at second base in 1927 and 1930. Frisch recorded the 6th highest rating in the century in 1927, but in this respect he was overshadowed by Freddie Maguire, who played second base for the Cubs in 1928. Maguire had the 4th highest rating in the century in 1928, the only year of his brief career of 6 seasons that he played for the Cubs.

Figure 3-23. AL/NL Errors Per Game 1920-30

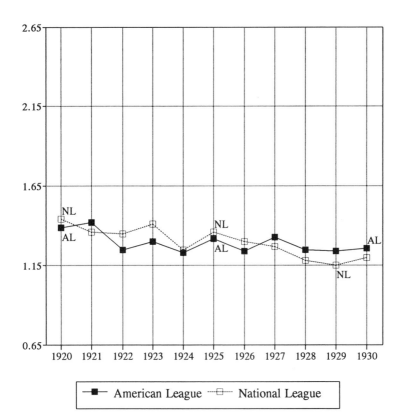

Year	AL Errors/Game	AL Leader	NL Errors/Game	NL Leader
1920	1.39	**Red Sox**	1.44	Pirates
1921	1.42	**Red Sox**	1.36	Cubs
1922	1.25	**White Sox**	1.35	Pirates
1923	1.30	**Yankees**	1.41	Giants
1924	1.23	**Yankees**	1.25	Braves
1925	1.32	**Yankees**	1.36	Cubs
1926	1.24	White Sox	1.30	**Cubs**
1927	1.33	White Sox	1.27	**Reds**
1928	1.25	Senators	1.18	**Cubs**
1929	1.24	**A's**	1.15	Cubs
1930	1.26	**A's**	1.20	Reds

Figure 3-24 shows errors per game by year for the American and National leagues from 1930 through 1940. The scale of the graph includes the highest and lowest values of errors per game in the century. The same scale is used for all decades except that after 1950 a maximum scale value of 1.00 is used to facilitate league comparisons. Thus, it is possible to see at a glance how errors in one decade compare to the highs and lows for the century. The exact values of errors per game for each year are shown below the graph together with the teams that led each league. Teams that led the majors are shown in bold.

Errors per game continued their slow downward movement in both leagues in the 1930s, and each league had nearly the same level of errors. The NL had fewer errors per game than the AL 8 times in the 11 years in the period, but this was the last decade in which the NL would record fewer errors per game more often than the AL. As discussed in the text accompanying Figure 3-21, after WWII the AL would have fewer errors per game than the NL nearly 90 percent of the time. The decline in errors was very slow in the 1930s, with the AL declining 7 percent between 1930 and 1940 and the NL declining 6 percent. The AL set what was then an all-time low in 1935 and the NL did so in 1933, and each league was at a higher level by the end of the decade. But the AL had its last mark above 1.20 errors per game in 1932 and the NL never rose above that level again after 1936. Overall fielding skills continue to improve.

The Tigers led the AL in fewest errors per game 3 times in the decade, while the A's, Senators, and Yankees each led twice. There was no dominant leader in the AL during the period. The Tigers led for the first time in franchise history in 1935, and after 1937 they did not lead again until 1958. The Browns also led for the first time in franchise history in 1938, and this was the only time the franchise led while it was in St. Louis. But after moving to Baltimore in 1954 and becoming the Orioles, the franchise led the league in fewest errors per game so many times from 1960 onward that it is at the top of the list for leading the AL the most times in the century (Table 4-8).

The Cubs led the NL in fewest errors per game 4 times in the period, while the Reds, Cards, and Braves all led twice. As in the AL, there was no dominant fielding team in the NL during the period. The Cards led for the first time in franchise history in 1931, but they led many times afterwards although they had a big gap between 1951 and 1984.

Ski Melillo, who played second base for the Browns, led the AL in fielding runs 3 times in the period. He led in 1930, 1931, and 1933. No other AL player led more than once. In the NL, Billy Jurges led at shortstop for the Cubs in 1932 and 1935, Hughie Critz led at second base for the Giants in 1933 and 1934, and Dick Bartell led at shortstop for the Giants in 1936 and 1937. In addition to leading the league for the Giants, Critz had the 7th highest rating in the century in 1933 and Bartell had the 9th highest rating in the century in 1936.

Figure 3-24. AL/NL Errors Per Game 1930-40

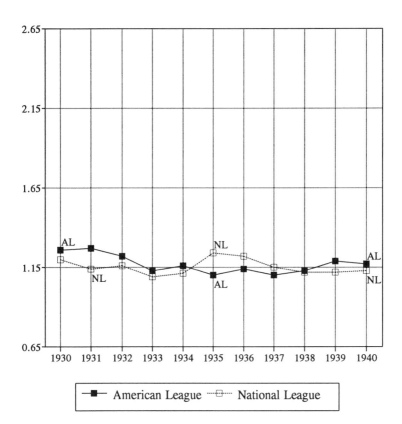

Year	AL Errors/Game	AL Leader	NL Errors/Game	NL Leader
1930	1.26	**A's**	1.20	Reds
1931	1.27	**Senators**	1.14	Cards
1932	1.22	**A's**	1.16	Braves
1933	1.13	**Senators**	1.09	Braves
1934	1.16	Yankees	1.11	**Cubs**
1935	1.10	**Tigers**	1.24	Cards
1936	1.14	Tigers	1.22	**Cubs**
1937	1.10	**Tigers**	1.15	Cubs
1938	1.13	Browns	1.12	**Cubs**
1939	1.19	**Yankees**	1.12	Giants
1940	1.17	Indians	1.13	**Reds**

Figure 3-25 shows errors per game by year for the American and National leagues from 1940 through 1950. The scale of the graph includes the highest and lowest values of errors per game in the century. The same scale is used for all decades except that after 1950 a maximum scale value of 1.00 is used to facilitate league comparisons. Thus, it is possible to see at a glance how errors in one decade compare to the highs and lows for the century. The exact values of errors per game for each year are shown below the graph together with the teams that led each league. Teams that led the majors are shown in bold.

There was a fundamental change between the leagues in errors per game in the 1940-50 period. For the first half of the decade, including the influx of "replacement" players during WWII, errors were nearly the same in each league, and they declined by about 10 percent between 1940 and 1946. But between 1946 and 1947, errors per game declined by 18 percent in the AL and 8 percent in the NL. In the AL, errors per game fell permanently below 1.00 after 1946. They did the same in the NL after 1948. But for most of the rest of the century, the AL kept the edge it had established over the NL in 1947.

As described in the text accompanying Figure 3-21, in the 46 seasons from 1901 through 1946, the NL had fewer errors per game than the AL 29 times while the AL had fewer errors than the NL 17 times. But in the 52 seasons between 1946 and 1998, the AL had fewer errors per game than the NL 46 times while the NL had fewer errors than the AL only 6 times. This rate is exactly the same before and after the DH. From 1947 through 1972, and from 1973 through 1998, both periods of 26 years, the AL had fewer errors per game 23 times and the NL had fewer errors per game 3 times. Something happened in 1947 that led to the AL becoming the better fielding league (or the NL the poorer fielding league) by a substantial margin for the rest of the century, even though the NL had been the better fielding league by a moderate margin in the 46 years before 1947. The nature of the change is unknown, but it appears to be permanent.

The Indians led the AL in fewest errors per game 6 times in the decade, while the Red Sox led 3 times and the Yankees twice. When the Indians led the league in 1940, it was the first time they had done so since 1906. In the NL, the Cards led 4 times and the Reds and Dodgers each led 3 times. The Dodgers led for the first time in franchise history in 1942, but after leading 8 times in the 19 seasons from 1942 through 1960, they never led again (Table 4-8).

Bobby Doerr, who played second base for the powerful Red Sox teams of the 1940s, led the AL in fielding runs in 1946, 1947, and 1949. No other AL player led more than once. In the NL, three players led the league twice in fielding runs and they did it in sequential order. Shortstops Buddy Kerr and Marty Marion led in 1944 through 1947 for the Giants and Cards respectively. Richie Ashburn, who played center field for the Phillies for 12 years, led in his rookie year of 1948 and also in 1949 (and in 3 years in the 1950s as well).

Figure 3-25. AL/NL Errors Per Game 1940-50

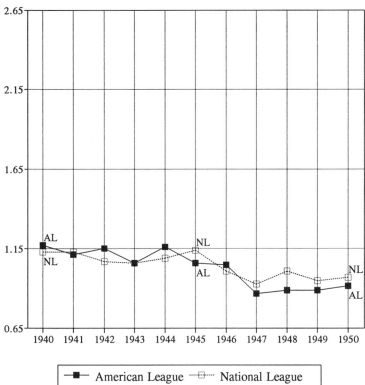

Year	AL Errors/Game	AL Leader	NL Errors/Game	NL Leader
1940	1.17	Indians	1.13	**Reds**
1941	1.11	**Indians**	1.13	Reds
1942	1.15	Yankees	1.07	**Dodgers**
1943	1.06	Red Sox	1.06	**Reds**
1944	1.16	Yankees	1.09	**Cards**
1945	1.06	Indians	1.14	**Cubs**
1946	1.05	Red Sox	1.01	**Cards**
1947	0.87	**Indians**	0.93	Cards
1948	0.89	**Indians**	1.01	Cards
1949	0.89	**Indians**	0.95	Dodgers
1950	0.92	**Red Sox**	0.97	Dodgers

Figure 3-26 shows errors per game by year for the American and National leagues from 1950 through 1960. The scale of the graph includes the highest and lowest values of errors per game in the century. The same scale is used for all decades except that after 1950 a maximum scale value of 1.00 is used to facilitate league comparisons. Thus, it is possible to see at a glance how errors in one decade compare to the highs and lows for the century. The exact values of errors per game for each year are shown below the graph together with the teams that led each league. Teams that led the majors are shown in bold.

A maximum of 1.00 is used for the first time in Figure 3-26. As discussed in the text accompanying Figure 3-25, neither league exceeded 1.00 errors per game after 1948. A maximum of 1.00 errors per game represents a decline of 62 percent from the record level of 2.62 recorded by the AL in 1901 (Figure 3-21). Thus, a scale maximum of 1.00 properly reflects the level of errors after 1948, and it also makes it possible to see the difference between the leagues much more clearly. Figure 3-26 shows that the AL not only had fewer errors per game than the NL 9 times in the 11 years in the period, it also had on average a much lower level of errors. The difference between the leagues grew even larger in the next decade. As discussed in detail in the text accompanying Figures 3-21 and 3-25, the AL had fewer errors per game than the NL 46 times in the 52 seasons from 1947 through 1998. The reason for the constant edge in fielding that the AL has compared to the NL is not known (the degree of difference before and after the DH is exactly the same).

The White Sox led the AL in fewest errors per game 4 times in the period and the Tigers led twice. But the most significant leadership came in 1960 when the Orioles led the league for the first time. In St. Louis the franchise led only once (1938). However, the Orioles led the AL 15 times from 1960 onward, giving the franchise first place in leading the league most often in fewest errors per game over the full century (Table 4-8). During the last 4 decades, the Orioles are easily the top fielding team in the AL. In the NL, the Dodgers led the league in fewest errors per game 6 times in the period, with the Reds leading twice. But the Dodgers never led again after 1960, while the Reds went on to lead 15 more times after 1958. Although the Orioles lead the majors from 1973 through 1998, the Reds lead the NL and the majors by a wide margin in most times leading in errors per game in the century (Table 4-8).

Even through the AL was the best fielding league overall, no AL player led in fielding runs more than once during the period, nor had an especially high rating. In the NL, Richie Ashburn led in center field for the Phillies 3 times, and Red Schoendienst led at second base for the Cards twice. But perhaps the best fielder ever to play at second base (certainly in terms of turning the double play) appeared on the list in 1960 when Bill Mazeroski of the Pirates led for the first time. He became a regular on the list, leading 6 more times in his career.

Figure 3-26. AL/NL Errors Per Game 1950-60

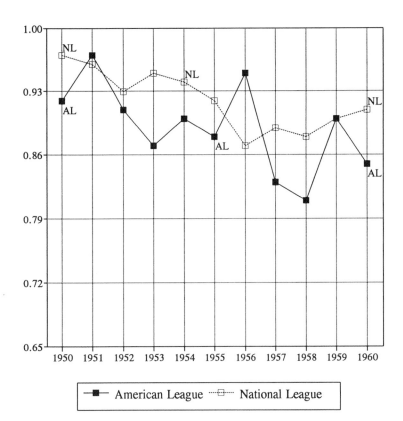

Year	AL Errors/Game	AL Leader	NL Errors/Game	NL Leader
1950	0.92	**Red Sox**	0.97	Dodgers
1951	0.97	Indians	0.96	**Cards**
1952	0.91	White Sox	0.93	**Dodgers**
1953	0.87	Senators	0.95	**Dodgers**
1954	0.90	**White Sox**	0.94	Braves
1955	0.88	**Indians**	0.92	Phillies
1956	0.95	White Sox	0.87	**Dodgers**
1957	0.83	**White Sox**	0.89	Reds
1958	0.81	Tigers	0.88	**Reds**
1959	0.90	Tigers	0.90	**Dodgers**
1960	0.85	**Orioles**	0.91	Dodgers

Figure 3-27 shows errors per game by year for the American and National leagues from 1960 through 1970. The scale of the graph includes the highest and lowest values of errors per game in the century. The same scale is used for all decades except that after 1950 a maximum scale value of 1.00 is used to facilitate league comparisons. Thus, it is possible to see at a glance how errors in one decade compare to the highs and lows for the century. The exact values of errors per game for each year are shown below the graph together with the teams that led each league. Teams that led the majors are shown in bold.

Continuing its edge over the NL as the best fielding league, the AL had fewer errors per game than the NL every year in the period (the AL was slightly better than the NL in 1968). This was the first time either league led every year in a decade, and the AL extended its streak to 15 straight years before the NL led again in 1975. There was an unusually large difference between the leagues from 1962 through 1965, and in 1964 the NL committed errors at a rate 27 percent above that of the AL. The huge difference resulted from the NL recording its highest levels of errors per game since 1948 while the AL set what was then an all-time low in errors per game. The low of 0.77 errors per game set by the AL in 1964 would last as the major league record until 1987. So 1964 represented an unusual combination of circumstances that had not happened before (and did not happen again), but the fact remains that for some reason errors were being committed at a much higher level in the NL than in the AL.

The Orioles asserted their position as the new fielding leader in the AL and led the league in fewest errors per game 5 times in the period. No other team led more than once. In an odd sequence, the Angels led for the one and only time in franchise history in 1967, while the Yankees led for the last time in 1961 and the Indians led for the last time in 1965 (Table 4-8). In the NL, the Braves led 4 times, the Reds 3 times, and the Phillies twice. But in a sequence similar to that in the AL, the Braves led for the last time in 1969, while the Dodgers opened the decade leading for the last time in 1960. Even the Cubs, who led in 1968, did not lead again until 1996.

Clete Boyer led the AL in fielding runs 3 times in the period at third base for the Yankees. Bobby Knoop led at second base for the Angels in 1964 and for the White Sox in 1970. But the real fielding story was in the NL. Bill Mazeroski led 7 times, the most often in the century, and his mark of 56.7 in 1963 is the second highest in the century. He was easily the best ever at turning the double play. The Pirates led the NL in double plays 9 straight years from 1959 through 1967, and they led the majors 7 straight years (Figure 3-37). The Pirates set the all-time NL double play record in 1966, a time of low offense when double plays were in decline. Mazeroski played nearly every game at second base for the Pirates when these records were set, and he holds the major league record for the most single season and lifetime double plays at second base.

Figure 3-27. AL/NL Errors Per Game 1960-70

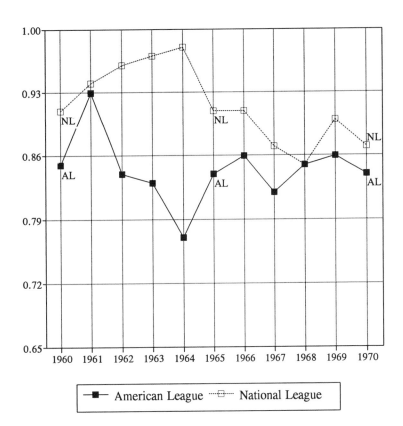

Year	AL Errors/Game	AL Leader	NL Errors/Game	NL Leader
1960	0.85	Orioles	0.91	Dodgers
1961	0.93	Yankees	0.94	**Braves**
1962	0.84	**White Sox**	0.96	Braves
1963	0.83	Orioles	0.97	Braves
1964	0.77	Orioles	0.98	Reds
1965	0.84	**Indians**	0.91	Reds
1966	0.86	Orioles	0.91	**Phillies**
1967	0.82	**Angels**	0.87	Reds
1968	0.85	**Tigers**	0.85	Cubs
1969	0.86	Orioles	0.90	Braves
1970	0.84	Rangers	0.87	**Phillies**

Figure 3-28 shows errors per game by year for the American and National leagues from 1970 through 1980. The scale of the graph includes the highest and lowest values of errors per game in the century. The same scale is used for all decades except that after 1950 a maximum scale value of 1.00 is used to facilitate league comparisons. Thus, it is possible to see at a glance how errors in one decade compare to the highs and lows for the century. The exact values of errors per game for each year are shown below the graph together with the teams that led each league. Teams that led the majors are shown in bold.

The AL adopted the designated hitter rule for the 1973 season, and with regard to errors the expectation was that errors would decline because in some cases the poorer fielders on the team would become the DH and would not play in the field. As so often happens in baseball, the result was exactly the opposite. Errors rose from sharply from 1972 through 1973 and up to a peak in 1975. Both leagues showed the same pattern even though the NL declined to use the DH. At the 1975 peak AL errors per game actually exceeded those in the NL for the first time since 1959. Errors in both leagues remained very close together after the 1975 peak, declining slowly through the end of the decade. The NL once again had fewer errors per game than the AL in 1979, but this failed to establish a trend because it did not happen again until 1992. After 1980 the AL regained it position as the better fielding league by a large margin.

The Orioles led the AL in fewest errors per game 5 times in the period. The Tigers led 4 times, and were the only other AL team to lead more than once. In the NL, the Reds led the league in fewest errors per game 7 times with the Phillies leading 3 times. The Reds and the Phillies were two of the best teams in the NL during the middle of the decade, confirming once again that often the best teams excel in every phase of the game. The Reds of the 1970s were known as the Big Red Machine because of their offensive prowess, but they were also the best fielding team in the league. The same was true of the Yankees during their long reign as the best team in baseball in the previous 5 decades. Their offensive output was famous, but it was little noticed that they were among the leaders in pitching and defense. It takes a balanced team to win regularly.

Freddie Patek led the AL in fielding runs in 1972 and 1973 as the shortstop for the Royals. Mark Belanger, who played 18 years in the majors even though he was the epitome of the "good field, no hit" shortstop, led the league in 1975 and 1978 for the Orioles. At the other end of the spectrum, Mike Schmidt led the NL 3 times in fielding runs at third base for the Phillies. During his career Schmidt led the NL in home runs 6 times while continuing to be a great fielder. Another "good field, no hit" shortstop, Dal Maxvill, led the NL for the Cards in 1970 and 1971. Belanger had a lifetime batting average of only .228, but Maxvill was even lower with a lifetime average of .217. Still, Maxvill played 14 years in the majors. Great fielding can take a shortstop a long way.

Figure 3-28. AL/NL Errors Per Game 1970-80

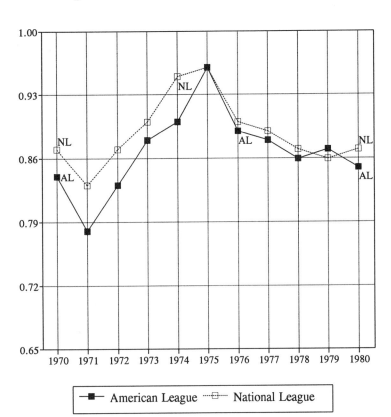

Year	AL Errors/Game	AL Leader	NL Errors/Game	NL Leader
1970	0.84	Rangers	0.87	**Phillies**
1971	0.78	Tigers	0.83	**Reds**
1972	0.83	**Tigers**	0.87	Reds
1973	0.88	**Tigers**	0.90	Reds
1974	0.90	Brewers	0.95	**Astros**
1975	0.96	Orioles	0.96	**Reds**
1976	0.89	Orioles	0.90	**Reds**
1977	0.88	Orioles	0.89	**Reds**
1978	0.86	Orioles	0.87	**Phillies**
1979	0.87	Tigers	0.86	**Phillies**
1980	0.85	**Orioles**	0.87	Reds

Figure 3-29 shows errors per game by year for the American and National leagues from 1980 through 1990. The scale of the graph includes the highest and lowest values of errors per game in the century. The same scale is used for all decades except that after 1950 a maximum scale value of 1.00 is used to facilitate league comparisons. Thus, it is possible to see at a glance how errors in one decade compare to the highs and lows for the century. The exact values of errors per game for each year are shown below the graph together with the teams that led each league. Teams that led the majors are shown in bold.

There was an offensive surge in both leagues in the 1980s that led to a new home run record for the AL in 1987 (Figure 2-29), but errors kept declining in both leagues, especially in the second half of the decade. The AL set what was then an all-time major league record for fewest errors per game in 1987, breaking the mark it had established in 1964. But the AL broke the record regularly through the end of the decade. The NL set an all-time league record in 1990, going below 0.80 errors per game for the first time. But it broke this record regularly in the next decade. All measures have limits they approach but do not reach. Thus, there is a limit on how long fielding skills can improve as new players come into the game, but that limit is not yet in sight for errors.

The Orioles and Twins each led the AL 3 times in fewest errors per game in the period, and the Blue Jays led twice. The Blue Jays led for the first and last time in franchise history in the period, and the Twins led for the last time in 1988. The Tigers also led for the last time in 1981 (Table 4-8). But with 14 teams in the league, nearly all of which are constantly improving in fielding, not leading in fewest errors per game for a long time is not necessarily an indication of a team moving into a cycle of poor fielding. If all teams among the 14 are reasonably good in fielding compared to prior years, then a typical leader will have to wait 14 years to reach the top.

In the NL, the Cards led 5 times and the Reds led 4 times. Even the Mets managed to lead for the first and only time in franchise history in 1988. The Phillies led for the last time in 1982. But the Reds, Cards, and Phillies rank at the top of the NL list for leading the league in fewest errors per game from 1973 through 1998 (Table 4-8).

Buddy Bell led the AL in fielding runs at third base for the Rangers in 1981 and 1982, and Spike Owen led at shortstop for the Mariners in 1985 and 1986 (playing part of the year for the Red Sox). In the NL, Ozzie Smith led the league 5 times, playing at shortstop for the Padres in 1980 and 1981, and for the Cards the rest of his career. Smith went on to set the lifetime major league double play record for shortstops. Glenn Hubbard of the Braves led 3 times at second base, and in 1985 he recorded the highest fielding runs mark (61.8) in history for any position. Hubbard was a fulltime player for only about 5 years, but he still ranks third in this century in lifetime fielding runs at second base.

Figure 3-29. AL/NL Errors Per Game 1980-90

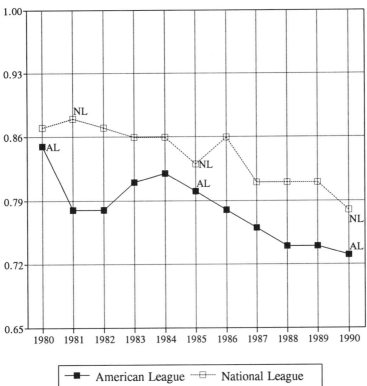

Year	AL Errors/Game	AL Leader	NL Errors/Game	NL Leader
1980	0.85	**Orioles**	0.87	Reds
1981	0.78	**Tigers**	0.88	Reds
1982	0.78	**Orioles**	0.87	Phillies
1983	0.81	**Rangers**	0.86	Reds
1984	0.82	Twins	0.86	**Cards**
1985	0.80	White Sox	0.83	**Cards**
1986	0.78	**Blue Jays**	0.86	Cards
1987	0.76	**Twins**	0.81	Cards
1988	0.74	**Twins**	0.81	Mets
1989	0.74	**Orioles**	0.81	Cards
1990	0.73	**Blue Jays**	0.78	Reds

Figure 3-30 shows errors per game by year for the American and National leagues from 1988 through 1998. The scale of the graph includes the highest and lowest values of errors per game in the century. The same scale is used for all decades except that after 1950 a maximum scale value of 1.00 is used to facilitate league comparisons. Thus, it is possible to see at a glance how errors in one decade compare to the highs and lows for the century. The exact values of errors per game for each year are shown below the graph together with the teams that led each league. Teams that led the majors are shown in bold.

At the beginning of the period AL errors per game were relatively constant, while NL errors per game steadily declined. Finally, in 1992, the NL recorded fewer errors per game than the AL for the first time since 1979 (and only the third time since 1959). The NL had to establish what was then an all-time league low for errors per game to beat the AL in 1992, and the effort obviously exhausted the league because errors per game soared 15 percent in the NL between 1992 and 1993. But the AL kept improving a little more every year, and in 1995 the AL set the all-time major league record for fewest errors per game in a season. The 0.68 mark recorded by the AL in 1995 is 74 percent lower than the level reached in the AL's first year in 1901.

The AL remained close to its all-time low for the rest of the decade. After setting its league low in 1992, the NL stayed well above the AL until 1998. Then the NL set a new all-time low for the league, nearly falling below the AL once more. Even after nearly 100 years, both leagues continue to show an improvement in fielding and a reduction in errors per game.

From 1991 onward, the Orioles led the AL in fewest errors per game 4 times while no other team was able to lead more than once. In a demonstration of how well all players are able to field today, the closest AL competitor to the Orioles for fewest errors per game in 1998 was an expansion team, the Devil Rays. Among other expansion teams, the Mariners led for the first time in franchise history in 1993, and the Royals led for the first time in franchise history in 1997 (Table 4-8). In the NL, from 1991 onward, the Cards, Giants and Reds each led twice. When the Giants led in 1993, it was the first time the franchise had led in fewest errors per game since 1939, a gap of 54 years.

Based on the data available at the time of the completion of this book, no player in either the AL or the NL led his league in fielding runs more than once in the period. This trend is likely to continue as it is more and more difficult for an individual player to stand out. Many starting players today are great fielders by the standards of a few decades ago. In 1998 the Orioles set a new major league record with only 0.50 errors per game, and the Braves just missed the NL record with 0.56 errors per game. It is not clear how low the level of errors per game can go. Although the ultimate limit of zero errors per game is not attainable, players generally continue to be better and better fielders.

Figure 3-30. AL/NL Errors Per Game 1988-98

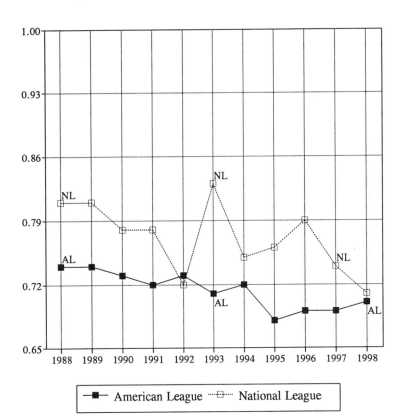

Year	AL Errors/Game	AL Leader	NL Errors/Game	NL Leader
1988	0.74	**Twins**	0.81	Mets
1989	0.74	**Orioles**	0.81	Cards
1990	0.73	**Blue Jays**	0.78	Reds
1991	0.72	**Orioles**	0.78	Cards
1992	0.73	**Brewers**	0.72	Cards
1993	0.71	**Mariners**	0.83	Giants
1994	0.72	**Orioles**	0.75	Giants
1995	0.68	**Orioles**	0.76	Reds
1996	0.69	**Rangers**	0.79	Cubs
1997	0.69	**Royals**	0.74	Reds
1998	0.70	**Orioles**	0.71	Braves

Figure 3-31 shows double plays per game by year for the American and National leagues from 1900 through 1910. The scale of the graph includes the highest and lowest values of double plays per game in the century. The same scale is used for all decades so it is possible to see at a glance how double plays in one decade compare to the highs and lows for the century. The exact values of double plays per game for each year are shown below the graph together with the teams that led each league. Teams that led the majors are shown in bold.

Double plays are a good indicator of the level of offense because the first requirement for a double play is a baserunner. Double plays increase with offense (more baserunners), walks (more baserunners in the prime position at first base), and improved fielding (although the overall level of fielding is not as important as the ability of the middle infielders to turn the double play). Double plays decrease with increased strikeouts. This is because there are fewer baserunners for a fixed number of outs, there are fewer balls put into play to turn into double plays, and strikeout pitchers bear down to get that crucial second out by a strikeout. After the second out a double play is no longer possible.

As an example of the importance of the level of offense in producing double plays, the Reds, Cubs, and Phillies set their all-time double play records in the 1920s (Figure 3-33) when the NL set its all-time records for runs, even though overall NL fielding was much better in the decades after 1920. The importance of walks to double plays is demonstrated by the fact that both leagues and many teams set all-time records for double plays in years close to 1950. This is because both leagues and many teams set all-time records for walks in years close to 1950 (Figures 3-35 and 3-36).

Because of the importance of baserunners and walks in producing double plays, the double play leaders in each league are often among the worse teams in the league. The poorest teams usually produce the highest number of opposing baserunners, and with nearly all teams steadily improving in fielding over the decades, the team with the most baserunners produces the most double plays. In spite of this relationship, the Yankees in the 1942-60 period were kings of the double play, and they were easily the best team in baseball in that period. They had a relatively low number of opposing baserunners, but they were good in all phases of the game including defense. As a result, the Yankees led the AL most often in double plays in the century (Table 4-9).

Both leagues had record lows in double plays in the first decade (the AL in 1905 and the NL in 1908) because of the low level of offense and the low level of defensive skills in the period. The Indians led the AL 4 times and the White Sox led twice. In the NL, the Reds and Braves led 3 times and the Cards twice. In spite of the famous verse about "Tinker to Evers to Chance" that was created in New York after the Cubs beat the Giants, the Cubs did not lead the NL in double plays any year in the decade.

Figure 3-31. AL/NL Double Plays Per Game 1900-10

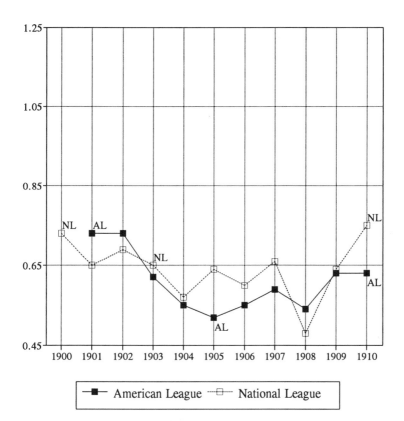

Year	AL DP/Game	AL Leader	NL DP/Game	NL Leader
1900	--	--	0.73	**Phillies**
1901	0.73	**Tigers**	0.65	Cards
1902	0.73	**White Sox**	0.69	Reds
1903	0.62	Indians	0.65	**Cards**
1904	0.55	**Senators**	0.57	Phillies
1905	0.52	White Sox	0.64	**Reds**
1906	0.55	Indians	0.60	**Pirates**
1907	0.59	**Indians**	0.66	Braves
1908	0.54	**Browns**	0.48	Braves
1909	0.63	Indians	0.64	**Reds**
1910	0.63	A's	0.75	**Braves**

Figure 3-32 shows double plays per game by year for the American and National leagues from 1910 through 1920. The scale of the graph includes the highest and lowest values of double plays per game in the century. The same scale is used for all decades so it is possible to see at a glance how double plays in one decade compare to the highs and lows for the century. The exact values of double plays per game for each year are shown below the graph together with the teams that led each league. Teams that led the majors are shown in bold.

Double plays increased slowly during the period even though offense fell sharply after 1912 as pitchers redoubled their efforts to "doctor" the ball to overcome the advantage given to hitters with the cork-center ball (Figure 2-2). The increase in double plays reflected the improvement of fielding skills and the decline in errors per game in the second decade (Figure 3-22). On average, double plays in the majors increased by 20 percent between the first and second decades even though runs increased by only 5 percent during the same period. Both leagues set what were then all-time highs for double plays in 1920, and they continued to set new records in the decades following 1920.

Confirming that low offense and high strikeouts will produce a decrease in double plays, the NL level of 0.82 double plays per game in 1920 was higher than that exhibited by the league 70 years later in any of the three years between 1989 and 1991 (Figure 3-39). NL defense was much better in 1990 than it was 70 years earlier in 1920, but no matter how talented the fielders are they cannot turn double plays without runners on base and less than two men out. Low offense and high strikeouts reduce the number of times this scenario occurs.

The NL led the AL in double plays 7 times in the period while the AL led the NL 4 times. In the 20 seasons from 1901 through 1920, the NL led the AL 13 times. But this edge lasted only through 1930. After that, the higher level of offense and walks in the AL gave it a big edge over the NL. The NL began to regain parity in the 1960s, but the birth of the DH in 1973 returned the edge to the AL. In the 67 seasons from 1932 through 1998, the AL led the NL in double plays 57 times, including 26 years in a row from 1972 through 1997.

The Browns led the AL in double plays per game 4 times in the period, while the Indians and White Sox led twice. The Browns were one of the worse teams in the league each year they led in double plays, putting them in the category of teams that lead mainly because the opposition puts lots of men on base. At the other extreme, the White Sox were an example of good teams that excel in all phases of the game. In the NL, the Braves and Reds each led 3 times. The Reds had mixed records, but the Braves twice were the worst team in the league. However, in 1914 the Braves led while winning the pennant by coming from last to first and sweeping the A's in the World Series. Shortstop Rabbit Maranville recorded the third highest level of fielding runs in the century in 1914, and was the major contributor to the top double play mark.

Figure 3-32. AL/NL Double Plays Per Game 1910-20

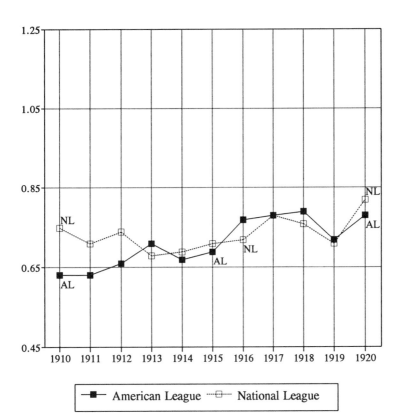

Year	AL DP/Game	AL Leader	NL DP/Game	NL Leader
1910	0.63	A's	0.75	**Braves**
1911	0.63	Indians	0.71	**Pirates**
1912	0.66	Browns	0.74	**Braves**
1913	0.71	Browns	0.68	**Dodgers**
1914	0.67	Indians	0.69	**Braves**
1915	0.69	Browns	0.71	**Reds**
1916	0.77	**White Sox**	0.72	Reds
1917	0.78	Browns	0.78	**Cards**
1918	0.79	**Yankees**	0.76	Reds
1919	0.72	**Red Sox**	0.71	Phillies
1920	0.78	**White Sox**	0.82	Giants

Figure 3-33 shows double plays per game by year for the American and National leagues from 1920 through 1930. The scale of the graph includes the highest and lowest values of double plays per game in the century. The same scale is used for all decades so it is possible to see at a glance how double plays in one decade compare to the highs and lows for the century. The exact values of double plays per game for each year are shown below the graph together with the teams that led each league. Teams that led the majors are shown in bold.

Double plays increased during the period as offense in both leagues soared to new highs (Figure 2-3). The AL climbed above 1.00 double plays per game for the first time in either league in 1925, while the NL topped the 1.00 mark in 1928 and then set what was then the all-time major league record of 1.07 double plays per game in 1930. This matched the all-time major league record for runs the NL also set in 1930. The AL did not top the NL record of 1.07 until the AL reached 1.09 double plays per game in 1948, and the NL did not top its 1930 mark until it set a new league record of 1.07 in 1951 (to three decimals, 1930 was 1.066 while 1951 was just below 1.075). But 1930 still remains as the second highest year in history for NL double plays per game.

The NL led the AL in double plays per game 7 times in the period while the AL led 4 times. In total, the NL led the AL 19 times in the 30 seasons between 1901 and 1930. However, as described in the text accompanying Figure 3-32, the AL led the NL in 57 of the 67 seasons from 1932 through 1998.

The Senators led the AL 3 times in double plays per game during the period while the White Sox and Indians led twice. All 3 leaders alternated between having good teams and bad during the years they led the league. The Indians and White Sox, in that order, rank second and third behind the Yankees in most times leading the league in double plays during the century (Table 4-9). The Cubs led the NL 3 times during the period while the Giants and Phillies each led twice. The Cubs and Giants had good teams while they were double play leaders, each winning the pennant once as a leader. In fact, every team that led the NL in double plays during the period had a winning record the year they led except for the Phillies. In the 2 years they led, the Phillies had winning percentages of .325 and .364, and finished last and seventh respectively. The Phillies clearly led due to the number of opposing baserunners their pitchers put on base.

The Reds led the NL in 1928 while setting an all-time team double play record. The Reds rank 3rd in the league in leading the NL in double plays most often (Table 4-9), but 1928 is still their top year for double plays. The Cubs also set their all-time team record in 1928, and the Reds, Cubs, and Phillies each set all-time team records in the 1920s for most double plays over a 5 year period. Each of these teams have had much better fielding teams since the 1920s, but the high level of offense (and low level of strikeouts) in the 1920s made this decade the most productive in team history for double plays.

Figure 3-33. AL/NL Double Plays Per Game 1920-30

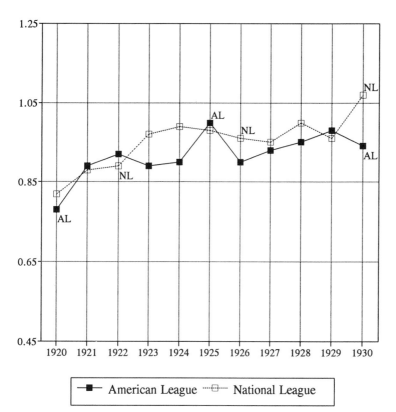

Year	AL DP/Game	AL Leader	NL DP/Game	NL Leader
1920	0.78	**White Sox**	0.82	Giants
1921	0.89	White Sox	0.88	**Giants**
1922	0.92	**Senators**	0.89	Cubs
1923	0.89	**Senators**	0.97	Phillies
1924	0.90	A's	0.99	**Phillies**
1925	1.00	Senators	0.98	**Pirates**
1926	0.90	Browns	0.96	**Cubs**
1927	0.93	Tigers	0.95	**Cards**
1928	0.95	Indians	1.00	**Reds**
1929	0.98	Indians	0.96	**Cubs**
1930	0.94	Red Sox	1.07	**Cards**

Figure 3-34 shows double plays per game by year for the American and National leagues from 1930 through 1940. The scale of the graph includes the highest and lowest values of double plays per game in the century. The same scale is used for all decades so it is possible to see at a glance how double plays in one decade compare to the highs and lows for the century. The exact values of double plays per game for each year are shown below the graph together with the teams that led each league. Teams that led the majors are shown in bold.

Runs were steady (Figure 2-4) and walks increased (Figure 3-14) during most of the decade in the AL, and this produced an increase in double plays from their already high levels entering the decade. There was a small decline in all three measures as the decade ended, just after the AL set a new league record for double plays per game in 1938. In the NL, runs and walks declined in the first half of the decade and double plays also declined. A recovery in runs and walks in the second half of the decade produced a corresponding recovery in double plays. The early NL decline took double plays down to 0.85 per game in 1935, the lowest level since 1920. The AL led the NL in double plays per game in 9 of the 10 years after 1931, a domination that continued the rest of the century.

The Senators led the AL in double plays per game 4 times during the period, while the White Sox and Browns led twice. Except for the 1936 White Sox, every team in the AL that led in double plays had a losing record the year they led. In the NL, the Braves led the league in double plays per game 3 times and the Phillies and Cubs each led twice. Among the leaders, the Braves and Phillies had losing records each year they led the league. But the Cubs led while winning the 1935 pennant and finishing third in 1933. The Cubs led the league only one more time after 1935 (in 1948), and of the 8 NL teams that existed in 1901, the Cubs led the league the fewest times in the century in double plays (Table 4-9).

Through 1940 no team dominated double play leadership. This is because of the complex relationship between the number of double plays a team turns in the field and the number of hits, walks, and strikeouts its pitchers record. The fielding skill of the team's infielders is also a key factor. Poor teams that create the most baserunners often alternate in leading in double plays with good teams that create fewer baserunners but have better infielders. Table 4-1 shows that double plays rank last in the AL in the number of times one team led, and they rank next to last in this respect in the NL. But in the next two decades three teams dominated in double play leadership in three different periods. The A's set all-time records near 1950 with a team of excellent infielders and poor pitchers who created a lot of baserunners. The Yankees dominated in the 1950s with the "disadvantage" of good pitching combined with highly skilled infielders. The Pirates had the highest level of double play domination in the century in the 1960s (when offense was near record lows) due to the unique skills of Bill Mazeroski, the best player in history at turning the double play.

Figure 3-34. AL/NL Double Plays Per Game 1930-40

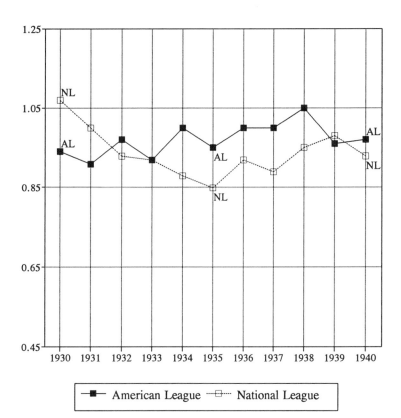

Year	AL DP/Game	AL Leader	NL DP/Game	NL Leader
1930	0.94	Red Sox	1.07	**Cards**
1931	0.91	Browns	1.00	**Reds**
1932	0.97	**White Sox**	0.93	Dodgers
1933	0.92	**Tigers**	0.92	Cubs
1934	1.00	**A's**	0.88	Phillies
1935	0.95	**Senators**	0.85	Cubs
1936	1.00	**White Sox**	0.92	Braves
1937	1.00	**Senators**	0.89	Phillies
1938	1.05	**Senators**	0.95	Pirates
1939	0.96	Senators	0.98	**Braves**
1940	0.97	**Browns**	0.93	Braves

Figure 3-35 shows double plays per game by year for the American and National leagues from 1940 through 1950. The scale of the graph includes the highest and lowest values of double plays per game in the century. The same scale is used for all decades so it is possible to see at a glance how double plays in one decade compare to the highs and lows for the century. The exact values of double plays per game for each year are shown below the graph together with the teams that led each league. Teams that led the majors are shown in bold.

In spite of declining runs in the first half of the 1940s due to the WWII draft, double plays stayed at high levels in the AL through 1946. Then they soared to an all-time major league record of 1.20 per game in 1949. This is because walks also reached all-time record levels at the end of the decade (Figure 3-15). Double plays in the NL changed very little from 1940 through 1948, then soared to a record high of 1.07 in 1951. The rise in double plays in the NL matched the rise in walks in the league shown in Figure 3-15. The clearest demonstration in the century of the relationship between walks and double plays came in the 1940s.

The Yankees led the AL in double plays per game 3 times during the period, while the Indians and A's led twice. In the NL, the Braves and Reds each led 3 times and the Dodgers led twice. As described in the text accompanying Figure 3-31, the Yankees were the best double play team in the majors between 1942 and 1960. They did not lead every year, but they led more often than any other team and were usually among the leaders. This is primarily a tribute to the skill of their infielders because, as usual, the Yankees also were among the leaders in pitching in this period. But the top story in double plays in this period belongs to the A's, who set all-time major league records for most double plays in one season as well as all-time records for consistency.

The A's led the AL in double plays only 7 times in the century, and after 1951 they did not lead again until 1996 (Table 4-9). But the A's of the 1949-51 period had both good infielders and pitchers who put lots of runners on base (especially in a period of a record number of walks). The primary A's infielders were Hank Majeski at third, Eddie Joost at short, Pete Suder at second, and Ferris Fain at first. They were aggressive in going for the double play, and they were extremely competent in turning the double play. The 1949 A's were the first team to record more than 200 double plays in a season, setting the all-time major league team record with 217. The A's exceeded 200 double plays 3 years in a row with 208 in 1950 and 204 in 1951. The A's are the only team to exceed 200 double plays in 3 different years, let alone 3 years in a row. The 1956 Yankees (214) and 1949 Red Sox (207) are the only other teams to go over 200 in 154 games. Thus, these teams join the A's at the top of the per game list. The 1979 Twins (203), 1980 Red Sox and Blue Jays (206 each), and the 1985 Angels (202) are the only other AL teams to go over 200. The 1966 Pirates hold the NL record with 215 while the 1997 Rockies had 202.

Figure 3-35. AL/NL Double Plays Per Game 1940-50

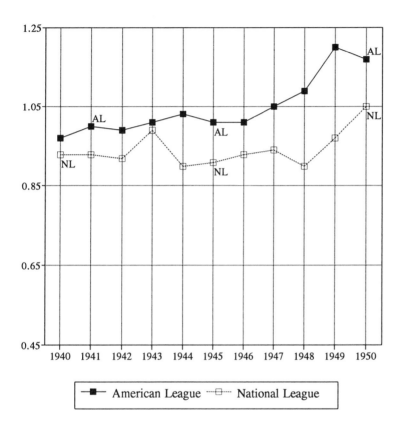

Year	AL DP/Game	AL Leader	NL DP/Game	NL Leader
1940	0.97	**Browns**	0.93	Braves
1941	1.00	**Yankees**	0.93	Braves
1942	0.99	**Yankees**	0.92	Reds
1943	1.01	Indians	0.99	**Reds**
1944	1.03	**Indians**	0.90	Cards
1945	1.01	**Red Sox**	0.91	Braves
1946	1.01	Yankees	0.93	**Reds**
1947	1.05	**White Sox**	0.94	Dodgers
1948	1.09	**Browns**	0.90	Cubs
1949	1.20	**A's**	0.97	Pirates
1950	1.17	**A's**	1.05	Dodgers

Figure 3-36 shows double plays per game by year for the American and National leagues from 1950 through 1960. The scale of the graph includes the highest and lowest values of double plays per game in the century. The same scale is used for all decades so it is possible to see at a glance how double plays in one decade compare to the highs and lows for the century. The exact values of double plays per game for each year are shown below the graph together with the teams that led each league. Teams that led the majors are shown in bold.

The 1950s featured lots of home runs, but both runs and walks declined (Figures 2-6 and 3-16), while strikeouts increased sharply (Figure 3-6). As a result, double plays declined from the record levels of 1949 and 1951. AL double plays fell below the 1.00 level in 1959 for the first time since 1942. Double plays in the NL declined a little more slowly than in the AL, and the NL had a higher level of double plays per game than the AL in 1954 for the first time since 1939. Between 1950 and 1960, double plays in the AL declined by 12 percent, and in the NL they declined by 13 percent. In the past 40 years, neither league has been able to get back to the level they posted in 1958.

The Yankees led the AL in double plays per game 6 times during the period, leading the majors 5 times. The A's were the only other AL team to lead more than once (after 1951 the A's did not lead again until 1996). In the NL, the Dodgers and Pirates led 3 times and the Giants and Reds led twice. For the Reds, 1954 was the last time in franchise history they led the league in double plays. The Dodgers were nearly the same as they led only one more time (1989) after leading in 1958. But the Pirates were just beginning the best run any major league team has had in leading their league in double plays per game. Bill Mazeroski was a rookie in 1956, and by 1959 he was leading the Pirates to an unprecedented string of double play titles. But this is mainly a story for the 1960s. The Yankees were the prime story of the 1950s after the A's finished their run of 3 straight years over 200 double plays in 1951.

Except for the Pirates of the 1960s, the 6 double play titles the Yankees won in the 1950s were more than any other major league team was able to record in one decade in the century. The Yankees won the AL double play title 10 times between 1941 and 1961, and this was the major contributor to the 15 titles they won in the century to put them at the top of the AL list (Table 4-9). The Yankees also led the majors 10 times, and only the Pirates at 12 led the majors more often. The Yankees led in double plays because of the great fielding skills they demonstrated year after year. The Yankees are famous for hitting home runs and scoring runs, but the key to their string of championships in the 1950s was pitching and defense. Infielders like Phil Rizzuto, Gil McDougald, Jerry Coleman, and Andy Carey kept turning double plays and helping the Yankees to stay on top. Even Yogi Berra played his part. He ranks 3rd on the lists for most double plays in a season and most double plays in a career for catchers.

Figure 3-36. AL/NL Double Plays Per Game 1950-60

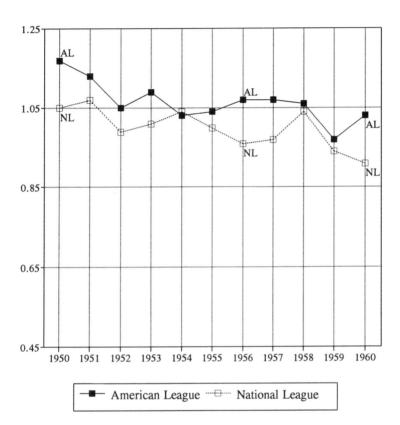

Year	AL DP/Game	AL Leader	NL DP/Game	NL Leader
1950	1.17	A's	1.05	Dodgers
1951	1.13	A's	1.07	Dodgers
1952	1.05	**Yankees**	0.99	Giants
1953	1.09	**Indians**	1.01	Reds
1954	1.03	**Yankees**	1.04	Reds
1955	1.04	**Yankees**	1.00	Pirates
1956	1.07	**Yankees**	0.96	Cards
1957	1.07	**Yankees**	0.97	Giants
1958	1.06	Yankees	1.04	**Dodgers**
1959	0.97	**Red Sox**	0.94	Pirates
1960	1.03	**White Sox**	0.91	Pirates

Figure 3-37 shows double plays per game by year for the American and National leagues from 1960 through 1970. The scale of the graph includes the highest and lowest values of double plays per game in the century. The same scale is used for all decades so it is possible to see at a glance how double plays in one decade compare to the highs and lows for the century. The exact values of double plays per game for each year are shown below the graph together with the teams that led each league. Teams that led the majors are shown in bold.

The strike zone change in the 1963-68 period resulted in lower runs and walks (Figures 2-7 and 3-17) while strikeouts soared (Figure 3-7). Double plays fell accordingly, with the AL reaching its lowest level since 1920 in 1968, and the NL reaching its lowest level since 1935 in 1963. Double plays were nearly the same in both leagues with the leagues alternating in leadership. When the 1963 strike zone change was reversed and the mound lowered in 1969, double plays in the AL increased by 12 percent from the 1968 level.

The Angels led the AL in double plays per game 3 times in the period, with the White Sox, Yankees, and Rangers each leading twice. In the NL, the Pirates capped a streak of leading 9 years in a row in 1967, and they led a total of 9 times in the period. The Pirates led the majors every year they led except 1960, and the 9 titles they won in the period were half the total of 18 they won in the century. They top the majors in leading in double plays most often (Table 4-9). The Pirates were king of the double play between 1959 and 1970, and this period matches the prime years Bill Mazeroski played for them at second base.

As described in the text accompanying Figure 3-27, Mazeroski set records in fielding runs in the period as well as in double plays. Mazeroski holds the major league record for most double plays in a season and most double plays in a career at second base. His peak season was 1966, when he took part in 161 of the 215 double plays (the NL record) turned by the Pirates. Mazeroski holds 3 of the top 8 positions on the single season list, and he is 87 double plays ahead of Nellie Fox, who is second on the lifetime list. The NL record of 215 double plays set by the Pirates trails only the 217 made by the 1949 A's, but the Pirates did it in 162 games. Thus, the Pirates rank only 5th behind the 1949 A's, 1956 Yankees, 1950 A's, and 1949 Red Sox in most double plays per game.

However, the 1966 Pirates played when runs were near record lows, walks were low, and strikeouts were high. The teams ahead of them in double plays per game played when runs were above average, walks were at record highs, and strikeouts were relatively low. Thus, there can be some argument about the best double play team in history. But there is no argument that Mazeroski was the best ever at turning the double play at second base. Dick Groat and Gene Alley, who played shortstop with Mazeroski, also rank among the top shortstops in double plays. Groat ranks 10th on the list of most double plays in a career, and Alley ranks 10th on the list for most double plays in one season (1966).

Figure 3-37. AL/NL Double Plays Per Game 1960-70

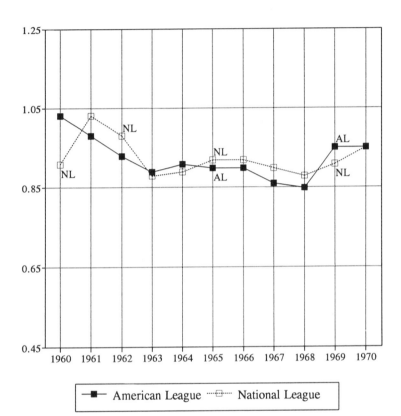

Year	AL DP/Game	AL Leader	NL DP/Game	NL Leader
1960	1.03	White Sox	0.91	Pirates
1961	0.98	Yankees	1.03	**Pirates**
1962	0.93	Twins	0.98	**Pirates**
1963	0.89	Rangers	0.88	**Pirates**
1964	0.91	Angels	0.89	**Pirates**
1965	0.90	Yankees	0.92	**Pirates**
1966	0.90	Angels	0.92	**Pirates**
1967	0.86	Rangers	0.90	**Pirates**
1968	0.85	Angels	0.88	**Phillies**
1969	0.95	Red Sox	0.91	**Expos**
1970	0.95	White Sox	0.95	**Pirates**

Figure 3-38 shows double plays per game by year for the American and National leagues from 1970 through 1980. The scale of the graph includes the highest and lowest values of double plays per game in the century. The same scale is used for all decades so it is possible to see at a glance how double plays in one decade compare to the highs and lows for the century. The exact values of double plays per game for each year are shown below the graph together with the teams that led each league. Teams that led the majors are shown in bold.

The arrival of the designated hitter in 1973 permanently changed the relationship between the leagues in double plays (as it did also in many other measures). With the DH the AL has more runs, more walks, and fewer strikeouts than the NL. As a result, the AL has more double plays than the NL. The AL led the NL in double plays per game every year after the DH was born until the NL finally edged the AL in 1998. This means the AL led for 26 straight years from 1972 through 1997. It can be expected that AL will turn more double plays than the NL for as long as the AL has the DH and the NL does not.

The Al responded with its highest level of double plays per game since 1960 when the DH was introduced in 1973. AL double plays increased by 8 percent between 1972 and 1973, and by 1980 AL double plays were 11 percent higher than they were when the period began in 1970. NL double plays, however, slowly decreased during the period and were 5 percent lower at the end than at the beginning. In 1978 NL double plays per game reached their lowest level since 1935. In the next 10 years NL double plays fell even farther.

Four teams (White Sox, Royals, Orioles, and Twins) led the AL in double plays per game two different times in the period. The Royals led for the only times in franchise history in 1971 and 1973, and the Twins, who led 11 times in the century (most often when they were the Senators), led for the last time in 1976. The Tigers, who led only 4 times in the century, the fewest of any of the original 16 teams, led for the last time in 1978 (Table 4-9). In the NL, the Cards led 3 times in the period, while the Pirates and Expos led twice. The Expos led for the last time in 1976, and the Mets led for the one and only time in franchise history in 1979. Perhaps the most notable event in the period from the standpoint of turning double plays occurred in 1978 when the Padres led the league in double plays for the first time in franchise history. This was the first year that rookie Ozzie Smith played in the majors at shortstop for the Padres.

Smith was traded to the Cards by the Padres for Gary Templeton before the 1982 season. There were other players involved, but the key part of the trade was the exchange of shortstops Smith and Templeton. By the end of his career the name "Ozzie Smith" was recognized to the same degree in terms of turning double plays at shortstop that the name "Bill Mazeroski" was recognized for turning double plays at second base. Smith ranks first in total career double plays for shortstops (as well as in career somersaults).

Figure 3-38. AL/NL Double Plays Per Game 1970-80

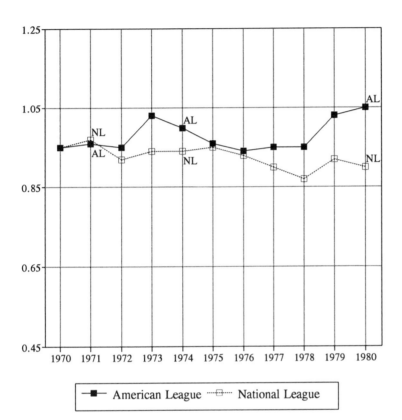

Year	AL DP/Game	AL Leader	NL DP/Game	NL Leader
1970	0.95	White Sox	0.95	**Pirates**
1971	0.96	Royals	0.97	**Braves**
1972	0.95	**Yankees**	0.92	Pirates
1973	1.03	**Royals**	0.94	Phillies
1974	1.00	White Sox	0.94	**Cards**
1975	0.96	Orioles	0.95	**Expos**
1976	0.94	**Twins**	0.93	Expos
1977	0.95	**Orioles**	0.90	Cards
1978	0.95	**Tigers**	0.87	Padres
1979	1.03	**Twins**	0.92	Mets
1980	1.05	**Red Sox**	0.90	Cards

Figure 3-39 shows double plays per game by year for the American and National leagues from 1980 through 1990. The scale of the graph includes the highest and lowest values of double plays per game in the century. The same scale is used for all decades so it is possible to see at a glance how double plays in one decade compare to the highs and lows for the century. The exact values of double plays per game for each year are shown below the graph together with the teams that led each league. Teams that led the majors are shown in bold.

With the DH, the AL stayed well ahead of NL in double plays per game for the full period. There was a home run outburst in 1987 (Figure 2-29), but the level of home runs has very little effect on double plays. Runs also increased (Figure 2-9), but walks were little changed (Figure 3-19) and strikeouts rose to what were then record levels (Figure 3-9). The net result was a small decline in double plays in the AL during the period, but, after exhibiting little change through 1987, NL double plays fell sharply as runs declined in the league after the home run outburst in 1987. From 1989 through 1991, double plays per game in the NL were at their lowest level since 1919. In terms of low offense and low double plays, the NL returned to "dead ball" days at the end of the 1980s and the beginning of the 1990s.

The Angels led the AL in double plays per game 3 times in the period with the Brewers and Yankees each leading twice. The Brewers led for the first time in franchise history in 1981, but the Brewers and Angels are at the top of the league list in leading the league in double plays most often between 1973 and 1998 (Table 4-9). In the NL, the Braves led 4 times and the Cards and Padres led twice. The Braves were at the top of their division the first two years they led, and at the bottom of the division the last two years they led. But the one constant for the Braves each of the 4 times they led was Glenn Hubbard at second base.

Hubbard had the highest level of fielding runs for any player in the century in 1985 (see text accompanying Figure 3-29). The Braves had the highest level of double plays per game in franchise history that year, and their leadership in 1985 was not an isolated event because the Braves rank second in the NL in leading the league most often in double plays during the century (Table 4-9). The Braves also set their franchise mark for most double plays per game over a five year period between 1982 and 1986, and Hubbard was at second base every year in that period. Hubbard and the Braves are a good example of the importance of an excellent middle infielder in producing double plays. In the 1980s the NL was in a down period in double plays, and the Braves, who often led the NL in double plays during the century, oscillated between being a good team at the top of the division and a bad team at the bottom of the division. But among all these variables, they had an exceptional player at second base. As a result they set all their franchise double play records in the period.

Figure 3-39. AL/NL Double Plays Per Game 1980-90

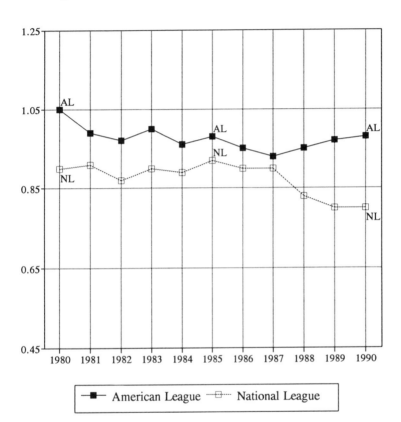

Year	AL DP/Game	AL Leader	NL DP/Game	NL Leader
1980	1.05	**Red Sox**	0.90	Cards
1981	0.99	**Brewers**	0.91	Padres
1982	0.97	Brewers	0.87	**Braves**
1983	1.00	**Angels**	0.90	Braves
1984	0.96	Yankees	0.89	**Cards**
1985	0.98	**Angels**	0.92	Braves
1986	0.95	**Mariners**	0.90	Braves
1987	0.93	Orioles	0.90	**Giants**
1988	0.95	**White Sox**	0.83	Padres
1989	0.97	**Yankees**	0.80	Dodgers
1990	0.98	**Angels**	0.80	Phillies

Figure 3-40 shows double plays per game by year for the American and National leagues from 1988 through 1998. The scale of the graph includes the highest and lowest values of double plays per game in the century. The same scale is used for all decades so it is possible to see at a glance how double plays in one decade compare to the highs and lows for the century. The exact values of double plays per game for each year are shown below the graph together with the teams that led each league. Teams that led the majors are shown in bold.

In the AL there was a moderate increase in double plays after 1993 as runs and walks increased sharply (Figures 2-10 and 3-20). But the huge surge in strikeouts (Figure 3-10) that accompanied the surge in runs and walks held down the increase in double plays. In the NL, double plays fell substantially as the league returned to "dead ball" days at the beginning of the decade. In 1991 NL double plays fell to only 0.79 per game. This was the lowest level in the NL since 1919. The AL had 24 percent more double plays per game in 1991 than the NL, the largest difference between the leagues in the century. NL double plays then rose in concert with the increase in offense following the 1993 expansion and the beginning of arcade baseball in Denver.

The margin between the leagues narrowed in 1994 as offense soared in both leagues. But the AL was pulling away again until interleague play started in 1997. The AL loss of the DH and the NL gain of the DH in interleague play reduced the difference between the leagues again. NL double plays were nearly constant from 1994 onward (and at their highest sustained levels in 20 years), but in 1998 the AL had its lowest level of double plays in 30 years. The result was that the NL led the AL in double plays in 1998, breaking the AL streak of leading the NL in double plays for 26 straight years from 1972 through 1997.

From 1991 onward, the Indians and Brewers each led the AL twice in double plays per game. When the Indians led in 1992, it was the first time they led since 1953, a gap of 39 years. But the A's had a bigger gap. When they led in 1996, it was the first time the franchise led since 1951, a gap of 45 years. In 1951 the A's completed a run of 3 straight years above 200 double plays, a major league record. In 1996 the A's came close with 195 double plays, but with the longer season the 1996 A's only had 1.20 double plays per game compared to 1.32 for their 1951 counterparts. The 1949 A's hold the franchise (and major league) record with 1.41 per game.

The Giants led the NL in double plays 3 years in a row from 1991 through 1993, while the Rockies led both the NL and the majors in double plays in 1997 and 1998. When the Rockies led in 1997, they turned 202 double plays. It was the first time since the Pirates set the NL record at 215 in 1966 that an NL team got above 200 double plays in one year (the Rockies could not quite make it to 200 in 1998). The Rockies have the advantage of a high level of offense in Coors Field, but they also have had reasonably good fielding teams.

Figure 3-40. AL/NL Double Plays Per Game 1988-98

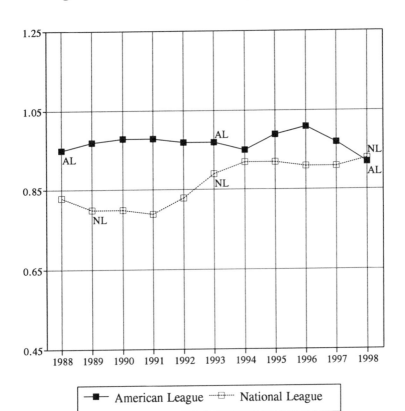

Year	AL DP/Game	AL Leader	NL DP/Game	NL Leader
1988	0.95	**White Sox**	0.83	Padres
1989	0.97	**Yankees**	0.80	Dodgers
1990	0.98	**Angels**	0.80	Phillies
1991	0.98	**Mariners**	0.79	Giants
1992	0.97	**Indians**	0.83	Giants
1993	0.97	**Indians**	0.89	Giants
1994	0.95	Brewers	0.92	**Pirates**
1995	0.99	**Brewers**	0.92	Cards
1996	1.01	**A's**	0.91	Marlins
1997	0.97	Red Sox	0.91	**Rockies**
1998	0.92	Devil Rays	0.93	**Rockies**

Part IV
Leaders and Records

Leaders Summary

Figure 4-1 shows the top three leaders from each league for the measures in the book ranked by the number of years each team led the specific measure in the century. Ties are broken based on which team led the majors most often. The discussion for each measure identifies the table in which all 30 teams are listed. This detailed table also has results before and after the DH was born in 1973.

Runs--The Yankees led the AL and the majors most often, but the Tigers and Red Sox are the leaders in the 1973-98 period (Table 4-2). The Giants are the NL leaders, but none of the top 3 NL teams rank high in the 1973-98 period, and all trail their AL counterparts in number of times leading the league.

Batting Average--The Cards are the century leaders, but the Red Sox led the majors the most often. The Red Sox are kings of the 1973-98 period while the Cards led the NL in both parts of the century (Table 4-3).

Home Runs--The Yankees led the majors in home runs most often in the century, but they have not led since 1961, the longest any leading team has gone without winning a home run title (Table 4-4). The Tigers are not in the top 7 teams for the century, but they led the majors most often in the 1973-98 period. The Giants easily lead the NL, but they last led in 1972. The Dodgers and Braves are the NL leaders in the 1973-98 period.

Stolen Bases--The White Sox lead the majors for the century by a large margin, but the last year they led was 1966 (Table 4-5). The A's are the AL leader for the 1973-98 period. The Dodgers edge the Cards for the NL title for the full century by leading the majors more often, but the Dodgers have not led since 1970. The Cards lead the NL and the majors in the 1973-98 period.

Strikeouts--The Dodgers led their league and the majors by the largest margin for any measure in the century (Table 4-6). Their 34 titles are also the most for any measure, just edging out the 33 home run titles won by the Yankees. The A's barely lead the AL for the century, and they last led in 1971. Expansion teams are at the top in both leagues in the 1973-98 period, with the Angels and Mariners leading the AL and the Mets leading the NL.

Walks--The White Sox easily top the majors in leading most often in fewest walks per game in the century, while the Pirates top the NL with only 17 titles, the lowest number to lead any measure in the NL in the century (the AL has 3 categories in which the leader has 17 titles or less). The Brewers lead the AL and the Expos lead the NL in the 1973-98 period (Table 4-7).

186

Errors--The Reds lead in most years leading their league in fewest errors per game, but the Orioles, the AL leaders, led the majors most often during the century (Table 4-8). Both the Reds and the Orioles also easily led their leagues in the 1973-98 period. The Orioles are the top team in the majors since 1960. Their predecessors, the Browns, led only once in the history of the franchise.

Double Plays--The Yankees had great defense to go along with their big hitters, and they led the AL in double plays during the century. But the Pirates led the NL and the majors most often (Table 4-9). The Pirates owe their lead to Bill Mazeroski, the best ever at turning the double play at second base.

Table 4-1. Teams Leading Most Often 1901-98

	American League		National League	
	Team	Years Led	Team	Years Led
Runs	Yankees	27	Giants	20
	Tigers	19	Cards	14
	Red Sox	16	Pirates	13
Bat Avg	Red Sox	21	Cards	22
	Tigers	16	Pirates	19
	Yankees	14	Giants	13
Home Runs	Yankees	33	Giants	27
	A's	16	Dodgers	17
	Red Sox	13	Phillies	14
Stolen Bases	White Sox	30	Dodgers	21
	Twins	13	Cards	21
	A's	12	Pirates	15
Strikeouts	A's	16	Dodgers	34
	Yankees	16	Mets	11
	Indians	11	Cards	11
Walks	White Sox	24	Pirates	17
	Twins	13	Giants	15
	Red Sox	12	Reds	12
Errors	Orioles	17	Reds	23
	White Sox	15	Cubs	17
	Tigers	11	Cards	14
Double Plays	Yankees	15	Pirates	18
	Indians	13	Braves	15
	White Sox	12	Reds	13

Table 4-2 shows the number of times each team led its league in runs per game during different periods (the Diamondbacks and Devil Rays are not listed because they did not lead in 1998). The first set of columns covers the 1901-98 period, the second the 1901-72 period, and the third the 1973-98 period (when the AL had the DH). The heading "Led Both" shows the number of times a team led both its own league and the majors. Years in bold under the "Last Led" heading identify teams that have gone the longest without leading. In Table 4-2, the Royals, Expos, and Padres have no years in bold because they never led in runs. But all were born in 1969 and thus have gone the longest without leading.

In nearly every measure the original 16 teams lead the list both for the century and the 1901-72 period because the expansion teams were not in existence long enough to accumulate a high number of leading years by 1972. But comparing the leaders before 1973 and after 1972 provides good insight into which of the original 16 teams were regular leaders during the century and which have been supplanted by other teams in the last quarter of the century.

The Yankees easily lead all teams in the number of times leading the league and the majors in runs. The Giants lead the NL. But the Yankees led as recently as 1998, while the Giants last led in 1970. The top 4 teams in the AL are the top 4 in all three periods, with the Tigers taking the lead after 1972 (as previously noted, ties in the rankings are broken by the number of times a team led the majors). The top 4 teams in the NL are the same for the century and the 1901-72 period, but none of these teams rank high after 1972.

The top 3 AL teams led the league 62 times in the century, or 63 percent of the 98 available seasons. But the top 3 NL teams led only 47 times or 48 percent of the available seasons. Further, the top 3 AL teams before 1972 led 13 times or 50 percent of the available seasons after 1972, while the top 3 NL teams before 1972 led only 5 times or 19 percent of the available seasons after 1972. Thus, at any time in the century, the Yankees, Tigers, and/or Red Sox have been scoring leaders in the AL. But in the NL, the Giants, Cards, and Pirates, who led most often before 1972, were replaced in the 1973-98 period.

A key problem for nearly every expansion team is scoring runs. It takes time to build a team that can execute the serial offense needed to generate runs on a consistent basis (the Colorado Rockies are an exception, but they had the advantage of coming into existence one mile up in thin air). This is a prime reason why the top 4 teams in the AL remained unchanged before and after 1972. It is only recently that AL expansion teams like the Mariners and Rangers became scoring leaders. In the NL, the Mets and Rockies had enough high scoring teams to become league leaders after 1972, but 7 original teams fill the next 7 places. In most other measures expansion teams routinely appear in the top part of the leader list after 1972, but runs are the most fundamental measure and expansion teams usually take a long time to catch up.

Table 4-2. Runs Leaders

American League

Team	1901-98 Led AL	Led Both	Last Led	Team	1901-72 Led AL	Led Both	Team	1973-98 Led AL	Led Both
Yankees	27	19	1998	Yankees	24	17	Tigers	5	5
Tigers	19	13	1993	Tigers	14	8	Red Sox	5	3
Red Sox	16	9	1989	Red Sox	11	6	Indians	3	3
Indians	9	5	1995	Indians	6	2	Yankees	3	2
A's	6	4	1973	A's	5	4	Brewers	2	2
Twins	5	2	1977	Orioles	5	1	Mariners	2	2
Orioles	5	1	**1971**	Twins	4	1	Angels	1	1
White Sox	4	4	1983	White Sox	3	3	Rangers	1	1
Brewers	2	2	1982				Twins	1	1
Mariners	2	2	1997				White Sox	1	1
Angels	1	1	1979				A's	1	0
Rangers	1	1	1991				Blue Jays	1	0
Blue Jays	1	0	1990				Orioles	0	0
Royals	0	0	--				Royals	0	0

National League

Team	1901-98 Led NL	Led Both	Last Led	Team	1901-72 Led NL	Led Both	Team	1973-98 Led NL	Led Both
Giants	20	7	**1970**	Giants	20	7	Mets	4	1
Cards	14	1	1985	Cards	12	1	Reds	3	2
Pirates	13	4	1992	Pirates	10	4	Braves	3	1
Dodgers	11	7	1978	Dodgers	9	6	Phillies	3	0
Reds	10	7	1994	Cubs	8	3	Pirates	3	0
Cubs	10	3	1989	Reds	7	5	Rockies	3	0
Braves	6	4	1983	Braves	3	3	Dodgers	2	1
Phillies	5	0	1993	Phillies	2	0	Cards	2	0
Mets	4	1	1990	Astros	1	1	Cubs	2	0
Rockies	3	0	1997				Astros	1	0
Astros	2	1	1998				Expos	0	0
Expos	0	0	--				Giants	0	0
Marlins	0	0	--				Marlins	0	0
Padres	0	0	--				Padres	0	0

Table 4-3 shows the number of times each team led its league in batting average during different periods (the Diamondbacks and Devil Rays are not listed because they did not lead in 1998). The first set of columns covers the 1901-98 period, the second the 1901-72 period, and the third the 1973-98 period (when the AL had the DH). The heading "Led Both" shows the number of times a team led both its own league and the majors. Years in bold under the "Last Led" heading identify teams that have gone the longest without leading.

In nearly every measure the original 16 teams lead the list both for the century and the 1901-72 period because the expansion teams were not in existence long enough to accumulate a high number of leading years by 1972. But comparing the leaders before 1973 and after 1972 provides good insight into which of the original 16 teams were regular leaders during the century and which have been supplanted by other teams in the last quarter of the century.

The Red Sox lead the AL in the number of times leading the league and the majors in batting average. The Cards lead the NL and the Red Sox in number of times leading the league, but the Red Sox are far ahead in number of times leading the majors. The Red Sox were only third in the AL in the 1901-72 period, but the Red Sox are runaway leaders from 1973-98. The Cards lead the NL both before 1973 and after 1972, but the Red Sox lead the Cards after 1972 by as big a margin as they lead the second place team in the AL. The edge held by the Red Sox after 1972 is so large it gives them the lead for the full century.

The top 3 AL teams before 1973 are the same 3 (Tigers, Yankees, and Red Sox) that led the AL in runs during the same period (Table 4-2). But only the Red Sox continued to be a leader in batting average after 1972. The Yankees are tied for fourth place far behind the Red Sox, and the Tigers last led the league in 1961. Only the White Sox, who last led in 1960, have gone longer than the Tigers without winning the AL batting title.

A similar pattern holds in the NL. The top 3 NL teams before 1973 are the same 3 (Cards, Pirates, and Giants) that led the NL in runs during that period. The Cards continue to be the NL leader after 1972, and the Pirates tie for third place. But the Giants were able to lead in batting average only once in the 1973-98 period. The Dodgers have gone the longest time in the NL (and the majors) without leading in batting average. They last led in 1955 during a period when they had the highest scoring teams in the majors.

The Rockies took advantage of their thin air and led the NL in batting average 4 years in a row from 1995 through 1998 (in 1998 they were the first NL team to lead the majors in batting average since the Reds did it in 1976). But losing Andres Galarraga to the Braves in 1998 cost the Rockies a chance to lead in runs and home runs 4 straight years as well (Tables 4-2 and 4-4). They continue to lead the NL in batting average because pitchers lose a lot of "bite" on their breaking pitches in Denver.

Table 4-3. Batting Average Leaders

American League

Team	1901-98 Led AL	Led Both	Last Led		Team	1901-72 Led AL	Led Both		Team	1973-98 Led AL	Led Both
Red Sox	21	16	1997		Tigers	16	10		Red Sox	10	10
Tigers	16	10	1961		Yankees	12	4		Twins	5	4
Yankees	14	6	1994		Red Sox	11	6		Indians	3	3
Indians	12	8	1996		Indians	9	5		Royals	2	2
Twins	11	6	1992		A's	8	3		Yankees	2	2
A's	8	3	1968		Twins	6	2		Rangers	2	0
White Sox	5	1	**1960**		White Sox	5	1		Blue Jays	1	1
Orioles	4	2	1971		Orioles	4	2		Brewers	1	1
Royals	3	2	1982		Royals	1	0		A's	0	0
Rangers	2	0	1998						Angels	0	0
Blue Jays	1	1	1983						Mariners	0	0
Brewers	1	1	1978						Orioles	0	0
Angels	0	0	--						Tigers	0	0
Mariners	0	0	--						White Sox	0	0

National League

Team	1901-98 Led NL	Led Both	Last Led		Team	1901-72 Led NL	Led Both		Team	1973-98 Led NL	Led Both
Cards	22	8	1992		Cards	17	8		Cards	5	0
Pirates	19	9	1991		Pirates	16	8		Rockies	4	1
Giants	13	8	1993		Giants	12	8		Pirates	3	1
Reds	11	8	1994		Reds	8	7		Reds	3	1
Dodgers	8	3	**1955**		Dodgers	8	3		Cubs	3	0
Cubs	8	1	1989		Cubs	5	1		Phillies	3	0
Braves	6	2	1983		Braves	4	2		Braves	2	0
Phillies	5	2	1984		Phillies	2	2		Mets	2	0
Rockies	4	1	1998						Giants	1	0
Mets	2	0	1987						Astros	0	0
Astros	0	0	--						Dodgers	0	0
Expos	0	0	--						Expos	0	0
Marlins	0	0	--						Marlins	0	0
Padres	0	0	--						Padres	0	0

Table 4-4 shows the number of times each team led its league in home runs per game during different periods (the Diamondbacks and Devil Rays are not listed because they did not lead in 1998). The first set of columns covers the 1901-98 period, the second the 1901-72 period, and the third the 1973-98 period (when the AL had the DH). The heading "Led Both" shows the number of times a team led both its own league and the majors. Years in bold under the "Last Led" heading identify teams that have gone the longest without leading.

In nearly every measure the original 16 teams lead the list both for the century and the 1901-72 period because the expansion teams were not in existence long enough to accumulate a high number of leading years by 1972. But comparing the leaders before 1973 and after 1972 provides good insight into which of the original 16 teams were regular leaders during the century and which have been supplanted by other teams in the last quarter of the century.

By a large margin the Yankees lead the AL in the number of times leading the league and the majors in home runs per game. The Yankees also lead the NL leader, the Giants, in both measures, but by a narrower margin. However, both teams are home run leaders only in the past. The Yankees have not led in home runs since 1961, when they set what was then the major league record behind Roger Maris and Mickey Mantle. Ironically, no AL team has gone as long as the Yankees without leading the league in home runs. But the Yankees continue to be big winners even if they are no longer home run leaders. They continue to score plenty of runs and have great pitching and defense. There's much more to winning than hitting it out.

Similarly, the Giants have gone longer than any NL team without leading in home runs (they last led in 1972). The Cards had held that distinction by not leading since 1944, but they led in 1998 behind the all-time record of 70 home runs hit by Mark McGwire. The Cards had a total of 223 home runs in 1998, the second highest total in league history behind the 239 hit by the Rockies in 1997. The Rockies appeared to be the new offensive leader in the NL. They led the NL in batting average 4 years in a row from 1995 through 1998 (Table 4-3), and they were expected to lead in runs and home runs as well. But losing Andres Galarraga to the Braves as a free agent greatly reduced home runs (and runs) for the Rockies in 1998, and they only ranked fourth in home runs and tied for third in runs. This is a good example of how hard it is to lead the league consistently in any measure. Being one of the top teams regularly is hard enough, but being the best every year is extremely difficult.

The Tigers are the AL leader in home runs since 1973, and the Dodgers lead the NL in spite of their reputation as a pitching team. Expansion teams rank third in each league, while the Yankees and Giants, who were the prior leaders by overwhelming margins, are still looking for their first titles in the period. Home run leaders have changed substantially since 1973.

Table 4-4. Home Run Leaders

American League

Team	1901-98 Led AL	Led Both	Last Led	Team	1901-72 Led AL	Led Both	Team	1973-98 Led AL	Led Both
Yankees	33	19	**1961**	Yankees	33	19	Tigers	6	6
A's	16	5	1981	A's	15	4	Indians	4	3
Red Sox	13	7	1979	Red Sox	10	5	Brewers	3	3
Tigers	10	9	1992	Indians	6	0	Orioles	3	3
Indians	10	3	1995	Tigers	4	3	Red Sox	3	2
Orioles	4	3	1996	Twins	3	3	Mariners	2	2
Brewers	3	3	1982	Orioles	1	0	A's	1	1
Twins	3	3	1964				Blue Jays	1	1
Mariners	2	2	1998				Rangers	1	1
Blue Jays	1	1	1988				Angels	1	0
Rangers	1	1	1993				White Sox	1	0
Angels	1	0	1989				Royals	0	0
White Sox	1	0	1974				Twins	0	0
Royals	0	0	--				Yankees	0	0

National League

Team	1901-98 Led NL	Led Both	Last Led	Team	1901-72 Led NL	Led Both	Team	1973-98 Led NL	Led Both
Giants	27	13	**1972**	Giants	27	13	Dodgers	6	1
Dodgers	17	9	1983	Phillies	13	7	Braves	5	1
Phillies	14	7	1984	Dodgers	11	8	Mets	3	2
Braves	12	6	1994	Braves	7	5	Cubs	3	0
Cubs	8	3	1987	Cards	5	3	Rockies	3	0
Cards	6	3	1998	Cubs	5	3	Reds	2	1
Reds	5	2	1991	Reds	3	1	Cards	1	0
Mets	3	2	1990	Pirates	2	0	Expos	1	0
Pirates	3	0	1975				Phillies	1	0
Rockies	3	0	1997				Pirates	1	0
Expos	1	0	1981				Astros	0	0
Astros	0	0	--				Giants	0	0
Marlins	0	0	--				Marlins	0	0
Padres	0	0	--				Padres	0	0

Table 4-5 shows the number of times each team led its league in stolen bases per game during different periods (the Diamondbacks and Devil Rays are not listed because they did not lead in 1998). The first set of columns covers the 1901-98 period, the second the 1901-72 period, and the third the 1973-98 period (when the AL had the DH). The heading "Led Both" shows the number of times a team led both its own league and the majors. Years in bold under the "Last Led" heading identify teams that have gone the longest without leading.

In nearly every measure the original 16 teams lead the list both for the century and the 1901-72 period because the expansion teams were not in existence long enough to accumulate a high number of leading years by 1972. But comparing the leaders before 1973 and after 1972 provides good insight into which of the original 16 teams were regular leaders during the century and which have been supplanted by other teams in the last quarter of the century.

The White Sox top the list by a large margin in most times leading their league and the majors in stolen bases. But this is a record of yesterday. The White Sox last led in stolen bases in 1966. In fact, the top 2 AL leaders are from the past. The Twins, who rank second, have not led since 1948, when they were the Senators. The Twins, in that sense, have never led the AL in stolen bases. The AL leaders since 1973 are the A's, Royals, and Brewers. The A's compiled the same record in the 26 seasons after 1972 as they did in the 72 seasons before 1973. Speed was a big part of their three straight championships in the 1970s.

The Red Sox are easily the worst team in the AL in stolen bases. In their 98 seasons in the AL, the Red Sox led in stolen bases only once (1935). The Red Sox are often last in the AL in stolen bases and that is exactly where they ranked in 1998. Their strategy does not include stolen bases. This is a tradition in Boston. The NL Braves also led only once in stolen bases (1945), and they took the tradition with them to Milwaukee and Atlanta. But the Phillies top both the Red Sox and the Braves. The Phillies have not led at any time in stolen bases, and thus they have gone 98 years without leading. The Phillies are the only one of the original 16 teams never to lead one of the measures in this book.

In spite of its common association with speed, the NL has an unusual collection of original teams that have gone a long time without leading in stolen bases. The Giants have not led since 1957, the Braves since 1945, the Cubs since 1939, and the Phillies since the century started.

The Dodgers and Cards both led the NL 21 times in stolen bases per game, but the Dodgers have a big margin in number of times leading the majors. Both teams, however, are far behind the White Sox. For the Dodgers, speed is also a thing of the past. They last led in stolen bases in 1970. But the Cards have continued to feature speed through the 1990s, and they are the major league leader in stolen bases since 1973. The expansion Expos rank second to the Cards in that period.

Table 4-5. Stolen Base Leaders

American League

1901-98				1901-72			1973-98		
	Led	Led	Last		Led	Led		Led	Led
Team	AL	Both	Led	Team	AL	Both	Team	AL	Both
White Sox	30	20	1966	White Sox	30	20	A's	6	3
Twins	13	4	1948	Twins	13	4	Royals	5	3
A's	12	6	1991	Yankees	7	4	Brewers	5	2
Yankees	8	4	1985	Tigers	6	4	Blue Jays	3	1
Tigers	7	4	1997	A's	6	3	Indians	3	0
Royals	6	4	1996	Orioles	3	1	Angels	1	1
Brewers	6	3	1992	Indians	2	0	Orioles	1	0
Indians	5	0	1995	Rangers	2	0	Tigers	1	0
Orioles	4	1	1973	Brewers	1	1	Yankees	1	0
Blue Jays	3	1	1998	Royals	1	1	Mariners	0	0
Rangers	2	0	1972	Red Sox	1	1	Red Sox	0	0
Angels	1	1	1975				Rangers	0	0
Red Sox	1	1	**1935**				Twins	0	0
Mariners	0	0	--				White Sox	0	0

National League

1901-98				1901-72			1973-98		
	Led	Led	Last		Led	Led		Led	Led
Team	NL	Both	Led	Team	NL	Both	Team	NL	Both
Dodgers	21	13	1970	Dodgers	21	13	Cards	9	6
Cards	21	8	1992	Giants	13	7	Expos	6	4
Pirates	15	8	1998	Pirates	12	7	Reds	5	3
Giants	13	7	1957	Cards	12	2	Pirates	3	1
Reds	12	7	1997	Reds	7	4	Padres	1	1
Expos	6	4	1994	Cubs	5	0	Rockies	1	1
Cubs	5	0	**1939**	Astros	1	0	Astros	1	0
Astros	2	0	1979	Braves	1	0	Braves	0	0
Padres	1	1	1980				Cubs	0	0
Rockies	1	1	1996				Dodgers	0	0
Braves	1	0	1945				Giants	0	0
Marlins	0	0	--				Marlins	0	0
Mets	0	0	--				Mets	0	0
Phillies	0	0	--				Phillies	0	0

Table 4-6 shows the number of times each team led its league in strikeouts per game during different periods (the Diamondbacks and Devil Rays are not listed because they did not lead in 1998). The first set of columns covers the 1901-98 period, the second the 1901-72 period, and the third the 1973-98 period (when the AL had the DH). The heading "Led Both" shows the number of times a team led both its own league and the majors. Years in bold under the "Last Led" heading identify teams that have gone the longest without leading.

In nearly every measure the original 16 teams lead the list both for the century and the 1901-72 period because the expansion teams were not in existence long enough to accumulate a high number of leading years by 1972. But comparing the leaders before 1973 and after 1972 provides good insight into which of the original 16 teams were regular leaders during the century and which have been supplanted by other teams in the last quarter of the century.

The A's edge the Yankees at the top of the AL list because the A's led the majors much more often than the Yankees. The Indians edge the Tigers for third place by also topping the Tigers in the number of times leading the majors. The top 4 teams are in the same order in the 1901-72 period as in the 1901-98 period. But of the 4 teams, only the Yankees led the league in the 1973-98 period, and they did so only twice. The A's last led in 1971, the Indians in 1970, and the Tigers in 1969.

Three expansion teams head the AL list in the 1973-98 period. The Angels are at the top thanks to Nolan Ryan. They led 7 times, but not since Ryan left as a free agent after the 1979 season. Similarly, the Mariners also led 7 times in the period behind Randy Johnson, who was in his free agent year in 1998 when he staked the Mariners to another title before going to Houston in mid-year.

The Dodgers lead the NL by a huge margin, and their 34 titles are the most for any team in any measure in the book (the Yankees are second with their 33 home run titles). The 22 times the Dodgers led the majors also tops the list for leading the majors most often (again the Yankees are second with 19 major league home run titles). Another key to the NL list is that an expansion team, the Mets, hold second place for the century. Strikeouts are the only measure in which an expansion team even cracks the top 5, let alone finishes second. The Mets are the NL (and major league) leader in the 1973-98 period, and, as in the AL, NL expansion teams have the top two places on the 1973-98 list.

The list features some original teams with long periods without a title. In the AL, the Orioles, who had some great pitching teams in Baltimore, never led in strikeouts. The last franchise strikeout title was won by the St. Louis Browns in 1944 when they won the only franchise pennant in St. Louis. The lack of a title for the Orioles shows there is much more to pitching than strikeouts. In the NL, the Cards have not won since 1947, the Giants since 1937, and the Pirates since 1921 (which is not long after Honus Wagner retired).

Table 4-6. Strikeout Leaders

American League

Team	1901-98 Led AL	Led Both	Last Led	Team	1901-72 Led AL	Led Both	Team	1973-98 Led AL	Led Both
A's	16	12	1971	A's	16	12	Angels	7	2
Yankees	16	6	1984	Yankees	14	5	Mariners	7	0
Indians	11	9	1970	Indians	11	9	Rangers	6	1
Tigers	11	8	1969	Tigers	11	8	Yankees	2	1
Twins	9	7	1962	Twins	9	7	Red Sox	2	0
Angels	9	2	1979	White Sox	4	0	Blue Jays	1	0
Mariners	7	0	1998	Red Sox	3	1	White Sox	1	0
Rangers	6	1	1992	Orioles	2	1	A's	0	0
Red Sox	5	1	1996	Angels	2	0	Brewers	0	0
White Sox	5	0	1985				Indians	0	0
Orioles	2	1	**1944**				Orioles	0	0
Blue Jays	1	0	1994				Royals	0	0
Brewers	0	0	--				Tigers	0	0
Royals	0	0	--				Twins	0	0

National League

Team	1901-98 Led NL	Led Both	Last Led	Team	1901-72 Led NL	Led Both	Team	1973-98 Led NL	Led Both
Dodgers	34	22	1997	Dodgers	31	20	Mets	8	7
Mets	11	9	1991	Cards	11	2	Astros	5	4
Cards	11	2	1947	Giants	9	1	Braves	4	4
Giants	9	1	1937	Cubs	6	1	Phillies	3	3
Cubs	8	2	1979	Reds	4	0	Dodgers	3	2
Astros	7	5	1987	Mets	3	2	Cubs	2	1
Phillies	6	3	1993	Pirates	3	2	Reds	1	1
Reds	5	1	1992	Phillies	3	0	Cards	0	0
Braves	4	4	1998	Astros	2	1	Expos	0	0
Pirates	3	2	**1921**				Giants	0	0
Expos	0	0	--				Marlins	0	0
Marlins	0	0	--				Padres	0	0
Padres	0	0	--				Pirates	0	0
Rockies	0	0	--				Rockies	0	0

Table 4-7 shows the number of times each team led its league in fewest walks per game during different periods (the Diamondbacks and Devil Rays are not listed because they did not lead in 1998). The first set of columns covers the 1901-98 period, the second the 1901-72 period, and the third the 1973-98 period (when the AL had the DH). The heading "Led Both" shows the number of times a team led both its own league and the majors. Years in bold under the "Last Led" heading identify teams that have gone the longest without leading.

In nearly every measure the original 16 teams lead the list both for the century and the 1901-72 period because the expansion teams were not in existence long enough to accumulate a high number of leading years by 1972. But comparing the leaders before 1973 and after 1972 provides good insight into which of the original 16 teams were regular leaders during the century and which have been supplanted by other teams in the last quarter of the century.

The White Sox lead the AL by a wide margin in the number of times leading in fewest walks per game, and they lead the top NL team, the Pirates, by a comfortable margin. But because the NL, for most of the century, issued far fewer walks than the AL, the AL leader rarely led the majors. The White Sox led the majors only 4 times during the 24 seasons they led the AL. But the White Sox only led twice after 1965 and not at all after 1983. The Twins and Red Sox are close together behind the White Sox for the century, and also close together behind the Brewers since 1973. The Tigers, who were close to the Twins in the 1901-72 period, have not led since 1961, the largest gap in the AL. But the Angels and Rangers, who were both born in 1962, have never led and thus are just one year behind the Tigers in the longest wait for a title.

The Pirates, Giants, and Reds cluster at the top of the NL list for the century, and the Giants lead both leagues in most years leading the majors in fewest walks per game. The same 3 teams cluster at the top of the list for the 1901-72 period, with the Giants on top. But the Giants and Reds are old news. The Giants have not led since 1968, and the Reds have not won a title since 1958, the longest wait in the NL for leading in fewest walks per game. The Pirates led as recently as 1990 and 1991, but they have only 3 titles in total since 1961. However, the leadership in fewest walks per game is so well divided in the NL since 1973 (just as it is in the AL), that the 3 titles won by the Pirates in the 1973-98 period ties them for second in the NL during this period.

The Expos lead the NL in the 1973-98 period, although in the past decade the Braves have led thanks to Greg Maddux, the best control pitcher of his generation. There is much irony in the leadership position held by the Expos because they set the NL record for most total walks issued in one season when they issued 716 in 1970 (the Marlins just missed the record with 715 in 1998). But 1970 was only one year after the birth of the Expos, and the walk record can be charged to growing pains. They certainly have improved since 1970.

Table 4-7. Walk Leaders

American League

1901-98 Team	Led AL	Led Both	Last Led	1901-72 Team	Led AL	Led Both	1973-98 Team	Led AL	Led Both
White Sox	24	4	1983	White Sox	22	3	Brewers	5	2
Twins	13	2	1998	Twins	9	1	Red Sox	4	2
Red Sox	12	4	1986	Tigers	9	0	Twins	4	1
Indians	10	1	1995	Red Sox	8	2	Indians	3	1
Tigers	9	0	**1961**	Orioles	7	3	Royals	3	1
Orioles	8	3	1994	Yankees	7	3	White Sox	2	1
Yankees	8	3	1973	Indians	7	0	A's	1	1
Brewers	5	2	1992	A's	3	0	Blue Jays	1	0
A's	4	1	1974				Mariners	1	0
Royals	3	1	1996				Orioles	1	0
Blue Jays	1	0	1990				Yankees	1	0
Mariners	1	0	1987				Angels	0	0
Angels	0	0	--				Rangers	0	0
Rangers	0	0	--				Tigers	0	0

National League

1901-98 Team	Led NL	Led Both	Last Led	1901-72 Team	Led NL	Led Both	1973-98 Team	Led NL	Led Both
Pirates	17	12	1991	Giants	15	13	Expos	5	4
Giants	15	13	1968	Pirates	14	10	Braves	3	2
Reds	12	11	**1958**	Reds	12	11	Cards	3	2
Dodgers	11	8	1977	Dodgers	8	7	Phillies	3	2
Phillies	10	9	1983	Phillies	7	7	Pirates	3	2
Braves	7	6	1997	Cubs	6	3	Dodgers	3	1
Cubs	8	4	1984	Braves	4	4	Mets	2	2
Cards	6	4	1993	Astros	3	3	Cubs	2	1
Expos	5	4	1994	Cards	3	2	Padres	1	1
Astros	4	3	1998				Astros	1	0
Mets	2	2	1995				Giants	0	0
Padres	1	1	1985				Marlins	0	0
Marlins	0	0	--				Reds	0	0
Rockies	0	0	--				Rockies	0	0

Table 4-8 shows the number of times each team led its league in fewest errors per game during different periods (the Diamondbacks and Devil Rays are not listed because they did not lead in 1998). The first set of columns covers the 1901-98 period, the second the 1901-72 period, and the third the 1973-98 period (when the AL had the DH). The heading "Led Both" shows the number of times a team led both its own league and the majors. Years in bold under the "Last Led" heading identify teams that have gone the longest without leading.

In nearly every measure the original 16 teams lead the list both for the century and the 1901-72 period because the expansion teams were not in existence long enough to accumulate a high number of leading years by 1972. But comparing the leaders before 1973 and after 1972 provides good insight into which of the original 16 teams were regular leaders during the century and which have been supplanted by other teams in the last quarter of the century.

The Orioles edge the White Sox for the overall lead in the AL during the century. The White Sox won all but one title before 1963, while the Orioles were the best team in the AL in the 1973-98 period by a wide margin. The Orioles became the class of the AL in fielding soon after the franchise moved to Baltimore in 1954. The St. Louis Browns led in fewest errors per game only once in 1938. The Orioles won their first title in 1960, then went on to win 16 titles in the 29 seasons from 1960 through 1998. Only the Reds, who led the NL in fewest errors per game 15 times during the same period, can come close to matching the Orioles. The Orioles and Reds together are far ahead of the rest of the teams in the majors over the last 3 decades in fewest errors per game, and it is this recent performance that gives both teams the lead in the century.

In the AL the Orioles are one of the few teams from the original 8 that are leaders in fewest errors per game in recent times. The A's last led in 1932, the longest gap in the AL, while the Red Sox last led in 1950, the Yankees in 1961, and the Indians in 1965. But every AL expansion team (except the Devil Rays) led the league in fewest errors per game at least once. This is the only measure for which this is true in either league. The original 8 teams have been more recent leaders in the NL, but the Pirates last led in 1922, the longest gap in the majors for fewest errors per game. This is also the longest gap in the majors for any measure except for strikeouts per game where the Pirates last led in 1921.

The Reds hold a large lead in the NL in fewest errors per game, and they were among the leaders during all periods in the century. The Cubs edged the Reds in the 1901-72 period, but the Cubs led only twice (1968 and 1996) after 1945. As in many measures, the Cubs were one of the elite teams before WWII, and one of the poorest teams after WWII. The Reds led for the first time when they won the pennant in 1919, and they led at least once in every decade after 1919. Being among the league leaders in fielding has been a tradition for the Reds for over 70 years.

Table 4-8. Error Leaders

American League

Team	1901-98 Led AL	Led Both	Last Led	Team	1901-72 Led AL	Led Both	Team	1973-98 Led AL	Led Both
Orioles	17	11	1998	White Sox	14	6	Orioles	11	7
White Sox	15	6	1985	Indians	10	6	Tigers	3	2
Tigers	11	6	1981	A's	9	7	Twins	3	2
Indians	10	6	1965	Red Sox	9	7	Blue Jays	2	2
A's	9	7	**1932**	Yankees	9	4	Rangers	2	2
Red Sox	9	7	1950	Tigers	8	4	Brewers	2	1
Yankees	9	4	1961	Orioles	6	4	Mariners	1	1
Twins	8	4	1988	Twins	5	2	Royals	1	1
Rangers	3	2	1996	Angels	1	1	White Sox	1	0
Blue Jays	2	2	1990	Rangers	1	0	A's	0	0
Brewers	2	1	1992				Angels	0	0
Angels	1	1	1967				Indians	0	0
Mariners	1	1	1993				Red Sox	0	0
Royals	1	1	1997				Yankees	0	0

National League

Team	1901-98 Led NL	Led Both	Last Led	Team	1901-72 Led NL	Led Both	Team	1973-98 Led NL	Led Both
Reds	23	8	1997	Cubs	16	9	Reds	10	3
Cubs	17	9	1996	Reds	13	5	Cards	7	2
Cards	14	5	1992	Braves	11	3	Phillies	3	2
Braves	12	3	1998	Dodgers	8	5	Giants	2	0
Phillies	8	6	1982	Cards	7	3	Astros	1	1
Dodgers	8	5	1960	Pirates	6	2	Braves	1	0
Giants	8	0	1994	Giants	6	0	Cubs	1	0
Pirates	6	2	**1922**	Phillies	5	4	Mets	1	0
Astros	1	1	1974				Dodgers	0	0
Mets	1	0	1988				Expos	0	0
Expos	0	0	--				Marlins	0	0
Marlins	0	0	--				Padres	0	0
Padres	0	0	--				Pirates	0	0
Rockies	0	0	--				Rockies	0	0

Table 4-9 shows the number of times each team led its league in double plays per game during different periods (the Diamondbacks are not listed because they did not lead in 1998). The first set of columns covers the 1901-98 period, the second the 1901-72 period, and the third the 1973-98 period (when the AL had the DH). The heading "Led Both" shows the number of times a team led both its own league and the majors. Years in bold under the "Last Led" heading identify teams that have gone the longest without leading.

In nearly every measure the original 16 teams lead the list both for the century and the 1901-72 period because the expansion teams were not in existence long enough to accumulate a high number of leading years by 1972. But comparing the leaders before 1973 and after 1972 provides good insight into which of the original 16 teams were regular leaders during the century and which have been supplanted by other teams in the last quarter of the century.

Double play leaders are widely distributed in both leagues because of the complex relationship between hits and walks given up and fielding skills. Sometimes the best teams lead and sometimes the worst teams lead. The Yankees lead the AL with only 15 leading years, the lowest number to lead any measure in the AL. The Pirates lead the NL (and the majors) with 18 leading years, the lowest number to lead any NL measure with the exception of walks. The Pirates lead in NL walk titles with only 17 leading years (Table 4-7).

The Yankees led the AL in the 1901-72 period because their peak period in leading in double plays came between 1941 and 1965. This period coincides with the peak for the Yankees in terms of winning the pennant consistently. This means the Yankees were double play leaders primarily because of their fielding skills (their great pitching resulted in few baserunners). The expansion Devil Rays led the AL in double plays in 1998. They had a poor record, as expected, but they had decent pitching and were second in fewest errors per game. Thus, their title was due to a mix of more baserunners than average and good fielding. The Rockies, who led the NL and the majors for the second year in a row in 1998, are a double play leader because they are a leader in opposing baserunners.

The Pirates led the NL in the century primarily because of the fielding skills of Bill Mazeroski, the best ever at turning the double play at second base. The Pirates led in double plays 9 straight years from 1959 through 1967, and this exactly matches the time Mazeroski played for them fulltime at second base. This period also includes the 1963-68 period when the strike zone was changed in favor of pitchers and baserunners were reduced to a minimum. In spite of this deficit, the Pirates set the all-time NL record for double plays in 1966 when Mazeroski was at his peak. Mazeroski's playing time was greatly reduced after 1968, but the Pirates led in double plays only once after he retired in 1972.

The Cubs have the longest gap in the NL (and the majors), winning their last double play title in 1948.

Table 4-9. Double Play Leaders

American League

Team	1901-98 Led AL	Led Both	Last Led	Team	1901-72 Led AL	Led Both	Team	1973-98 Led AL	Led Both
Yankees	15	10	1989	Yankees	13	9	Brewers	4	2
Indians	13	5	1993	Indians	11	3	Angels	3	3
White Sox	12	8	1988	White Sox	10	7	Orioles	3	1
Orioles	12	4	1987	Twins	9	6	Indians	2	2
Twins	11	8	1978	Orioles	9	3	Mariners	2	2
A's	7	5	1996	A's	6	4	Twins	2	2
Red Sox	7	4	1997	Red Sox	5	3	Red Sox	2	1
Angels	6	3	1990	Tigers	3	2	White Sox	2	1
Tigers	4	3	1978	Angels	3	0	Yankees	2	1
Brewers	4	2	1995	Rangers	2	0	A's	1	1
Mariners	2	2	1991	Royals	1	0	Royals	1	1
Royals	2	1	1973				Tigers	1	1
Rangers	2	0	**1967**				Devil Rays	1	0
Devil Rays	1	0	1998				Blue Jays	0	0
Blue Jays	0	0	--				Rangers	0	0

National League

Team	1901-98 Led NL	Led Both	Last Led	Team	1901-72 Led NL	Led Both	Team	1973-98 Led NL	Led Both
Pirates	18	12	1994	Pirates	17	11	Cards	5	2
Braves	15	6	1986	Reds	13	7	Braves	4	1
Reds	13	7	1954	Braves	11	5	Giants	4	1
Cards	12	6	1995	Cards	7	4	Padres	3	0
Phillies	9	2	1990	Phillies	7	2	Rockies	2	2
Giants	8	2	1993	Cubs	6	2	Expos	2	1
Dodgers	7	2	1989	Dodgers	6	2	Phillies	2	0
Cubs	6	2	**1948**	Giants	4	1	Pirates	1	1
Expos	3	2	1976	Expos	1	1	Dodgers	1	0
Padres	3	0	1988				Marlins	1	0
Rockies	2	2	1998				Mets	1	0
Marlins	1	0	1996				Astros	0	0
Mets	1	0	1979				Cubs	0	0
Astros	0	0	--				Reds	0	0

Table 4-10 shows all-time league and team records for the eight measures in the book. League records are listed on a per game basis while team records are listed on both a per game and total year basis. The years in which the various records were set are also shown.

Runs--The NL holds the all-time record at 5.68 runs per game in 1930. The AL just missed a tie with 5.67 runs per game in 1936. The Yankees set the per game record for a team in 1930 with 6.90 runs per game and the 1931 Yankees hold the total year record with 1,067 runs in 1931. The Cards set both the per game and total year records for the NL with 1,004 runs in 1930, an average of 6.52 per game. No other NL team has exceeded 1,000 runs in a year, but the Yankees did it four times in the 1930s and the Red Sox did it in 1950.

Batting Average--The NL peaked at .303 in 1930, the all-time major league record. The AL peaked at .292 in 1921, the year after the rule changes of 1920. In concert with their leagues, the Giants set the NL team high at .319 in 1930, and the Tigers set the AL high at .316 in 1921.

Home Runs--The AL set the all-time record in 1996 at 1.21 home runs per game, but, without the DH, the NL has not been able to top its 1955 peak of 1.03. The 1997 Mariners set both the AL per game and total year records with 264 home runs in 1997 for an average of 1.63 per game. The Rockies also set both NL records in 1997 with 239 home runs or 1.46 per game.

Stolen Bases--The AL set the all-time record in 1912 at 1.46 stolen bases per game, and the NL set its record at 1.39 in 1903. The 1911 Giants hold both team records with 347 stolen bases for an average of 2.25 per game. The 1976 A's hold the AL records with 341 stolen bases or 2.12 per game, but the A's in 1976 were much farther above the league average than the Giants were in 1911.

Strikeouts--All league and team records were set in the big swing era of the 1990s. The NL holds both the league and team records thanks to the DH in the AL. The NL set the all-time record in 1997 at 6.88 strikeouts per game, well ahead of the AL record level of 6.38 in 1997. The Braves hold the all-time team records with 1,245 strikeouts in 1996 for an average of 7.69 per game. The Mariners set the AL record in 1997 with 1,207 strikeouts or 7.45 per game.

Walks--League records for fewest walks were set when the foul strike rule was new. The AL set the all-time record at 2.05 in 1903, the first year the rule was in effect in the AL. The NL low is 2.33, a mark the league set in 1902, the year after the foul strike rule went into effect in the NL. The 1904 Red Sox set the all-time team record for fewest walks per game with a mark of 1.48. The 1904 Red Sox played 157 games (due to ties) and issued only 239 walks, the record low total for the AL. The 1933 Reds hold the NL per game mark at 1.68, issuing 257 walks in 153 games. But the 1918 Giants, in a season cut short due to WWI, issued an all-time low total of 228 walks in only 124 games. The per game mark for the 1918 Giants was a non-record 1.84 walks per game.

Errors--The AL set the all-time major league low in 1996 at 0.68 errors per game. The NL set its league record in 1998 at 0.71. The 1998 Orioles tied their all-time per game low of 0.50 set in 1995, but in the even shorter year of 1994 they had a record low total of 57 errors. Similarly, the 1995 Reds set the NL per game low of 0.55, but the 1994 Giants had fewer errors in the shorter season.

Double Plays--The AL set the all-time double play record at 1.20 per game in 1949, the same year it had a record high in walks. The NL set its league high at 1.07 in 1951, the year after it set a league walk record. As explained in the text accompanying Figure 3-15, it is not a coincidence both leagues set double play records in a time of record walks. The A's set the all-time team record in the AL league record year of 1949. The Pirates set the NL team record in 1966 when both runs and walks were very low, but Bill Mazeroski was at his peak.

Table 4-10. League and Team Records 1901-98

		League Records Per Game	Year	Team Records	Per Game	Total	Year
Runs	AL	5.67	1936	Yankees	6.90	1062	1930
				Yankees	6.88	1067	1931
	NL	5.68	1930	Cards	6.52	1004	1930
Bat Avg	AL	.292	1921	Tigers	.316	.316	1921
	NL	.303	1930	Giants	.319	.319	1930
Home Runs	AL	1.21	1996	Mariners	1.63	264	1997
	NL	1.03	1955	Rockies	1.46	239	1997
Stolen Bases	AL	1.46	1912	A's	2.12	341	1976
	NL	1.39	1903	Giants	2.25	347	1911
Strikeouts	AL	6.38	1997	Mariners	7.45	1207	1997
	NL	6.83	1997	Braves	7.69	1245	1996
Walks	AL	2.05	1903	Red Sox	1.48	239	1904
	NL	2.33	1902	Reds	1.68	257	1933
				Giants	1.84	228	1918
Errors	AL	0.68	1995	Orioles	0.50	81	1998
				Orioles	0.51	57	1994
	NL	0.71	1998	Reds	0.55	79	1995
				Giants	0.59	68	1994
Double Plays	AL	1.20	1949	A's	1.41	217	1949
	NL	1.07	1951	Pirates	1.33	215	1966

Table 4-11 shows data for the eight measures before and after the DH. Column 1 covers the 1901-72 period and column 4 covers the 1973-98 period during which the DH rule was in effect. Column 2 covers the 1901-45 period (the AL dominated) and column 3 covers the 1946-72 period (the NL dominated). Thus, columns 3 and 4 cover post-WWII periods of nearly equal length in which the major difference between the leagues was the use of the DH. The last column headed "DH Change" shows the difference between column 4 and column 3.

Runs--From 1901 through 1972 the AL scored 2.8 percent more runs than the NL. Dividing the 1901-72 period at 1945 shows that the AL led the NL by 4.9 percent through 1945 while the AL trailed the NL by 0.8 percent after 1945. With the DH the AL led the NL by 7.8 percent because the DH increased AL run scoring by 7.7 percent while the NL fell by 1.0 percent in the same period.

Batting Average--In the 1901-72 period the AL trailed the NL by 0.4 percent. The AL led by 0.4 percent in the 1901-45 period and trailed by 1.6 percent in the 1946-72 period. With the DH the AL led by 2.7 percent because AL batting averages increased by 4.6 percent while the NL went up 0.1 percent.

Home Runs--The AL trailed the NL by 3.5 percent in the 1901-72 period. The AL also trailed by 1.7 percent in the 1901-45 period and by 4.7 percent in the 1946-72 period. Thus, contrary to most perceptions, the NL regularly hit more home runs than the AL through 1972. But with the DH the AL leads by 17.0 percent because the DH increased AL home runs by 15.3 percent and the NL fell by 6.1 percent in the same period.

Stolen Bases--The AL led by 1.1 percent in the 1901-72 period and by 3.6 percent in the 1901-45 period. The AL trailed by 7.3 percent in the 1946-72 period, and the deficit increased to 16.5 percent during the period of the DH. AL stolen bases actually increased by 90.1 percent after the DH was born, but in the same period NL stolen bases increased by 111 percent.

Strikeouts--The AL led the NL by 0.9 percent from 1901 through 1972, and the AL led by 3.4 percent in the 1901-45 period. But the AL trailed the NL in the 1946-72 period by 1.9 percent, and the deficit increased to 6.5 percent in the 1973-88 period. This is because strikeouts increased by only 9.6 percent in the AL with the DH while strikeouts increased by 15.1 percent during the same period in the NL. Both leagues exhibit substantial increases in strikeouts in the last five decades, but the DH has muted the strikeout increase in the AL while producing more runs and many more home runs than in the NL.

Walks--The AL had more walks than the NL in all periods until the DH was born. Then AL walks decreased and NL walks increased, the reverse of what was expected. The AL led the NL by 11.5 percent in the 1901-72 period, by 12.2 percent in the 1901-45 period, and by 10.5 percent in the 1946-72 period. The edge has declined to 3.0 percent since the DH was born as AL walks fell by 6.4 percent and NL walks increased by 0.4 percent during the same period.

Errors--The AL had 0.3 percent fewer errors in the 1901-72 period, 1.7 percent more in the 1901-45 period, and 5.6 percent fewer in the 1946-72 period. The AL had a 5.5 percent edge in the 1973-98 period because AL errors fell by 9.7 percent and NL errors by 9.8 percent after the DH was born.

Double Plays--The AL led in double plays by 2.2 percent in the 1901-72 period, with an edge of 0.5 percent in the 1901-45 period and 4.7 percent in the 1946-72 period. The lead jumped to 9.3 percent in the 1973-89 period because AL double plays fell by only 2.8 percent after the DH was born, while NL double plays fell by 7.0 percent due to fewer baserunners without the DH.

Table 4-11. Before and After the DH

		73 Yrs. 1901-72	46 Yrs. 1901-45	27 Yrs. 1946-72	26 Yrs. 1973-98	DH Change
Runs	AL	4.39	4.50	4.22	4.55	+7.7%
	NL	4.27	4.29	4.26	4.22	-1.0%
	AL/NL	+2.8%	+4.9%	-0.8%	+7.8%	
Bat Avg	AL	.262	.268	.252	.264	+4.6%
	NL	.263	.267	.257	.257	0.1%
	AL/NL	-0.4%	+0.4%	-1.6%	+2.7%	
Home Runs	AL	0.50	0.33	0.77	0.89	+15.3%
	NL	0.52	0.34	0.81	0.76	-6.1%
	AL/NL	-3.5%	-1.7%	-4.7%	+17.0%	
Stolen Bases	AL	0.62	0.78	0.35	0.67	+90.1%
	NL	0.61	0.75	0.38	0.80	+111%
	AL/NL	+1.1%	+3.6%	-7.3%	-16.5%	
Strikeouts	AL	3.95	3.40	4.86	5.33	+9.6%
	NL	3.91	3.29	4.95	5.70	+15.1%
	AL/NL	+0.9%	+3.4%	-1.9%	-6.5%	
Walks	AL	3.32	3.17	3.58	3.35	-6.4%
	NL	2.98	2.82	3.24	3.25	+0.4%
	AL/NL	+11.5%	+12.2%	+10.5%	+3.0%	
Errors	AL	1.24	1.45	0.87	0.79	-9.7%
	NL	1.24	1.43	0.92	0.83	-9.8%
	AL/NL	-0.3%	+1.7%	-5.6%	-5.5%	
Double Plays	AL	0.90	0.83	1.00	0.98	-2.8%
	NL	0.88	0.83	0.96	0.89	-7.0%
	AL/NL	+2.2%	+0.5%	+4.7%	+9.3%	

The data and accompanying discussion on pages 206 and 207 confirm that the designated hitter had exactly the effect that was intended when the rule was adopted in the AL in 1973. The DH increased runs in the AL by 7.2 percent compared to the average for the 27 years prior to the implementation of the DH. This was accompanied by an increase of 4.4 percent in batting average and a huge 14.2 percent increase in home runs. The DH did not stop strikeouts from increasing by 8.8 percent in the AL, but this is much less than the increase of 14.2 percent in strikeouts in the NL during the same period.

In the simplest terms, by replacing the pitcher with a designated slugger, the AL has eliminated the uninteresting mismatch that occurs when a pitcher comes to bat and is blown away by the opposing pitcher. At the same time, the AL has greatly increased the number of times the ball is hit out of the park, by far the most appealing part of the game to many fans.

Interleague play shows it takes time to learn how to use the DH to increase offense. The approach used by the Dodgers when they had the chance to use the DH during the first year of interleague play in 1997 is a good example. The Dodgers used slugger Mike Piazza as the DH and replaced him in the lineup with Tom Prince, an excellent defensive catcher. They felt this was an opportunity to give Piazza a rest from the toils of catching while keeping his bat in the lineup. In their mind they were taking prime advantage of the DH rule.

But the Dodgers were actually replacing the pitcher with Tom Prince. The advantage of the DH was thus very marginal because Prince is hard pressed to keep his batting average above .200. If Piazza was the kind of hitter who does not do well in the DH role (he is essentially pinch hitting four times a game and this does not come naturally), then the Dodgers may well have had a less potent lineup on the field in games when they were able to use the DH. This is why the DH rule will be of little help to the NL unless they adopt the rule on a fulltime basis and develop players who can hit well in the role. Then more interleague play and realignment will be much simpler issues to resolve.

The key issue about the DH right now is whether or not the owners will succeed in eliminating the position. I doubt they are even serious about their stated intention to do so. It appears to be just another bargaining chip to use in negotiations with the union. The NL is essentially the only league in organized baseball (in the world) that still insists on banning the DH. All children who start out in baseball play with the DH for whatever time they stay in organized baseball. The DH not only eliminates the futility of pitchers at bat, it brings more baserunners to the basepaths, more runners crossing the plate, and more home runs leaving the park. It also can greatly extend the career of players who give us great pleasure in watching them continue to play. The real issue is when the NL will join the rest of the baseball world in the new century rather than staying buried in the past.

Index